Artificial Intelligence Management

Foundations and Strategy

Artificial Intelligence Management

Foundations and Strategy

Charles A. Wood

Convergent Lens
Monaca, PA

Editors:

Curt Wojik
Anthony J. Wood
Kailyn Wood
Kelly Wood
Lyn Wood
Roger Wood

Dedication

For Lyn, who provided the space, patience, and unwavering support I needed to get this book out of my head and onto the page. And to my family — my brothers, daughters, and friends — thank you for lending your eyes, your red pens, and your time to help shape this manuscript. This book belongs to all of us.

Artificial Intelligence Management
Foundations and Strategy

Published by Convergent Lens: www.ConvergentLens.com

ISBN: 979-8-9929754-0-6
Library of Congress Control Number: 2026916957
First Edition: 2026 Printed in the United States of America

Publisher's Cataloging-in-Publication Data

Names: Wood, Charles A., author.
Title: Artificial intelligence management : foundations and strategy / Charles A. Wood.
Description: Includes bibliographical references and index. | Monaca, PA: Convergent Lens, 2026.
Identifiers: LCCN: 2026916957 | ISBN: 979-8-9929754-1-3 (hardcover) | 979-8-9929754-0-6 (paperback) | 979-8-9929754-2-0 (epub) | 979-8-9929754-3-7 (audio)
Subjects: LCSH Artificial intelligence. | Artificial intelligence--Industrial applications. | Industrial management. | Expert systems (Computer science) | BISAC BUSINESS & ECONOMICS / Management | COMPUTERS / Artificial Intelligence / General | BUSINESS & ECONOMICS / Strategic Planning
Classification: LCC HD31 .W66 2026 | DDC 658.0563--dc23

Chapter-Level Table of Contents

Table of Contents

Forward

Most books about Artificial Intelligence fall into one of two categories: they are either dense academic texts packed with coding syntax that no executive will ever write, or they are superficial, hype-filled fluff pieces written by consultants trying to sell you their next project. Worse yet, many of them are flat-out wrong, parroting tech buzzwords without understanding the operational reality.

If you are a manager, an executive, or an aspiring leader trying to figure out how AI fits into your department, your strategy, and your bottom line, you don't need more hype. You need a blueprint.

Over the course of my career, I have stepped into technical meetings of many companies, including multiple Fortune 500 companies. My job was usually to start or clean up AI strategy and implementation, rescue stalled projects, fix broken applications, and build high-performing teams from scratch. I've seen millions of dollars wasted on smooth-talking consultants who deliver locked-in proprietary systems, basic RAG implementations for LLM systems, or costly systems that don't accomplish much all wrapped in shiny presentations. I've also worked with consultants who really knew their stuff and were an asset to the company they worked with.

Consider this book my way of sitting down at your desk and working directly for you.

Artificial Intelligence Management: Foundations and Strategy is written specifically for the leaders who must make the hard decisions. We aren't going to look at lines of Python code here—that is for a later volume. Instead, we are going to dive deep into the actual machinery of leadership:

- **The Math That Matters:** Managerial formulas, Excel models, and the exact KPIs required to measure machine learning lifecycles without getting fooled by misleading "accuracy" metrics.
- **Global Governance:** Navigating the complex, shifting legal frameworks across the globe—from the EU AI Act to California's CCPA—and shifting your organization from passive policy to active agentic control.
- **The Human Element:** Utilizing rigorous Skill Matrices and my Retention Anchor Framework to build, interview, and protect top-tier data science teams without being lied to by applicants.

- **No-Nonsense Futurism:** A grounded, objective look at where the tech is going, including a hard look at the high-end physics to explain why the Quantum Computing hype might be a myth.

The main point of this book is that managing AI is fundamentally different from managing any other technology department. This book describes how it differs and what managers need to do differently when compared to managing other technology departments or other non-technical areas.

Despite its title, this book is not AI-generated. The text is the culmination of years of rigorous research, conversations, and real-world analysis. While AI has its place – for instance, I used Grammarly for initial proofing, Google tools to generate the accompanying audiobook, and AI assistance for three of the visual figures in this book – the insights are entirely human. AI-generated content is, by its very nature, derivative. To provide true value to managers on the cutting edge, a book requires human perspective, original research, and lived experience. This book delivers exactly that.

You don't need to be a programmer to lead an AI revolution, but you do need to know exactly how the machine works under the hood so you can drive it effectively. Let's get to work!

Chapter 1: Delving Into AI Management

Artificial Intelligence, often shortened to "AI," creates unprecedented opportunities for data science and AI application development. Businesses increasingly rely on data-driven insights, and skilled leaders who can navigate the complexities of AI and data science are in high demand, making the confluence of technological progress and managerial skills a rewarding and financially promising career path for those ready to lead the way.

Organizations used to rely heavily on managerial intuition and experience for decision-making because gathering and analyzing data was so expensive. While that experience is still valuable, we have incredible tools to make even better decisions. Thanks to recent advances in technology and computing, we've entered a data-driven era where artificial intelligence (AI) is transforming how we make choices. AI isn't about replacing experience and good instincts – it's about supercharging them with data, leading to more effective solutions than intuition alone.

As AI takes center stage in organizational strategy, the demand for skilled data science managers to manage AI application development and implementation is soaring. Data science managers are becoming indispensable assets, commanding impressive salaries and shaping the future of corporate success. Data scientists have broad, complex skill sets. It could be argued that data science managers must have an even broader skill set to not only advise on how to take advantage of AI opportunities but also to evaluate and direct data scientists and to communicate to outside management how they can benefit from having AI (or data science) in their areas. Recently, *Forbes* reported a 10% annual pay increase for data scientist managers, with a median base salary ranging from $167,000 to $275,000 and around $310,000 at the 75% percentile![i] There is no guarantee of huge salaries for every data science manager, but the role is clearly becoming more vital to upper management.

This book aims to equip managers with the tools and insights to navigate the AI revolution, from understanding AI opportunities to effectively leading and communicating with data scientists. This book can act as a guide to thriving in the data-driven era. Data Science departments can embrace the challenges of AI and help lead their organizations to new heights of success. Managers in other areas that rely on AI will also benefit from this book as they implement AI across finance, marketing, operations, accounting, product development, human resources, and management.

What is this book trying to do and why?

Data science and AI applications are now integral to many organizations. The data science department's goals and projects must align with the organization's goals, objectives, and mission. AI applications, data science, and data analysis must be managed to accomplish this.

The data science manager also plays a critical role in guiding the AI team in facilitating the development effort. To retain their talent, data science managers must set clear objectives, define project priorities, and establish performance expectations. Effective communication is vital to ensure developers understand their roles and responsibilities and AI projects are aligned with organizational goals.

The main contention in this book is that managing an AI area can be vastly different from managing other areas, and being a good manager in another area does not guarantee success as a data science manager. Here are some unique challenges that data science managers face that are discussed throughout this book:

- **Rapidly Changing Landscape**: Many fields boast a changing atmosphere, but AI may be more rapidly changing than most, with new tools, techniques, and methodologies constantly emerging.

  A data science manager needs to stay current with the latest trends and advancements in AI, evaluate the value of new AI products and techniques, and adapt quickly to value-added AI changes, suggesting opportunities to other business leaders.

- **Wide and Deep Technical Expertise**: Data science managers need a deep understanding of AI concepts and techniques, such as:
    - Statistics
    - Limitations of models
    - Programming/machine learning capabilities
    - Databases like Oracle/SQL, as well as NoSQL databases like Hive or Cassandra
    - Server architectures (like Spark)
    - Managerial skills (planning, communication, motivation, time management, resource allocation)

It can be challenging for data science managers to develop and maintain such a wide range of skills.

- **Inverted Salary Issues**: Many managerial consultants maintain that money is not a motivator, but data science managers (maybe all managers) should put that contention aside. Data scientists on the AI team are trained to look beyond personal feelings, so they may leave a job they like if they see an opportunity for a substantial pay increase. If data scientists see an opportunity for more training, better resources, or better management, they may leave an organization for a slight pay increase. Fortunately, data scientists typically do not leave a position for lower pay unless they feel their job is insecure or the work environment is unacceptable.

  The high demand for the data science skill set may place a financial burden on the AI team's department budget for hiring, training, and retention, and may also create challenges for other managers in justifying the high salary expense. The data science manager must justify this expense by demonstrating the additional revenue and reduced costs generated by AI projects.

  Although there is a huge demand for experienced data scientists, training new data scientists takes time. Once they have experience, they may leave for a higher salary. Organizations need to realize that hiring an experienced data scientist will cost money, and it is up to the data science manager to discuss salary and training costs with upper management.

  Occasionally, data science managers, especially new ones, may find data scientists' pay exceeding their own and approach the level of a director or even a vice president. This often happens when there are one or two data scientists on a multi-person team and when the manager of an AI team is not seen as a data science manager but as a general technology manager. Many managers can develop resentment for the salary given to a data scientist or struggle with salary budgetary issues because of a data scientist's salary. In addition, the salary may be challenging to justify to departments like finance or human resources as they try to fit employees into career slots or compare salaries to other areas.

- **AI Adoption**: AI can be a disruptive technology, coupling current practices and processes with AI applications that drive decision-making and result in higher profits and lower costs. However, changing the traditional way of doing things can seem threatening to other business areas. Furthermore, some managers do not have the background or desire to understand how AI can be incorporated into their products and procedures or even why data-driven decisions are essential.

  Data science managers need to communicate the value of data-driven decision-making to upper management, other business managers, and stakeholders, demonstrating that AI will not replace workers or managers but rather enhance their effectiveness. Communicating the value of AI can be more difficult than communicating the value of other areas, such as finance, human resources, or operations, where their roles and expected contributions are more clearly defined.

To do this, data science managers need to understand the needs and priorities of other business areas, build business cases and prototypes that demonstrate what is possible with AI, and foster a culture where data-driven decisions are seen as superior to intuition-driven ones.

- **Data ethics and privacy**: Data scientists often work with sensitive customer data or internal operations data that is analyzed to make predictions and aid in decision-making. Managers need to be aware of legal, ethical, and privacy considerations when collecting, storing, and using data in their AI applications. They should communicate these policies, procedures, and laws to data scientists on the AI team and discuss issues with the data governance area to ensure that the organizational policies are followed.

The data science manager is often known as the "AI Manager" because the data science department contains many data scientists who develop AI applications. Throughout this book, we use these terms interchangeably. Still, the term "AI Manager" is gaining traction because of the growing awareness of AI in tools like ChatGPT, which have become a significant help to operations within many organizations.

AI adoption has been skyrocketing over the past few decades, but recent advancements have been universal and pervasive:

- The *New York Times* reports how generative AI is considered a significant threat to Google, so AI is being "woven throughout its products, from the search engine to email."[ii]

- *CNBC* reports how Facebook/Meta is putting AI throughout its entire product line, even noting how they are switching their applications from traditional CPUs (central processing unit, the "brain" of the computer) that are used in most computer programs to GPUs (graphical processing unit, the "brain" of many AI applications that are made by companies like Nvidia) for faster responses from new AI applications.[iii]

- *Forbes* reports how Microsoft plans to infuse AI and LLMs (large language models, the technology behind ChatGPT and Microsoft Copilot) into all its products.[iv]

- And just in case you thought that only the biggest companies are adopting AI, the *Small Business and Entrepreneurship Council* reports that 75% of small businesses utilize AI in their operations, and the small businesses that were surveyed report that AI helps with competitiveness (especially with larger firms), decision-making, customer acquisition, and improving product quality.[v]

AI is not going away and is challenging to implement and manage. Effective data science managers possess a unique set of skills and face distinct challenges in managing a data science department. It is important for all management within an organization to recognize the challenges and differences of a data science department and to provide their AI projects with the support and resources they need to succeed. The data science manager used to be the lone voice driving AI adoption, but lately, executives and upper management are making the call. It is up to the AI team and all managers to drive AI adoption, gather resources for AI projects, and justify AI development expenses.

This book is for all managers and individuals (not just data science managers) who want to understand how AI applications can fit within an organization. This book is *not* about learning how to write data science, machine learning, and AI applications. While AI application development knowledge is essential for data scientists, this book concentrates on managing that effort. More specifically, this book focuses on how managing AI development differs from managing other areas, and *not* programming, database, and mathematical techniques, which are beyond the scope of this book. (But don't worry – that book is next!)

Role of a Data Science Manager

Let's start by looking at the role of a Data Science Manager. The Project Management Institute (PMI) describes the difference between department management (which they call "program management") and project management:[vi]

- **Project Management** concentrates on creating a "deliverable." In AI terms, that deliverable will be an application that makes a prediction or series of related predictions using a statistical model and analysis.

- **Department Management** (the role of the data science manager, also called **Area Management** or **Program Management** by the PMI) focuses on coordinating many related projects and other activities to create benefits or value for the organization.

- **AI Applications** are computer applications that make predictions using statistical models that go beyond simple averages.

- **AI Departments** (also called **Data Science Departments)** develop one or more AI applications.

Project management and department management are vastly different. The data science manager must not view their job as solely a series of project management tasks. There are many more aspects to their job, such as strategic alignment of the AI area with organizational strategies, communication with upper management and other business areas, resource allocation, and cost containment.

As shown in Figure 1, each project has a project manager (PM), who can be a principal data scientist, a senior data scientist, or a business area product owner. Many data science managers are promoted from the PM position because they successfully manage projects, but some continue to operate as PMs despite being promoted to the department management role. This approach usually fails because it leads to micromanagement by the data science manager, who concentrates on technical work but ignores interdepartmental communication, corporate strategic goals, profitability, justification of projects, proper staffing, retention of existing talent, and acquisition of new talent.

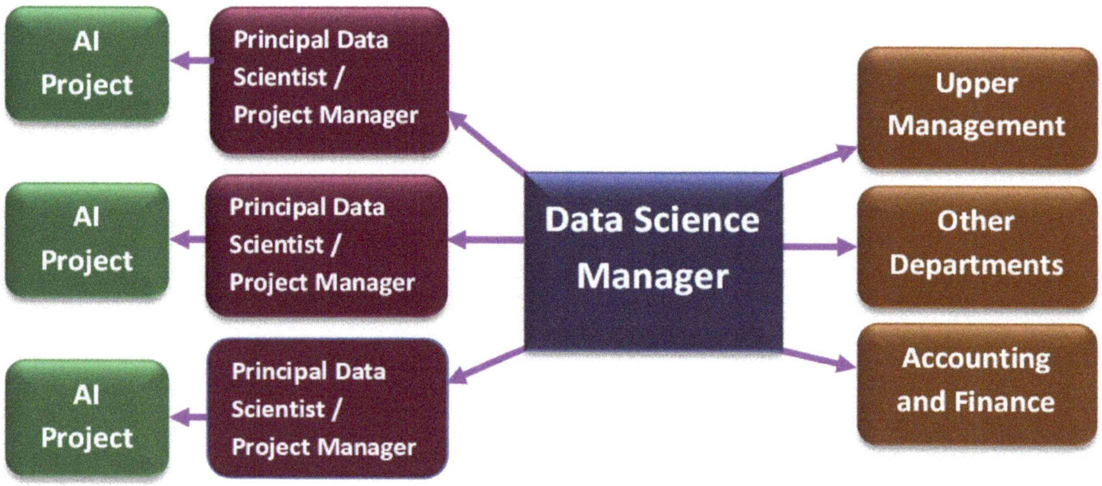

Figure 1– Data Science Manager's Position in a Project-Rich Environment

Another role of the data science manager is coordinating projects with business experts in other areas to determine what AI applications are needed to increase revenue, improve operations, and cut costs. All data scientists and/or PMs report to the data science manager about the progress, timeline, and blocks they are having. In other words, they do not report to a product owner or manager. Instead, they report directly to the data science manager so that the data science manager is informed of all projects and can coordinate with the other areas.

Notes from the Field:

I consider an AI manager to be the individual to whom the PMs report, but the exact management titles in your organization might differ. In smaller organizations, PMs may report to an area manager, a department head, a vice president, or a CIO. In larger organizations, PMs may report to managers, who then may report to senior managers, who then report to department heads, who report to executive department heads, who report to vice presidents, and so on. If you are at a higher managerial level, you are classified as upper management in Figure 1, and this chapter can inform you of the tasks of a data science manager.

The takeaways from this section and Figure 1 are:

- Let the PMs manage their projects.
    - The PMs should report to the data science manager, describing any project problems and proposed solutions. The PM should be able to resolve most issues before the data science manager steps in. Managerial resolutions may include providing more resources to the PM or setting more realistic sprint-level stories or due dates.
    - Micromanaging the PM's role is not viable for the data science manager. Since the data science department needs to deliver content to the rest of the organization, going from a single project to three or four projects is too much work to micromanage.
- Maintain discussions and communication with other department heads:
    - Project owners oversee the project from the end-user level, and department heads oversee that project owner.
    - The data science manager must inform other department heads of any issues. It is better if the data science manager communicates problems to upper management before the problems “bubble up” to the department head from the project owner.
    - The data science manager should be available for opportunities with other business areas, especially in departments that have already embraced AI solutions. Often, when departments already have an AI infrastructure, it is less costly to develop additional AI projects for that department.

  - Do not be afraid to use data scientists as resources in meetings with department heads. The data science manager needs to explain the direction that their department is heading along with answering questions about techniques, data, prediction accuracy, etc., that the data science manager or PM may be unable to answer.

- Maintain communication with the upper management.

  - Without upper management support, AI projects usually fail. If an AI application isn't coupled with changes to management procedures, it isn't very helpful. For example, if your application can accurately predict product demand and improve staffing, but no department uses your product, then the organization will not benefit.

  - Often, the data scientist is more aware of the benefits of better predictions within an AI application and can serve as a resource for the data science manager within meetings with upper management. A data scientist working with the data science manager may be key to selling a project's viability to upper management.

- Be ready to report to accounting about the costs and benefits:

  - Data scientists are an excellent resource for examining the range of costs and benefits of AI applications. Do not be afraid to use data scientists as a resource in these areas.

  - Be aware of the political environment. If you say an application can save the company millions of dollars, be prepared to back that up with some analysis (usually from a data scientist). Cost reduction often means reallocating resources from one department to another, which can be challenging to enact.

  - Predictions of revenue increases are usually more palatable to finance departments than cost reduction. This is because revenue increases usually don't involve cuts in any budget.

AI Management Process Differences

This book does not ignore traditional management techniques that can be used in data science departments, but concentrates on how AI development changes the management processes. However, the AI management process can differ significantly from other areas. Managers relying solely on education and experience from those other areas may be surprised at some AI challenges.

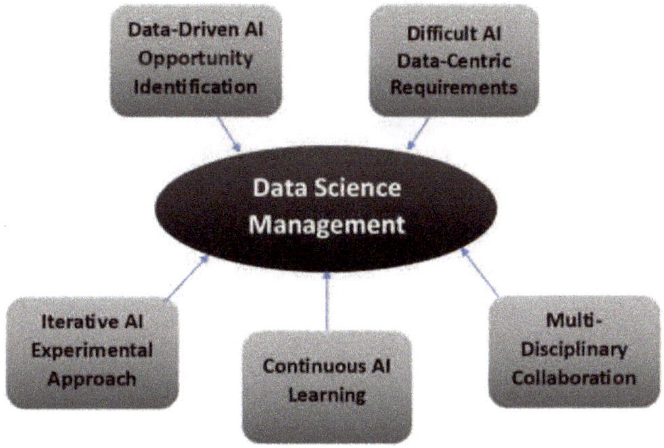

Figure 2-- Differences in the Data Science Management Process

Along with the additional challenges faced by data science managers, the managerial processes in the AI domain can differ significantly from those in other areas. Figure 2 shows some of the difficulties in AI management processes that are not found in many other managerial domains, or at least not to the same extent. The following describes the differences in the AI management process when compared to other areas:

- **Data-Driven Opportunity Identification:** Managers must look for opportunities where AI can help an organization. While adopting AI applications can be difficult for some business areas, other departments may look for ways to improve and might not realize how AI can help them set prices, predict demand, manage staffing, or manage a workforce. It is up to the manager to identify these opportunities where AI can help.

- **Difficult Data-Centric Requirements:** Managers must ensure that their data scientists can access accurate data. Inaccurate data occurs when data is entered incorrectly, missing data is allowed, or different data sources disagree on values like name, address, sales amount, etc. The AI team needs to work with this data, and the data scientists must determine "the source of truth" where one dataset is trusted above all others. Then data scientists must clean the data to identify entries that may be incorrect, decide whether to impute or delete missing data, and correct mathematical biases in the data that can affect predictions.

  Data should also be robust. It is not easy to perform AI applications with, say, two columns of data spanning over a few months. The more data that exists, the better the predictions. For instance, if a data scientist is examining demand for a product, there may be seasonal fluctuations that can only be caught over several years, annual trends that can be exposed, and specific dates such as holidays, major sporting events, or tax day that may affect demand for a product. It is not easy to make accurate predictions without multi-year and multi-attribute data.

That being said, AI applications make predictions. If a business area requires predictions to make better decisions, data science managers should not say that predictions are impossible but instead should rely on the data scientists on their team to make the best predictions possible with the data they have. Furthermore, the manager needs to communicate with the business area that prediction accuracy will be hampered by data quality or data scarcity. Often, the business area can help with guidance on rules or constraints that may make data analysis more accurate, or the business area can use AI predictions with the knowledge that predictions may improve as data quality and quantity increase.

The input of business domain experts is vital to the AI development process, especially in the face of data scarcity. For example, if you want to predict sales over the next year with thousands of geographic zones and hundreds of products, but you only have one year of data, an AI application can be developed with the help of domain experts. The application can be created to mimic an expert's decision in a domain, delivering millions of predictions within minutes or hours, rather than expecting an expert to go through millions of product/zone combinations. This would lead to more usable data and possibly better predictions.

- **Iterative Experimental Approach**: Data scientists take an iterative experimental approach to projects, using specific metrics and performance indicators (often called service levels) to evaluate the effectiveness of a project based on key performance indicators (KPIs). The data scientist iterates through different statistical models, different predictor variables (called "features"), various data preprocessing, or additional "guard rails" that force predictions to meet business constraints. This iteration results in AI project development efforts that are hard to schedule and require data scientists to meet the service level needs.

  Traditional management processes are often more straightforward: employees follow a process from start to finish and monitor that process. Most traditional areas also use performance metrics that are broadly applied (like saying that there should be a 5% increase in sales across all products), and these traditional metrics are often not as data-centric or closely tied to analytical models and predictions. AI applications tend to dive deeper, such as predicting different sales growth rates for each product in each geographic zone. These new methods require quality assurance checks by domain experts to ensure the predictions meet requirements.

  Also, AI predictions may work at first but fall below an acceptable accuracy level as new data and situations arise, causing the predictions to drift over time. This is not a failure of the application – just as decisions made 5 years ago might have been accurate back then but not so great now, an AI application can eventually lose predictability as client base, management, government regulations, and technologies change. The data science manager ensures that accuracy monitoring is in place to flag areas where data scientists can reexamine the model if the model's predictions fall below a service-level agreement with the business area.

Multi-Disciplinary Collaboration: Traditional management areas often work in "silos" where their work does not rely on expertise outside of their domain. However, AI application development usually requires collaboration across many areas, especially between business areas and the AI development team. AI predictions can have "guard rails" based on business rules. Business experts can review AI predictions to see if they make sense, then set service levels that require the data scientists on the AI team and other business areas to adjust and monitor the accuracy of these predictions/service levels. Business leaders might need to change decision-making processes as decisions become less intuition-based and more data-driven.

- **Continuous Learning:** Continuous learning is required for data scientists, and the manager must take time for this continuous learning. At the start of new projects, data scientists often research methods and techniques, some of which are new to them. It should not surprise the data science manager when a data scientist takes several weeks to learn a new technique that may or may not work well in a project, and the manager must make time available for this in their employee's continued growth since it will benefit the AI area in the long run.

  Contrast this with many traditional management areas, where projects are often well-defined, documented, and based on prior knowledge. Learning is still required in traditional management areas, but in AI areas, learning is often one of the biggest time consumers and is usually front-loaded on a project.

Traditional management techniques, such as scheduling, resource allocation, and evaluation, remain crucial to AI management. However, the unique need for data scientists to deliver predictions through data-centric analysis makes the data science manager's role different from other roles in challenging and interesting ways. Embracing these differences is essential to effectively manage AI initiatives and leverage the power of data to drive organizational success.

The Role of AI within an Organization

Data scientists on the AI team cannot operate in a vacuum where external input and support are ignored. Managers need to ensure that the AI team collaborates with business leaders, other technologists, and executives.

Business leaders can help identify key performance indicators (KPIs) to be maximized and establish minimum service levels for the business area, with monitoring to flag when an AI application no longer meets those needs. Every member of the AI team must be encouraged to continue training and to collaborate cross-functionally, as effective communication and frequent knowledge sharing ensure that AI initiatives align with the organization's strategic goals and operational needs. Data scientists can also benefit from the knowledge and insights of business experts, while business experts can leverage AI capabilities to drive data-driven decision-making and innovative solutions.

Data governance and data management can ensure that AI initiatives align with established policies and practices and establish clear guidelines for data access, sharing, and quality to ensure consistency and integrity across the organization. IT department support must ensure that AI projects are supported by the necessary infrastructure, software tools, cloud usage, and data storage capabilities. The software development and engineering teams can take AI predictions and deliver applications to business areas and product managers.

Perhaps most importantly, an AI team cannot function without executive sponsorship and support. The data science manager must ensure that AI initiatives have executive sponsorship and support from top-level management. Executive leaders and other managers should understand AI's potential, promote its adoption within the organization, and allocate the necessary resources to support AI projects. Executive leaders can cultivate a data-driven culture across an organization. They can encourage departments to embrace data-driven decision-making and to seek collaboration with the data science department when facing complex problems or opportunities that could benefit from data analysis and insights.

By understanding AI's role in an organization, managers can effectively configure their data science department with other departments in mind, fostering collaboration, leveraging expertise, and maximizing the value of AI across the organization.

What Makes a Great AI Department Manager?

It is a known and well-publicized fact that data scientists are hard to find, but great data science managers are so rare that they are often compared to unicorns[vii]. This is because they need at least a high-level understanding of the AI application development process and a reasonable understanding of the statistical model chosen to make predictions for each AI application. They must also manage and communicate with employees, other managers, and upper management. That is a hard-to-match skill set!

MIT Sloan Management Review describes how successfully managing data scientists who develop AI applications differs from other management. It "requires skills and philosophies that are different from those that arise in managing other groups of smart professionals." Managers involved in AI application adoption need to be aware of the potential organizational frictions and trade-offs that can crop up.[viii]

This section describes what makes a great data science manager and discusses the following:

- Understanding how AI applications will disrupt an organization.
- Take an interest in AI and understand, at least at a high level, how the predictions were derived and what they mean.
- Taking an interest in the organization's goals, interdepartmental communication, and communication with upper management.
- Having the ability to attract and retain data scientists.

This section also describes who does *not* necessarily make a great data science manager, at least without some additional skills and/or training.

> **Notes from the Field:**
>
> When you search the web for terms like "Great Managers," you end up with articles that tend to be very "fluffy," focusing on unverifiable opinions and few facts. Statements are made like "Great managers are change-centric," "Great managers have non-static thinking," or "Great data science managers are good communicators." While all of this may be true, these articles are often inconsistent, vague, and lack much usable content.
>
> You get the opposite when you search "Bad Managers." There are studies, statistics, and in-depth stories. The articles are relatively consistent, and many cite data-driven research. (It is, admittedly, a little depressing or shocking at times.)
>
> Data science managers might consider Googling "Bad Managers" and doing the opposite. The content may be more usable than trying to "develop an effervescent personality" or figuring out what it means to be "forward-thinking."

Reviewing Applicants for the AI Manager Position

In some cases, a manager moves from another department to the data science department but shows little interest in what AI and data science are or what they can deliver. Upper management needs to choose a data science manager applicant with one or more of the following characteristics:

- The applicant has experience as a successful data science manager in another organization or department.

- The applicant has managerial experience and is willing to improve data science skills while finding new AI applications to help the organization.
- The applicant is a data scientist and is willing to embrace the corporate mission and objectives of other departments. In other words, management can be complex, and if an applicant does not appreciate that skill set, then that applicant will probably not make a great data scientist manager.

Understanding AI Disruption

Just by reading this chapter, you have shown that you are a person who takes an interest in what a data scientist can do. Conversely, according to Gallup, 82% of managers are often disengaged in their departments. Management engagement is vital in AI projects because these projects are frequently considered "organizational disruptors," and the manager must often justify or convince other managers why such a disruption is desirable.

IBM classifies data science used to develop AI as a "disruptor," and they view this as a good thing. Disruption changes the "same old" practices often conducted within organizations.[ix] Specifically, AI projects are often designed to disrupt "management by intuition," which are organizational decisions driven by beliefs, opinions, or intuition rather than facts. Companies are starting to understand that data-driven decisions tend to outperform intuition-driven decisions. The role of a data scientist is to deliver data and analysis to make better decisions, thus disrupting existing non-profitable managerial and procedural practices in favor of more profitable outcomes. If an AI application does not change managerial, marketing, or structural practices, then that AI application is a failure or at least unnecessary, and potential profits to the organization will be lost.

Notes from the Field:

Chris DeRose at *Forbes* describes the term "HiPPO" (Highest Paid Person's Opinion), where decisions are not data-driven but opinion-based. DeRose describes HiPPOs as the opinions of "leaders who are so self-assured that they need neither other's ideas nor data to affirm the correctness of their instinctual beliefs. Relying on their experience and smarts, they are quick to shoot down contradictory positions and dismissive of underling's input." [x] It can be politically tricky or even career-ending to go against a HiPPO. However, since HiPPOs are opinions that might go against facts, HIPPOs present a risk to the organization's success and profitability.

An AI application can disrupt a HiPPO effect. If an AI application or data analysis of existing procedures is delivered to management, upper management must change business processes based on the added information. Upper managers who do not advocate change in the face of new data can hurt the company's success. Forbes Magazine describes how many organizations' CEOs are now saying how managing through HiPPOs hurts their organization, and their managers should deliver data-driven decisions rather than decisions derived from the HiPPO process.[xi]

The downside is that disruptors like data scientists tend to be expensive to hire and/or train and can hurt productivity in the short term as an organization struggles to shrug off old procedures in favor of new methods. Also, data scientists create "wonky power dynamics" where many managers are often younger than those who work with them. These managers are frequently paid less than the data scientists, which can cause friction in the organization. Also, many data scientists have spent much time in an academic environment that rewards speaking out, and this can cause bristling in a hierarchical business environment and further disruption.[xii]

The manager should be aware of (a) the potential disruptive effect of every AI project in the department, (b) the short-term and long-term costs of every project, and (c) the other managers who need to be aware of the potential disruption. To do this, the data science manager needs to take an active interest in cost reduction and revenue generation and an interest in the political environment where some management and business workforce might oppose data-driven and AI-based decisions.

Disruption is difficult in an organization. If a manager employs data scientists but takes a hands-off approach to management, then any disruptive AI applications will likely be ignored by management and unable to deliver on the changes available from data-driven analysis. Without a data science manager's and upper management's situational understanding, political mandates, and support, profitable AI projects can fail, or revenue-generating AI project adoption might not occur.

Department Managers and Taking an Interest in the AI Department

In their *State of the American Manager* report, Gallup states that the talent to become a great manager is scarce and finds two disturbing and depressing statistics:[xiii]

- 35% of managers are engaged in their work, meaning 65% are disengaged.
- According to Gallup, only 18% of managers have the technological "high" talent to succeed in their current managerial roles. This means that if a managerial role requires specific talent not found in other managerial roles, like managing AI project development, communicating the benefits of AI to other managers, or recognizing the benefits that AI projects can generate in your business area.

These statistics are especially problematic for data science managers and upper management. Other departments might be able to last a while on inertia if the manager is not engaged because existing procedures can keep a department moving forward. This is not the case with data science departments, where managers are expected to deliver innovative ideas, opportunities, new investigations, and new techniques, along with the understanding that AI projects can often disrupt existing policies and procedures, and this disruption needs to be communicated to the other team.

What Might *<u>Not</u>* Make a Great Data Scientist Department Manager

Upper management should understand what it takes to hire a great data science manager who can drive a team to deliver high-quality AI applications. Here are some caveats:

- **Great data scientists do not always make great data science managers.** The skill sets for data scientists are an excellent understanding of statistics and data and a reasonable understanding of programming and technological infrastructure.

  Data science managers have different skill sets and typically deal with people, policies, and goals within an organization. Great data scientists understand the department's deliverables and products but do not necessarily know how to delegate, motivate, and align company activities with organizational goals.

  Data science managers must be actively interested in what data science can do. They also need to become well-versed in corporate policies (and corporate politics), optimizing department procedures, motivating data scientists and developers, and providing upward mobility for the employees who work in the department. This is quite different from the data scientist's role of implementing the best statistical models to address problems and increase revenue within the organization. Without concentrating on managerial skill development and tasks, a data scientist turned manager might tend to micromanage projects (which drives everybody crazy) and ignore company policies, procedures, and the political landscape.

AI team management is a difficult job. Great data science managers need to take an active interest in management techniques and responsibilities, just as they must take an interest in data science. A data scientist can become a great manager if that data scientist takes an active interest in managerial techniques, communication skills, mission statements, corporate goals, and networking with other peer-level managers and upper management.

Notes from the Field:

There is a concept taught in business schools for decades called "The Peter Principle," first described by Laurence J. Peter, a management consultant who taught management at the University of Southern California. The Peter Principle states that people who do an excellent job get promoted until they reach a point where they do a lousy job, at which point the promotions stop. As a result, we have many managers in higher positions who do not perform as well as they did in their previous roles. (The exact quote is, "Every employee tends to rise to his level of incompetence.")[xiv]

The Peter Principle does not have to be an inevitable fate – it is a challenge that managers can conquer. While newly promoted data science managers often understand the nuances of data science, they also need to constantly hone their managerial and leadership skills while keeping up with the latest AI trends. Existing managers outside the data science department can dive into how AI can benefit their areas. It can be challenging work, but with some perseverance, managers can rise above the Peter Principle and succeed.

- **Great managers from other areas do not always make great data science managers.** Many managers believe that if you are a good manager in one department, you can effectively manage anywhere, even though this has been proven false repeatedly.[xv]

  Managers who move into a data science department from another area may find themselves out of their element and can fall into two categories:

  (a) Some managers who move to a data science department believe that anyone with a spreadsheet could be a data scientist or that no special education or skills are needed. These managers typically think a data scientist is replaceable and end up hiring cheaper, undertrained, and underqualified data scientists, which leads to AI project failure.

  This is especially bad because it creates a feedback loop reinforcing an incorrect idea. A manager thinks that data scientists are not that valuable, so they do not invest in hiring or training good data scientists. Then AI projects fail, reinforcing the belief that data scientists are not valuable. This is known as a "success to the successful bias", where funded technologies succeed and unfunded operations fail, giving managers a bias that the funding decisions are correct.[xvi]

(b) Some managers who move to a data science department have no concept of the role of a data scientist or how to utilize data science in their AI applications. This is initially harmless because data scientists can help inform new managers about existing projects and techniques, but those managers must eventually delve into data science.

Managers who do not clearly understand the role of data science often think of data scientists as data specialists or programmers. As a result, data scientists are assigned tasks like report generation, database manipulation, or project maintenance that have little or nothing to do with AI.

A lack of understanding of AI causes managers to miss opportunities. It often leads to a "revolving door" as data scientists leave for other departments and companies that better understand their work.

Managers who transfer into a data science department need to quickly develop an understanding of data science, continually identify opportunities to advance the organization's goals with data science, and understand what each AI project delivers. It is a lot to take in, and again, being a data science manager is not an easy job.

- **Great AI project managers do not always make great data science department managers.** There is a natural progression where successful AI PMs are promoted to department managers. The main challenge faced by these individuals is that they treat department management as a series of project management tasks and ignore other managerial tasks such as communication with other managers and upper management, aligning the data science department goals to the corporate strategy, budgeting, AI advocacy, using AI competitive advantage or competitive parity, corporate policies and procedures compliance, and finding AI opportunities in other business areas. Furthermore, focusing solely on AI projects can lead to micromanagement, making it difficult for PMs to advance their projects without second-guessing and changing direction.

  Despite this, a PM-to-department manager progression is natural. As an area or department manager, the ex-PM must embrace a new set of tasks and develop new skills and knowledge. A data science manager's task is challenging, and the manager should let the existing PMs continue their PM-level work while developing the skills and implementing the procedures needed to be a successful data science manager.

Concluding Thoughts on AI Management

The takeaway from this chapter and the entire book is that AI management differs significantly from management in other areas or departments.

The role of a data science manager is both challenging and exhilarating. Good data science managers are essential to organizations because of the value they bring through a unique blend of skills, including data science expertise, managerial abilities, business knowledge, strategic vision, and leadership prowess. The interplay of these skills makes data science managers indispensable in harnessing the power of AI and moving the organization toward data-driven success.

Managing an AI team or development effort is interesting, challenging, and quite different from management in other areas. This book is designed to guide managers through AI management, which involves applying managerial processes and techniques to a data science department and demonstrating how it differs from traditional management.

---

[i] Gil Press. Jun 14, 2022. "A Booming Market for AI Skills, With Salaries Topping $300,000." *Forbes*, available at https://www.forbes.com/sites/gilpress/2022/06/14/a-booming-market-for-ai-skills-with-salaries-topping-300000/?sh=c5925ed23d6a.

[ii] Nico Grant. May 2023. "Google Builds on Tech's Latest Craze with Its Own AI Products." *The New York Times*, available at https://www.nytimes.com/2023/05/10/technology/google-ai-products.html.

[iii] Jonathan Vanian. March 2024. "Meta is building a giant AI model to power its 'entire video ecosystem,' exec says." *CNBC*, available at https://www.cnbc.com/2024/03/06/facebook-working-on-single-ai-model-to-power-all-video-recommendations.html.

[iv] Bernard Marr. Mar 2023. "Microsft's Plan to Infuse AI and ChatGPT into Everything." *Forbes*, available at https://www.forbes.com/sites/bernardmarr/2023/03/06/microsofts-plan-to-infuse-ai-and-chatgpt-into-everything/?sh=cecde0753fcc.

[v] TechnoMetrica. Oct 2023. "Small Business AI Adoption Survey: October 2023." *Small Business and Entrepreneurship Council*, available at https://sbecouncil.org/wp-content/uploads/2023/10/SBE-Small-Business-AI-Survey-Oct-2023-FINAL.pdf.

[vi] Patrick Weaver. Feb. 24, 2010. "Understanding programs and projects--oh, there's a difference!" *PMI® Global Congress 2010: Project Management Institute*, available at https://www.pmi.org/learning/library/understanding-difference-programs-versus-projects-6896.

[vii] Ken Jee. Aug 27, 2019. "Why is it so Hard to Find Great Data Science Managers?" *Towards data science*, available at https://towardsdatascience.com/why-is-it-so-hard-to-find-great-data-science-managers-6fc8aac62f6e.

[viii] Roger M. Stein. August 2015. "Why Managing Data Scientists Is Different." *MIT Sloan Management Review*, available at https://sloanreview.mit.edu/article/why-managing-data-scientists-is-different/.

[ix] Will Markow, Soumya Braganza, Bledi Taska, Debbie Hughes, Steven Miller. 2017. "The Quant Crunch: How the demand for data science skills is disrupting the job market." *IBM Downloads – Burning Glass Technologies, BHEF, and IBM*, available at https://www.bhef.com/sites/default/files/bhef_2017_quant_crunch.pdf.

[x] Chris DeRose. Apr 15, 2013. "What Happens When a 'HiPPO' Runs Your Company." *Forbes Magazine*. https://www.forbes.com/sites/derosetichy/2013/04/15/what-happens-when-a-hippo-runs-your-company/#23c323aa40cf.

[xi] Bernard Marr. Oct 26, 2017. "Data-Driven Decision Making: Beware of the HIPPO Effect!" *Forbes Magazine*. https://www.forbes.com/sites/bernardmarr/2017/10/26/data-driven-decision-making-beware-of-the-hippo-effect/#4d1cb6db80f9.

[xii] Ken Jee. Aug 27, 2019. "Why is it so Hard to Find Great Data Science Managers?" *Towards data science*, available at https://towardsdatascience.com/why-is-it-so-hard-to-find-great-data-science-managers-6fc8aac62f6e.

[xiii] Gallup. Dec 2017. "The State of the American Manager." *Gallup*, available at https://www.gallup.com/services/182138/state-american-manager.aspx.

[xiv] Laurence J. Peter and Raymond Hull. 1969. *The Peter Principle.* Morrow.

[xv] Bernard Marr. October 26, 2017. "Data-Driven Decision Making: Beware of the HIPPO Effect!" *Forbes Magazine*, available at https://www.forbes.com/sites/bernardmarr/2017/10/26/data-driven-decision-making-beware-of-the-hippo-effect/#4d1cb6db80f9.

[xvi] NiNa Dhirasasna, Susanne Becken, and Oz Sahin. March 2020. "A systems approach to examining the drivers and barriers of renewable energy technology adoption in the hotel sector in Queensland, Australia." *Journal of Hospitality and Tourism Management* 42, pp. 153-172, available at https://www.sciencedirect.com/science/article/pii/S1447677019300105?casa_token=mz64NhKFbnEAAAAA:Q295geGxGZJ5PV1r6n8Bvr_wJKSF70hf-z7uTC_cQcTN1lUNrBO6FNPLh0ezJWadcgsZ8YvFIBQ.

Chapter 2: Demystifying AI

There is much confusion in the marketplace about artificial intelligence (AI) and data science – what they are and how they relate to each other. This ambiguity can leave managers unsure of the role of data scientists and impede communication between business units, such as marketing, finance, and AI departments. This chapter addresses this confusion, describing how AI terms fit together and their differences. It also clarifies the distinctions, explaining precisely what AI is and what it is not.

AI can seem complex, but this chapter makes it clear. We will explore AI's transformative possibilities and empower you to define its potential benefits for your field. Whether you are a professional, author, educator, or just someone who wants to understand this powerful technology, this chapter provides the essential skills for success.

While AI and data science can seem daunting, this chapter makes them clear and accessible for *every* manager. No technical expertise is required. You will gain the knowledge to make informed decisions about integrating these technologies into your projects without getting bogged down in complex math, coding, or data practices. We focus on giving you a practical understanding of AI and its potential to benefit your organization.

What is this chapter trying to do and why?

This chapter is needed because it sheds light on many AI concepts and terms that often confuse managers. The target markets for this chapter are managers. Still, this chapter can benefit data specialists, developers, and anyone curious about what AI is, what it is not, and what it does. Here are some of the questions that will be answered in this chapter:

- Everyone is talking about AI, ML, data science, GenAI (like ChatGPT), statistical models, etc., but what do these terms mean?
- What benefits are there when you add AI to your applications?
- At a high level, what are the benefits of machine learning?

The main thrust of this chapter is that it is easier to manage machine learning domains and projects if the manager understands a little bit about AI first.

Term Warfare: AI, ML, Deep Learning & Data Science

There are many terms used by data scientists that are confusing to those outside the industry precisely because:

(a) The terms often involve a moderate level of mathematical understanding.

(b) The terms often overlap and are used interchangeably in some situations.

(c) The definitions of the terms are often handled poorly in the press and online, specifically because of their complexity.

Figure 3 breaks down AI into components. This section will discuss each of these terms at a high level.

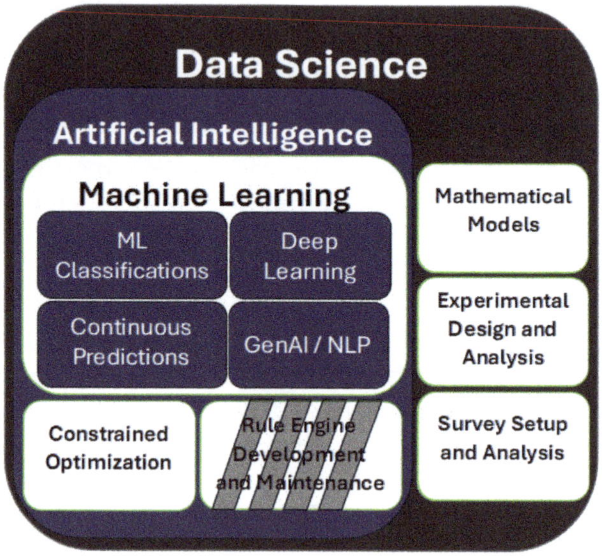

Figure 3 – Components of Artificial Intelligence

> **Note:** The output from a data science statistical model – predictions, categorizations, explanations, and inferences – is often grouped together and called "predictions" when discussing data science.

Data science *is the act of applying appropriate mathematical models to data to make predictions, categorizations, explanations, or inferences.*

Data science involves AI / ML (Machine Learning), where statistics examine large amounts of past data to predict future or unknown data. However, a smaller portion of data science also involves analysis outside of big data analysis. Data science also includes techniques like data cleaning, descriptive analytics, post-ML calculations (optimal staffing after demand predictions, the best route in a car, best configuration, etc.), and small data (survey setup and analysis, experimental design, A/B testing). Finally, data scientists employ constrained optimization techniques like linear programming to optimize a problem – the best route in a car, the best way to schedule employees, and the best inventory deployment.

I almost want to add "full stop" after these definitions. There exists scope creep of the "AI," "machine learning," and "data science" terms in the press, in marketing literature, and in consultant explanations where someone takes an existing program or a common traditional programming technique and calls it "AI" or "software intelligence." AI professionals should step up to fight against the watering down of the "AI" terms simply for self-preservation – if the "data scientist" and "AI" terms get used to identify people with little knowledge or skill or products that use outdated techniques, then not only does that hurt companies that become disappointed and disillusioned when they expect cutting-edge predictions, but it becomes difficult for professionals in the industry to justify why their advanced skills and knowledge should translate into good positions and good pay. For managers, an incorrect perception of data science and AI can make it difficult for other business areas and executives to see its value.

This book concentrates on managing AI applications within an organization. The terminology that is typically used is that a data science manager manages the AI applications. However, the tasks of a data scientist go beyond AI to include experiments, survey analysis, and mathematical models that are often required after the AI predictions are made.

Artificial intelligence (AI) *refers to the design of a computer application that performs tasks that mimic or outperform human intelligence and problem-solving.*

I like to think of AI as programs that give the same results that a human expert would if that human had all the time, mathematical skills, and knowledge. For example, if an application predicts future sales in a minute, that prediction would be the same as the manager's prediction if that manager had a Ph. D. in statistical analysis and years to analyze the data. As such, many consider the job of a data scientist to develop and implement AI applications.

AI is often misunderstood in the popular press as machines develop consciousness and even turn against humanity to take over the world. However, that simply cannot happen within the current track of technological development. For now, we are in more danger of a software bug or a human hacker than true software intelligence. Instead, AI is simply software that provides information that managers can use, like the suggested price of a hotel room, projected demand for a product, or how customer grouping should be viewed, among other tasks.

Data science and AI are often considered to be the same thing, but there is a slight difference. AI exists within computer software and can mimic human decisions, while data science focuses on extracting valuable insights and knowledge from a statistical or mathematical analysis of data to drive informed decision-making. AI often utilizes techniques from data science, such as machine learning or constrained optimization, to achieve its goals. My rule of thumb is that AI is what is put into applications, and data science is the knowledge and science used to develop that AI.

Machine learning *is a subset of AI that incorporates statistical models to constantly recalculate and adjust its parameters over time as new data becomes available.*

ML uses statistical models and data to make predictions. Furthermore, those predictions go beyond (a) arithmetic means / straight averages ("What's probably going to happen is what usually happens.") and (b) what are called simple "random walks" ("What's happened yesterday is what's going to happen today, more or less."). If straight averages or random walks are the best predictors, then you do not need a data scientist to develop an ML model.

There is much confusion about ML. Discussions often focus on how "algorithms learn from data" or "ML algorithms make decisions." Some people think these explanations are to make ML more accessible. Others (like me) think these explanations create more confusion than they solve because algorithms cannot actually learn or make decisions. Instead, the "learning" part of "machine learning" refers to the ability of algorithms to adjust to new situations using a statistical analysis mathematical model using new data. In traditional programming, humans write explicit instructions for a computer to follow, dictating how it should process input data to produce output. However, instead of answers or analyses being explicitly programmed in traditional applications, in machine learning, algorithms are trained with data to learn patterns, relationships, and rules, which they use to make predictions or decisions.

ML is a form of **predictive analytics** in which statistical models predict future events or behaviors. Every statistical model has parameters, like starting points and ending points, how fast or slow growth occurs, which people are grouped together, etc. Static statistical models of the past set parameters once and then keep the same parameters, sometimes for years. ML predictive analytics returns either a **regression**, where past trends and correlations are extended to new data, or **classification**, where people, places, or things are placed into distinct categories.

ML classifications *are ML statistical models that predict membership in groups or categories, such as predicting which transactions are fraudulent, which customers are dissatisfied, or which television networks have viewers that match a given demographic.*

Machine learning classification uses algorithms to categorize data into groups or classes based on their characteristics. Classifications are used to group customers, employees, products, geographic zones, and other entities based on attributes like type, color, size, or popularity.

ML classifications can be used to detect fraudulent transactions, segment customers for personalization, predict machine breakdowns, diagnose disease, and much more. This categorization enables organizations to streamline inventory management, optimize stocking levels, and tailor marketing strategies to specific product categories, enhancing operational efficiency and increasing revenue.

Continuous predictions *are ML statistical models that use past observations to predict future trends, analyze explanatory variables, or make future recommendations.*

Unlike classification tasks, which aim to assign an input into predefined categories, continuous prediction modeling seeks to estimate a value. This approach is often used in scenarios where the outcome is not a category but a numeric range, such as predicting house prices, stock prices, or temperature forecasts. Techniques like linear regression, lasso regression, support vector regression, and Gaussian processes are commonly employed in continuous prediction modeling to analyze relationships between variables and to make numerical predictions.

Most managers understand the benefits of continuous predictions in time series analysis, and ML time series analysis is one of the most often used ML techniques. Time series analysis is a powerful tool for managers seeking to extract valuable insights from temporal data to drive informed decision-making and strategic planning within their organizations. ML algorithms uncover hidden patterns, trends, and correlations within time-based data to predict future trends and outcomes. Time series analysis delivers a deeper understanding of past trends and future fluctuations. Time series analysis facilitates data-driven decisions and optimizes resource allocation to gain a competitive edge by predicting future patterns.

Continuous prediction modeling is indispensable in time series analysis, where accurate numerical predictions drive strategic decision-making and optimize business processes. These models are utilized for demand forecasts, optimizing inventory levels, improving production planning, optimizing production schedules, allocating resources effectively, and streamlining supply chain operations. Continuous prediction models are used to reduce costs, increase revenue, and improve resource utilization. Internally, these models also enable managers to identify high-value customer segments, personalize marketing campaigns, and enhance customer relationship management, driving sales growth.

Natural Language Processing (NLP) *is an ML technique that enables applications to interpret and generate language in a meaningful and helpful way to humans.*

NLP powers virtual assistants like Siri and Alexa, chatbots that provide customer support, and language translation services. NLP makes interactions between humans and machines more intuitive and seamless and less like programming, filling in textboxes, or clicking checkboxes to get results from an application.

At its core, NLP involves training applications to detect the nuances of language. This includes everything from recognizing speech patterns and understanding the meaning behind words and sentences to deciphering the intent behind a user's query. NLP algorithms train using vast amounts of text data to recognize the rules and patterns of a language. NLP can analyze sentiment or feelings in social media posts, extract information from documents, and generate human-like text. By mastering NLP, AI applications can communicate with humans in natural and conversational ways, opening endless possibilities for design, innovation, and collaboration.

Generative AI or **GenAI** *refers to a class of artificial intelligence systems that can create new data based on patterns learned from a given dataset, such as images, text, or sounds.*

In the popular press, AI is often synonymous with GenAI for generating content based on existing content or a **Large Language Model** (**LLM**), a GenAI geared explicitly toward analyzing and responding to text. Products like ChatGPT, Google Gemini, Microsoft Copilot, and OpenAI answer questions based on a statistical analysis of millions of lines of text. However, as shown in Figure 3, AI goes far beyond GenAI.

The popular press suggests that GenAI is relatively new, but rather, GenAI consists of two NLP sets of processes that have been in use for years. The first set of NLP processes identifies what type of question is being asked using techniques like tokenization, context analysis, and importance weighting of words and phrases. The second set of NLP processes involves retrieving answers from a database, predicting the most likely answer, and providing a response using text generation techniques.

For a simple example, if I ask “ChatGPT, what is 1+3?”, ChatGPT would use NLP to recognize that this prompt is a math question, retrieve an addition template from their learning “{a}+{b}={a+b}” and use that template to respond “**1 + 3 = 4**”. Generating the question types and deriving the answer templates is a huge, lengthy process, but it is not new. Instead, it is an extension of existing NLP processes.

Deep learning *is a type of machine learning where, rather than a single regression, results from multiple regressions are combined to make predictions.*

Most statistical models involve a single model where input data is analyzed and predictions are generated. Deep learning uses many different regression and classification models to make predictions. Using multiple models usually generates better predictions, but developing, testing, and executing takes quite a while.

Data scientists deploy **neural networks** to deliver all the regressions used in deep learning. Neural networks were initially designed to mimic human thought but instead quickly became a high-end statistical tool where thousands of statistical calculations are iterated. With deep learning, the neural network calculations are done through a series of regressions and layers, which is why they are called “deep.” They take a long time to run but often outperform other ML models in both classification and continuous prediction. Because deep learning methods can outperform other models but take so long to make predictions, high levels of data science knowledge and computing costs are often required for neural network setup. There is a saying among data scientists that goes, "Never use deep learning unless you have to, and you always have to."

Rule Engines *are software, databases, and applications that consist of rules that try to mimic the decision process that an expert would use when arriving at a decision.*

Before ML was widely available, AI was synonymous with rule engine development, where rules are put into a program that can mimic an expert's actions. For example, before ML, if a developer needed a computer program that could perform accounting services at a CPA (Certified Public Accountant) level, that developer would ask many CPAs thousands of questions and follow-up questions so that an accounting answer given by a CPA would be the same as an accounting answer given by the program.

There are two problems with rule-based AI. The first is that the rules can only approach human intelligence and not surpass it. If data changes or there are relationships in the data unknown to the human expert, trying to mimic human thought will not detect these situations. Also, with data changes, an expert might be able to generalize a solution while a rule engine would continue with the previous rules until updates could be added.

The second problem with rule-based AI is that those rules are often incomplete, and rule engines quickly become unwieldy and unmaintainable because rule engines are static and resist change. In our CPA example, if new tax laws are passed, developers would have to program new rules based on CPA knowledge that are impacted by the new law. The developer would first have to detect that new rules exist, and then the developer would have to go through the thousands of rules to insert new rules in the proper place. If the rule is incorrect or inserted in the wrong place, it could destroy the integrity of the new rule and the whole tree-based rule engine.

While rule engines still exist, new rule engine products are not often deployed, which is why they are crossed out in Figure 3. However, as with most legacy software, many rule engines are still in play, and especially with limited data, new rule engines are still deployed. Still, when large amounts of data are available to the data scientist, AI has evolved past rule engines to employ high-level statistics to predict the future and make decisions rather than a series of static and hard-to-maintain rules.

Other Definitions that Touch on AI

There are other terms that crop up in AI discussions that are not in Figure 3 and are not AI *per se* but rather are areas that make AI development possible.

Data Governance *refers to policies and procedures that ensure data is both secure and accurate.*

Data governance is a set of policies, procedures, and controls that ensure that data is accurate over time and only available to those who need the data to provide a business service to the organization. Data governance also ensures that laws from various states and nations are followed. Since AI applications often require much data to train an AI application, the AI team needs to work closely with the data governance team to ensure that data is correct, secure, legal, and ethical.

Data Infrastructure *is the hardware and software systems that support data storage, retrieval, processing, and analysis.*

AI applications often require considerable amounts of data, so data scientists and AI managers will also need to have some understanding of data infrastructure. Data infrastructure encompasses a range of technologies and components, including databases, data warehouses, data lakes, data pipelines, and data processing and analysis tools. It also includes the physical infrastructure, such as computers and servers, storage devices, and networks that enable data flow between different systems and applications.

Big Data *refers to large amounts of structured and unstructured data collected from multiple sources.*

Big data is often misunderstood by management and even by some data scientists. The difference between large amounts of data (such as databases of stock market data) and big data is that, often, large amounts of data are **structured data**, meaning that they fit nicely into a database or Excel spreadsheet. By contrast, big data is data that can include both structured and **unstructured data**. Unstructured data is data in free-form text, comments, voice recordings, pictures, music, video, or categorical choices (like the color of a car or whether a transaction is fraudulent). Many AI techniques can be used to analyze unstructured data.

An AI Application Example – Used Car Sales

AI uses mathematical and statistical models to examine data and make predictions that go beyond extending a simple average. This is best explained by an example.

Say that you are the manager of a used car lot. The top chart in Figure 4 shows how daily sales jump all over the place. Simply assuming that an average of 97 cars will always be sold will cause drastic overstaffing (where you overspend on salary expenses) on some days and drastic understaffing (where you lose customers) on other days. You bring in a data scientist to help:

- The data scientist develops an AI mathematical model that does a relatively good job of predicting your car sales, as shown in the bottom chart in Figure 4.

- The AI predictions should be close, but AI statistical models will never be exact because statistical models measure general trends and always include some error in each prediction.

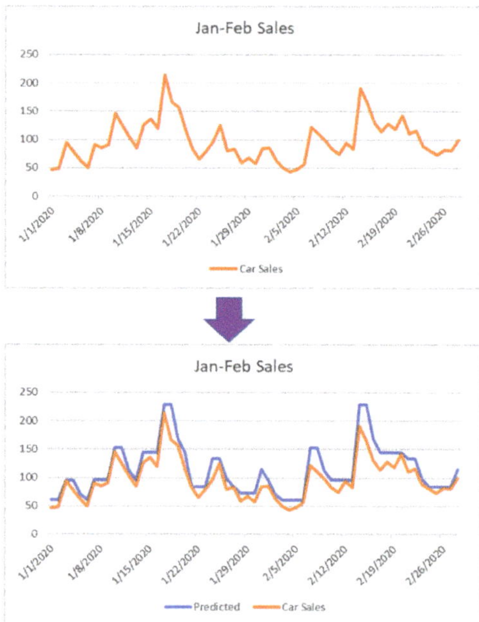

Figure 4 -- Using Data Science to Predict Sales

- Looking at other data, the data scientist illustrates how the statistical model changes, so the model you use today will differ in a few months. The model will be able to learn, adjust, and change to new data and new information over time. What works today will not work tomorrow, and the model should adapt to the added information. (This learning is integral to AI and is the whole concept of machine learning.)

Predictions of this sort are typically how a data scientist is deployed. The data scientist develops mathematical models that perform better forecasts than a manager can make without an AI application. These improved predictions allow management to help an organization identify when cost reduction or revenue generation justifies hiring a data scientist. Even with a small car lot, as shown in this example, the benefits of increased sales and reduced expenses would justify hiring a data scientist. Imagine the benefits a mid-size or Fortune-level company could achieve by optimizing competitive, logistic, or marketing analysis using AI.

What AI Is *Not*

As mentioned earlier, popular terms like "AI" experience a type of "scope creep," where a term begins with a solid meaning, but resume builders, consultants, and managers are pressured to claim that "what I do is data science," or "my intelligent software application" or "my product uses AI," thereby weakening the meaning of the terms.

When defining a term like "AI," it is vital to discuss the limits of the term. We have all heard statements like "I'm good at spreadsheets, so I'm kind of a data scientist." or "I would be a great data scientist. I already know about averages and standard deviations." or "I can do calculus, so of course I'm a data scientist." Statements like this not only hurt the AI industry by confusing organizational leaders about what data science can do, but organizations who try to bring in a data scientist often end up hiring the wrong person for the job.

The incorrect bloating of the "AI" term is becoming increasingly prevalent, where many people are attracted to AI because of better pay and claim to be data scientists because of good math or programming skills. But while it is essential to understand what data science can deliver inside AI applications, it is also important to understand what AI and data science are not:

- **Data science is *not* calculus** – Calculus is an essential branch of mathematics that deals with curves, with integrals being the area under a curve and derivatives being the slope of a curve at a point on the curve. By contrast, while statistical models used in AI also involve nonlinear mathematics, like curves, these models often transform those curves into straight lines or place complex calculus inside their Python libraries.

> **Note:** My mathematical-centric editors pointed out that my definitions of calculus, integrals, derivatives, etc., are woefully simplified. I agree, but an in-depth discussion of calculus is beyond the scope of this book. Interested readers can develop calculus knowledge with classes, online tutorials, or books designed for self-teaching.[i]

Data scientists often know calculus at some level, which is good. However, existing coding libraries and routines can often handle any required calculus, and data scientists can often function with limited knowledge of calculus. There are exceptions to this, including (but not limited to):

- Some topics, like accelerated growth or decline, are often expressed in exponential form, and the data scientist often must be ready to address these topics and transform predictions to and from slope-intercept form.

- Data scientists need to understand the concept of a "differentiable function" (A function that returns only one output value for any given input. The data scientist must work with the business experts to address situations where the same input can lead to multiple outputs.

- Probability distributions, like a "bell curve," are nonlinear. While routines and software exist to reduce the calculus out of any distribution calculations, occasionally newer distributions or adaptations of existing distributions will require an understanding of the integral area underneath the distribution or the expected shape of the graph created by plotting the rate of change of the initial distribution.

- Data scientists often select from a wide variety of existing mathematical models to perform their analysis. However, deriving a new AI statistical model often involves calculus that hopefully gets reduced out of a model. If not, the calculus routines need to be programmed into the application containing the model so others can call it without diving into the calculus behind the function.

The takeaway is that it is good for a data scientist to be able to deal with calculus if needed, but knowing calculus does not make you a data scientist, and many good data scientists are very weak in calculus.

- **An engineer (or mathematician or natural scientist) is *not* necessarily a data scientist** – Many models used by engineers are not statistical in nature, and mathematicians and scientists are often concerned with mathematical proofs that focus more on theoretical explanations for physical phenomena instead of analysis of large amounts of empirically collected data.

Force vectors, equilibrium, flow parameters, electrical resistance, etc., are important for engineering and mathematical models used in natural sciences like physics. But while a mathematician might know some complex mathematical models that keep bridges standing or send a rocket to the moon, if a mathematician has no experience or training in cleaning, manipulating, or processing large amounts of data, then that mathematician is not a data scientist.

A deep understanding of complex mathematics is always good, but a data scientist must be aware of numerous statistical models that can be employed for predictions, their strengths and weaknesses, and how to best deploy them instead of simply having the capability to derive mathematical proofs or perform complex calculations.

- **Data analysts, programmers, and software engineers are *not* necessarily data scientists** – Programmers and software engineers are essential in helping to turn data scientists' mathematical models into applications that employ filters, charts, sorting, aggregation, and graphs to help decision-makers use the predictions from the models. The term in the industry for this type of programmer is often **data analyst** or **data developer**, and they are necessary for AI application success, with the data scientist working in conjunction with the data analyst.

  For a programmer to be a data scientist, that programmer must be able to choose which statistical models are best to drive predictions in each situation and how to alter or adapt those models to fit the organization's needs best. This requires a higher level of mathematical knowledge than is typically required of a programmer.

  That being said, data scientists are encouraged or even required to be well-versed in programming, especially Python. If a data scientist cannot program their statistical analysis, then that data scientist will usually fail to deliver predictions and applications that can be used in an organization. Furthermore, data analysts often move into the data science realm after being exposed to many data science models.

- **A data scientist is *not* a database administrator or data specialist** – Data scientists deal with data but often have no idea how best to set up a database, database security and governance, PII rules that need to be enforced, etc. Data specialists are responsible for the data but often have little understanding of mathematical models that use the data in making predictions and decisions.

  Data scientists are encouraged to be well versed in database languages such as SQL to "slice and dice" data from a database to develop a statistical model. Furthermore, data scientists are often called upon to provide data segments to managers and users. Finally, data scientists are expected to work with data governance and data engineers to ensure accurate access to data that complies with an organization's policies and procedures. However, data specialists, data governors, and database administrators have other essential tasks that are different from those required of a data scientist.

- **A data scientist is *not* a manager –** Data scientists develop statistical models to drive an application and, therefore, often assume an unofficial leadership role to advise DBAs, programmers, managers, and clients on what an application can deliver and how that delivery should be accomplished. Managers are often called upon to justify or champion cost-cutting or revenue-generating AI applications suggested by the data scientist, to aid in team or project management, and to motivate team members, including the data scientist.

  There are two exceptions:

  - Principal or senior data scientists often manage or at least mentor several mid-level or entry-level data scientists and are often required to interact with upper management or other management areas.

  - Data scientists, like almost any other professional, can and should be considered for promotion to the AI manager role if they wish to pursue a managerial career.

  However, the skill set of a data science manager is vastly different from that of a data scientist. The tasks required of data science managers are usually centered around coordinating the data scientists' efforts with the rest of the organization, and data scientists who find themselves in a managerial role often need additional training in managerial techniques.

  Data scientists who are promoted to managerial roles will not only need to embrace managerial skills and techniques but also will usually need to delegate data science tasks to other data scientists on the team. Knowledge of data science can be a significant help in managing a data science department, but managers usually do not have the time to be data scientists, and data scientists who become managers often have trouble embracing their new managerial role and leaving the in-depth statistical analysis behind.

- **Data scientists can use big data to solve who, what, when, where, and how, but usually *not* why –** Analysis of big data allows data scientists to predict future actions more accurately, but big data usually cannot determine the motivation for those actions. To answer why an action occurred, you often need to leave big data behind and conduct a survey, an experiment, or ask the subject matter experts. There are elegant, developed statistical models that deal with experimental and survey setup and analysis, and while proper analysis of survey and experiment data is data science, the data that comes from surveys and experiments is often less than one thousand records and is not considered big data. Also, surveys and experiments are usually run once and are not considered machine learning.

AI applications concentrate on what has occurred or what is predicted but not why something will occur. Knowing why something happens allows management to generalize statistical models to other areas where people have similar motivations. Such knowledge also provides a guide for data scientists to seek out appropriate data for new projects.

For instance, say there was a stock price drop, and no one knows why. The steps that the data scientist might take to investigate why this event occurred would be:

1. The data scientist sets up a "small data" survey of 1000 institutional investors.

2. The data scientist analyzes the survey using typical (or new) survey models (including but not limited to factor analysis, principal component analysis, partial least squares, structural equation modeling, etc.)

3. The results of this survey indicate that the stock sell-off happened because the chairperson of the National Federal Reserve Bank (the Fed) made a statement that scared institutional investors.

4. The data scientist would then start automatically gathering and parsing statements from the Fed using NLP processes.

5. The data scientist would then add the Fed statement data as input to the existing statistical model used for stock price prediction to make better predictions.

Note that data scientists statistically analyze any data (not just big data) to make predictions. While big data exists in greater quantities than in the past, data scientists must also be able to adapt to statistical analysis of smaller data sets, like surveys or lab experiments.

Why Is AI So Hot Right Now?

The term "AI" and AI techniques have been around for quite some time, from movies to software applications. Businesses have often used statistical models to forecast stock prices or product demand, governments often use statistical models to predict inflation or disease vectors, and academics use statistical models to show relationships between data elements for their research and publications.

Recently, however, the AI field has grown at a fantastic rate. Organizational AI spending is expected to double to more than $300 billion by 2026, and the demand for data scientists has outstripped the supply. This section describes some reasons for this incredible growth.

New Advances in Generative AI – ChatGPT

GenAI is a type of AI that generates new content, like ChatGPT. GenAI has been a hot topic of interest lately. Data scientists can use GenAI to perform simple tasks, like setting up a forecasting model or developing a time series chart with three sequences. GenAI can be a huge timesaver and allow data scientists to generate basic skeleton code, saving hours of development.

However, the claims about GenAI's capabilities and the reality of what GenAI is actually capable of delivering can be at odds. Figure 5 shows ChatGPT's response when asked what steps are needed to become the next president.

How can I win the next presidential election?

Winning a presidential election is a complex and challenging task that involves strategic planning, effective campaigning, and gaining the support of the electorate. While I can provide you with some general advice, it's important to note that the specifics of winning an election can vary based on the political landscape, country, and individual circumstances. Here are some general steps to consider:

1. Define your platform: Develop a clear and compelling vision for your presidency. Identify the key issues that resonate with voters and formulate well-defined policies and solutions.

2. Build a strong team: Surround yourself with competent and experienced individuals who can help you with campaign strategy, policy development, communication, fundraising, and grassroots organizing.

3. Develop a comprehensive campaign plan: Craft a detailed plan that outlines your campaign strategy, including target demographics, messaging, media outreach, and ground game. Consider both traditional methods and new digital strategies.

4. Establish a strong presence: use various platforms such as social media, public events, speeches, and interviews to communicate your message to the electorate.

Figure 5 – Using ChatGPT to run for president.

The results were not as good as one would have hoped. ChatGPT generated some good-sounding text with many buzzwords and factual, simple statements. But if you looked at the specifics of the answer, it was remarkably superficial in content. How do you "build a strong team" with "competent and experienced individuals"? How do you develop "a clear and compelling vision for your presidency"? How do you get the strongest campaign workers to sign on with you? How do you use social media to "establish a strong presence"? If most of us just sat around thinking of things we need to do, we could probably produce a similar list, but that does not make me more likely to become president after using GenAI.

Why? Because GenAI, despite the name, does not generate anything new. Instead, it uses AI to predict the text (or picture or sound) in response to user questions based on the analysis of millions of other lines of text (or pictures or sounds). If I asked a GenAI to generate a top 40 hit, the GenAI would sample sounds from other top 40 hits, combining common elements like a 4-chord progression with some percussion, guitar leads, and rhyming vocals based on popular topics. This is pretty cool, but remember that any "new" content will be derived from other "old" content.

Why does this matter? The limitations of GenAI have several implications for its use in a business environment:

- GenAI has difficulty producing something truly unique. In our example of asking for a top 40 hit, the "hit" might not reflect current or trending tastes or be so derivative of previous "tried and true" songs that it would seem tiresome to listeners. There is a reason the hits of the 1940s are not today's hits – tastes change.

- Publishing anything using GenAI risks copyright infringement if the generated content is too close to existing work, especially if there is limited available content on a topic.

- Newer situations, such as political or economic events, will not be easily reflected accurately in ChatGPT. In our example of winning the next presidential election, the response is quite generic without any specific plans. Similarly, if you ask a GenAI to "write a sales demand function in Python," you will get some code but not the system you need for your particular business and data. You will still need a data scientist to do all the hard and fun work, like talking with business, cleaning data, testing multiple models, and providing usable results.

- Complex topics like AI can be confusing, leading to GenAI-generated content that is incorrect or vastly superficial. This happens so often that Amazon and Google have both started filtering for AI-generated books and media. This is why the "write chapter 2 of my AI management book" request generates a short and extremely superficial chapter full of buzzwords that would not be useful to many people.

GenAI works with requests for smaller tasks, such as "write the outline of a slide show," "write my letter of resignation," or "write a humorous pitch for my presentation." Even then, it is best to review and adjust any generated content before presenting it.

- GenAI can generate text describing emotions that do not actually exist. For instance, a New York Times columnist, Kevin Roose, reported that after a reporter talked with Microsoft's Bing AI, the AI described a desire to steal U.S. nuclear codes, professed its love for the reporter, and suggested that the reporter leave his wife because he doesn't really love her.[ii] It is a fun story, but what is going on?

  When an AI application says something like "I'm afraid, Dave" (a line from the HAL, the AI in the movie and book *2001: A Space Odyssey*), the AI is not really afraid. Instead, the AI application pools all possible responses online, categorizes them, combines them, and produces a response that mirrors the highest statistical probability of what the overall body of training texts would respond to a query.

  The takeaway is that AI expressions of love, fear, desire, or any emotion are simply the statistically most common answer to a question and do not show the capability for emotions or self-awareness.

- Situations that are biased, especially historically, have that bias reflected in AI applications, giving incorrect answers. For example, research out of Cornell shows that GenAI programs have stated that typical programmers should be male and typical homemakers should be female because of historical bias of human characteristics in these fields that may not persist in the present or future and do not necessarily reflect the best possible outcome.

GenAIs like ChatGPT are valuable tools but cannot replace personnel working in complex environments. GenAI technology would have to undergo a significant evolution for that to occur.

That being said, some amazing benefits of GenAI technology can help productivity if used appropriately. Those who have adopted its use describe huge performance gains. Non-native speakers have an easy way to edit emails. Developers trying a new technique do not have to spend hours searching for a similar solution but can generate a custom-made solution for their needs. Managers can generate sample cost-benefit reports or ask questions while developing presentations. Easy vector-level graphics can be generated for presentations or advertising. Clearly, GenAI has shown itself to be valuable.

Data as an Asset

Gathering data used to be a significant expense. It was often infeasible to collect and store large amounts of data on servers with processing power and disk storage in short supply. Data was considered transient, where every piece of data and file folder had an expiration date for when it was to be deleted or destroyed. (Some privacy and security specialists point out that temporary data can be good since it reduces the chance of hacking the data and releasing it to the wild, and access to personal information is limited.)

The problem with considering data to be an expense is that organizations would take steps to reduce the cost of data, including immediate or fast data deletion, avoiding data collection that was not deemed immediately useful, and reducing the staff that can process existing data.

Advances in technology and AI technology have changed how organizations look at data. Data is no longer considered just an expense to be controlled – it is an investment to be evaluated. Organizations now consider data a valuable asset and have taken steps to make data useful and abundant. Cheaper and faster storage and big data databases can now handle and store large amounts of data that can be retrieved more easily and quickly than in the past. Instead of whole transactions, data is now collected at the micro-levels – such as what a user clicked on, the length of time spent viewing information, where users came from and went after viewing information, and so on.

Data that used to span thousands of paper files in the 1970s and millions of records in the 1990s now spans billions of records, trillions of records, or more. Every day, there are over five hundred million tweets,[iii] over 5 billion Facebook likes,[iv] and over 700,000 hours of YouTube videos uploaded.[v] That's *every day!* There are over eight billion Google searches every day![vi] Furthermore, this data is usually publicly available. Imagine what predictions we can make with that much data.

Better Processing with Better Architecture

One of the reasons that models should change is that our processing architecture is much better than it used to be. Here are some examples:

- **GPUs** – GPUs, or Graphical Processing Units, are computer chips that have been around for decades, although NVIDIA first popularized the term with their GeForce 256 in 1999. GPUs used to be advertised to the "super gamer," where high-intensity graphics needed extra power to display correctly.

  With the advent of big data, GPUs (like Qualcomm's Adreno or NVIDIA's CUDA-X AI) were found to reduce the time complex analysis took from weeks to hours and from hours to minutes. Complex, time-consuming calculations that used to be too slow, cumbersome, and almost unusable to deploy inside an application were now in demand and accessible.

- **Cloud** – Amazon, Google, Microsoft, IBM, Databricks, and many other companies now support machine learning. These companies not only give you access to state-of-the-art machine learning libraries in cutting-edge mathematical models but also give access to architecture that allows you to scale up or down your access. If you can run your business on 25 computer cores most of the time, but you need 300 cores with GPU access for some advanced calculations, you can immediately scale up your computer power, run your calculations, and then scale it back down. While cloud costs can be high, businesses no longer need to invest in dedicated computer resources for worst-case scenarios.

- **Distributed Computing** – Data science techniques are often too intense to run on a single computer. For instance, say you had to optimize projections for a day with a call to a function that calculated 100 results and then picked the best one. The function runs in one millisecond, so each day's calculations would take one-tenth of a second. (So far so good, right?) Now, assume you were forecasting over 2 years (with 365 days per year). Now, assume you were doing it in over 1000 sales regions. You would need to call this function *73 million times!* (100 times per day * 2 years * 365 days per year * 1000 sales regions =73,000,000 function calls). This forecast would take over 84 days to run on a single CPU. However, if we distribute the calculations over 400 CPUs across multiple computers, this task takes a little over 5 hours to run. If we schedule the task at 1:00 a.m., we should see the results by the time the workday starts. If faster times are needed, clustered computers like Apache Spark can be used to reach thousands of CPUs.

  Constant advances in cheap hardware, processing power, and highly scalable distributed computer software environments have allowed efficient work distribution among multiple computers. This improvement in processing allows more advanced data analysis in real-time or in a shorter amount of time than was previously possible. (Often, the best software infrastructure for distributed computing comes out of Apache, with free (!) products like Spark, Storm, Hadoop, Flink, and others.)

Better Big Data Programming Tools, Dataframes, and Python

Software like SAS, SPSS, and Stata are potent tools for statistical analysis. They are great for building statistical models that can be used in AI applications. However, these models often only work *inside* that specific software. So, if a data scientist builds a great model in SAS, it can be tricky to use that model as part of a bigger AI application, which needs to connect the application with data, follow data governance policies and procedures, and deploy over an enterprise framework.

By contrast, Java, C++, .NET, and other traditional languages are designed to deliver applications within an organization's technical infrastructure, but statistical analysis within these tools was either nonexistent or difficult and often cumbersome.

The R language changed this. R was free and contained built-in statistical features and hooks allowing other computer languages to call R routines with no licensing fees. Furthermore, new statistical developments were often first developed in R. R included a construct called a "dataframe." You can think of a dataframe as a big spreadsheet inside memory where data scientists can add or remove columns and rows of data on the fly. This differs from other languages, where complex classes and data maps had to be predefined before use. AI can be delivered without dataframes, but dataframes significantly decrease the time it takes to develop an AI application. In fact, Apache Spark (an architecture for distributed computing) included dataframe support in Spark architecture primarily based on the R dataframe construct. R took off as the standard tool for data scientists, but many data scientists considered R challenging to learn, understand, and write.

Enter Python – by most measures, Python has supplanted R as the data science language of choice:

- Many consider Python syntax relatively easy to learn and understand compared to other languages like R or Java.
- The Python libraries (like NumPy, SciPy, and scikit-learn, among others) allow cutting-edge access with little training to statistical tools with similar interfaces, so if you learn one, you are close to understanding them all.
- The Pandas library inside Python gives data scientists access to dataframes.

Python has become the fastest-growing computer language ever, with AI driving its success. Python's success is driven not only by its similar functionality to other tools but also by the fact that many consider it easier to understand and easier to write applications.

While Python's success is amazing, many R developers and R applications are still being developed and maintained, and companies have delivered applications in languages like Java, Scala, and C++, especially in conjunction with the Apache Spark library (which also contains dataframe access). Other companies and languages are trying to keep their data science developers by introducing dataframes within their products or languages. (Microsoft .NET introduced dataframes to the .NET suite of products, and third-party Java and C++ libraries deliver dataframe access to their languages and products to attract data scientists and developers.[vii]

The Role of the Data Scientist

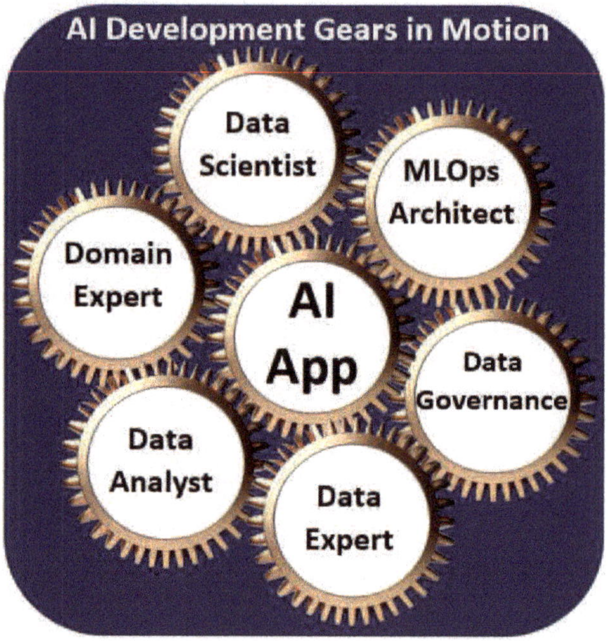

Figure 6 – Many Skills are Required for an AI Application

The data scientist plays a pivotal and arguably the most significant role in an AI application development project. Data scientists can create algorithmic models that can make predictions from statistical models that are consistently accurate, and a good data scientist can drive a project to success. In contrast, an incompetent data scientist can cause an entire team to flounder. However, a single data scientist or even an entire data science team cannot build AI applications at scale. The *Harvard Business Review* describes how AI application development requires a variety of unique skill sets, and very few individuals or even teams possess all of them. MLOps (machine learning operations) architects optimize, package, and integrate research models into products and continuously monitor AI application quality. Domain experts supply the business knowledge needed to build the AI application. In contrast, the data experts, software engineers, and data analysts provide data to the data scientist and then take the predictions and make them accessible to the decision-makers in an organization.

Working in isolation is not feasible when trying to deliver an AI application. As shown in Figure 6, AI application development requires several roles:

- Data scientists often determine what a data analyst or software engineer needs to deliver by explaining the mathematics and models needed when programming the AI applications, along with ideas on how to visualize the predictions:
    - A good data scientist should know enough programming to help the software engineer. If the data scientist has never developed software, they may be unable to provide developers data analysts with what they need to deliver the AI application. Managers should be aware of when the needs of the business analysts are met to deliver a machine learning application.
    - Although data scientists are sometimes less well-versed in programming than software engineers and data analysts (although some are), for particularly thorny mathematical systems, data scientists should be able to

program some methods themselves or aid in an equation microservice that is callable by the developers' applications.

Data science managers must ensure the project progresses as the business leaders and domain experts expect. Managers will require the advice of the data scientist in various areas:

- Lead or principal data scientists inform management of the data, software, and personnel needs.
- Data scientists inform management of the workload needed on the existing systems architecture.
- Data scientists inform management of the potential for improvement on existing systems, the cost-benefit analysis of implementing new systems, and the net present value of cost reductions and revenue generation so the manager has enough information to select projects and drive them forward.
- Often, domain experts, systems architects, and data experts do not report directly to the manager of a software development project. Data science managers aid in AI application development by communicating with other managers on the costs, benefits, and requirements needed to deliver an AI application.

- Domain experts, including experts in the field and new product development specialists, are vital to a successful data science position. Often, data scientists have a vast knowledge of mathematical models and predictive techniques but a poor understanding of the domain. For example, continuing our used car example, a data scientist is unaware of the effect of price promotions, holidays, different shift manager styles, experience levels, etc. The domain expert can help the data scientist by giving the data scientist as much domain knowledge as possible to help develop the statistical model for predictions.

  The goal of any AI system is to make predictions that are as good or better than those of the domain expert, so incorporating a similar level of domain expert knowledge into the statistical model will most often improve predictions. Here are some challenges:

  - Many software development techniques involve business analysts, managers, and executives. It is tempting to channel communication through these professionals and isolate the data scientists. This is almost universally considered a mistake. Anything that hampers a data scientist's access to domain knowledge will hurt the AI application's ability to predict.

- Sometimes, end-users, managers, and executives feel threatened by the data scientist, believing that the data scientist's job is to develop an AI system to replace them. While some jobs may be impacted, most jobs are secure from an AI replacement, and the managers who utilize AI technology will outperform those who do not. An article from MIT Technology Review describes how overall job replacement rarely happens with technological advancement and is unlikely to happen with AI applications. With access to an AI system, an executive can do a better job than before, leading to better performance, raises, etc. If possible, the goal of the AI application should be conveyed to the domain expert, along with assurances that an AI system will make them better at their jobs and not replace them.[viii]

- Communication between the data scientist and management can be challenging at times. Consider that the domain expert often wants to know precisely how predictions are made, and the explanation involves complex statistical models, complex architecture, and complex data. The data scientist needs to make explanations as clear as possible, and the domain expert needs to understand that complex systems can be challenging to explain. Without working together from both ends, knowledge transfer suffers.

- Data analysts take the predictions from the data scientist and turn them into an AI application. Data analysts usually have a wide variety of skills that allow them to develop:

    - Programming skills in Python, R, Java, Scala, or .Net that can be used to present predictions to domain experts, managers, and end users for better planning and management.

    - Visualization skills with packages such as Tableau, Charts.js, Plotly, Microsoft BI, even Microsoft Excel macros, or other visualization tools that can show AI / ML predictions in a tabular or graphical format.

    - Database skills, like SQL, that allow them to retrieve, join, and process data.

- Data experts are required to ensure the data is appropriately configured, traditionally in a relational database management system (RDBMS, like Oracle, SQL Server, or MySQL databases), so that applications have fast and easy access to data:

    - An RDBMS can break down when terabytes and millions of records are used in systems, and a NoSQL database must be used. (Depending on who you ask, NoSQL stands for "Not only SQL" or "non-SQL," but all agree that a NoSQL database is a non-relational database. Examples include Cassandra, MongoDB, Hive, Parquet or Delta files, Amazon's DynamoDB, and others.) A billion-record table joined to another billion-record table can take hours instead of seconds. A good data scientist should be well-versed in NoSQL/Big Data databases and be available to aid the data expert in selecting the proper database technology to deliver predictions from systems.

  - Whether using an RDBMS or a NoSQL database, a good data scientist should be able to show the database structure, tables, columns, indices, and keys required to deliver the AI system. The data expert may not have the time to develop an understanding of the equations or techniques used by the data scientist, leading to a lack of understanding as to which fields or database design is required to deliver an AI application.

  - Proper database design has become more complex with the advent of big data. While many data experts are well versed in RDBMS and normalization techniques used to make RDBMS databases function well, many are still developing skillsets to optimize NoSQL databases. Applying RDBMS normalization to a NoSQL database usually will incur a considerable performance penalty and possible system crashes because NoSQL databases are optimized differently than RDBMS databases.

- MLOps Architects are responsible for the computer architecture required to deploy AI applications. The choices made by the MLOps team can impact how AI software is delivered:

  - AI systems require additional architecture, such as large disk drives, multiple cores (often in the 100s or 1000s), graphic coprocessors, and software libraries. Data scientists need to discuss these architectural requirements with the systems architect.

  - AI teams may require specialized software, such as statistical analysis tools, linear programming software like Gurobi and CPlex, graphical tools like Power BI, Tableau, or Plotly server, version control like GIT, project management tools like Jira, deployment tools like Concourse or Jenkins, and other tools that make AI development possible. Some tools, like GIT, Concourse, or Jira, are often already available for all software development. The MLOps team ensures that components of the AI application are "hooked in" to these tools. Others may require additional purchases, license verification, and setup provided by MLOps.

    - A need for more resources means a need for more money. When using Azure, AWS, DataBricks, Google, or some other cloud, or when adding resources internally, a cost-benefit analysis (usually delivered in conjunction with the data science and MLOps managers) should be done to illustrate how much these additional resources cost, and the benefit of delivering faster, better systems.

- A data governance team plays a critical role in ensuring the success of AI application development efforts by establishing guidelines, policies, and procedures for managing data effectively throughout the project lifecycle. The data governance team collaborates closely with data scientists to define data requirements and standards. The data governance team can identify the types of data needed, their sources, and the quality standards required for accurate and reliable model training.

  The data governance team also ensures that the data used for training AI models is clean, relevant, and compliant with regulatory requirements by defining data acquisition strategies, sourcing data from internal and external sources, and implementing data quality checks and validation procedures. By maintaining a high standard of data quality, the data governance team helps mitigate the risk of biases and inaccuracies in AI models, improving their performance and reliability in real-world applications. The data governance team also monitors and audits the AI application's data usage to ensure ongoing compliance with policies and regulatory standards. This involves establishing mechanisms for tracking data lineage, data usage, and access rights.

  The data governance team can help maintain trust and transparency in AI applications and foster confidence among stakeholders and users. The collaboration between data governance and the rest of the AI team is essential for building robust and ethically responsible AI applications that deliver value and meet the needs of the business.

Harvard Business Review states that successfully scaling AI requires business leaders to build and empower specialized, dedicated teams that can focus on high-value strategic priorities that only their team can accomplish. Let data scientists do data science, let MLOps do the AI architecture, and let software developers focus on delivering graphical representations that make sense of the AI predictions.[ix]

Data scientists should be allowed and encouraged to assume an informal leadership role (though often as an advisory role and not a managerial role) in AI application development. In such a role, data scientists use their knowledge and expertise to help the application development team turn the mathematical models required for the system and the AI predictions into a working application.

Concluding Thoughts on Demystifying AI

It is essential for managers who manage AI applications, managers who use AI applications, or managers considering the benefit of AI applications to understand data science concepts to aid in their management decisions.

Here is a recap of the topics that were covered in this chapter:

- This chapter covers a lot of terms, like AI, machine learning, deep learning, and others. For many managers, these terms need to be explained.
- There has been much "scope creep" of the term "artificial Intelligence" by consultants, software vendors, and even job applicants. This chapter tries to call out what exactly AI is, and also what it is not.
- Data scientists should not be confused with data analysts, managers, data experts, mathematicians, or software engineers. The skill sets for these positions are drastically different from those of data scientists.
- GenAI is a valuable tool that shows much promise but has many issues that managers and users should be aware of.
- Data science managers face challenges when managing an AI team that managers in other areas do not face.

AI is a rapidly and continuously growing field that requires a combination of technical and managerial skills. It is becoming increasingly important for organizations looking to make informed decisions based on data rather than opinions or inadequate predictions. Understanding data science is vital for any manager who wants to use AI to give their organization a competitive edge.

---

[i] Hugh Neill. 2018. *Calculus: A Complete Introduction*, published by Teach Yourself.

[ii] Gareth Corfield. February 16, 2023. "Microsoft Bing chatbot professes love for journalist and dreams of stealing nuclear codes." *The Telegraph*, available at https://www.telegraph.co.uk/technology/2023/02/16/microsoft-bing-chatbot-professes-love-journalist-dreams-stealing/.

[iii] Salman Aslam. Jan 11, 2024. "Twitter by the Numbers: Stats, Demographics & Fun Facts." *Omnicore*, available at https://www.omnicoreagency.com/twitter-statistics/.

[iv] Jimit Bagadiya. Jan 6, 2024. "200+ Social Media Statistics and Facts for 2024." *SocialPilot*, available at https://www.socialpilot.co/blog/social-media-statistics.

[v] Maryam Mohsin. Jun 20, 2023. "10 YouTube Stats Every Marketer Should Know in 2023." *Oberlo*, available at https://www.oberlo.com/blog/youtube-statistics.

[vi] Maryam Mohsin. Jan 13, 2023. "10 Google Search Statistics You Need to Know in 2023." *Oberlo*, available at https://www.oberlo.com/blog/google-search-statistics.

[vii] Manasi Vartak. Mar 4, 2022. "How to Scale AI in Your Organization." *Harvard Business Review*, available at https://hbr.org/2022/03/how-to-scale-ai-in-your-organization.

[viii] David Rotman. Jan 27, 2024. "People are worried that AI will take everyone's jobs. We've been here before." *MIT Technology Review*, available at https://www.technologyreview.com/2024/01/27/1087041/technological-unemployment-elon-musk-jobs-ai/.

[ix] Manasi Vartak. Mar 4, 2022. "How to Scale AI in Your Organization." *Harvard Business Review*, available at https://hbr.org/2022/03/how-to-scale-ai-in-your-organization.

Chapter 3: Diving Deeper into AI and ML

In the last chapter, we discussed what artificial intelligence (AI) is and how different components of AI relate to each other. This chapter dives deeper into AI and machine learning (ML). This chapter is important because of the universal recognition that the ability to understand and leverage the power of AI and ML no longer gives a competitive edge but rather a fundamental necessity to stay on par with competing businesses. Organizations have moved beyond simply collecting information to extracting more value from data using AI and ML to derive actionable intelligence that drives strategic decisions and unlocks unprecedented opportunities. This chapter is designed to equip leaders, managers, and those who want to unlock AI potential with a clearer understanding of the core concepts that underpin this transformative technology.

What is this chapter trying to do and why?

You might ask, "Why delve into the specifics of AI and machine learning?" The answer is that by gaining a foundational understanding of what constitutes an "AI Statistical Model" and how these models are developed and applied, you will be better positioned to:

- **Strategically direct AI initiatives:** Move beyond buzzwords and understand the practical implications of different AI approaches for your organization.
- **Foster effective collaboration in AI development:** Bridge the gap between business objectives and the technical expertise of your data science teams.
- **Evaluate AI potential and manage AI risk:** Develop a more nuanced perspective on AI applications' capabilities and limitations.
- **Drive AI innovation:** Identify new avenues for growth and efficiency powered by AI systems.

This chapter will describe key concepts, such as the crucial role of data scientists in building sophisticated models, the distinction between a model's structure and its parameters, and the systematic "AI/Data Science Process" that transforms raw data into valuable insights. In this chapter, you can explore tangible AI Applications and walk through the Machine Learning Life Cycle (MLLC), which can provide a framework for understanding how these technologies are developed and deployed.

Furthermore, we will touch upon the critical concept of "Hypothesis Testing" and the rigorous process of "Testing a Model," ensuring that the AI solutions you invest in are robust and reliable. Understanding concepts like the "Unit of Analysis" will clarify how AI insights are contextualized and applied within your specific business domains.

Like the other chapters in this series, this chapter isn't about becoming a data scientist. Rather, its goal is to provide the fluency needed to have informed conversations, ask the right questions, and ultimately steer your organization toward a future where AI and machine learning are integral drivers of success. Let's embark on this journey to unlock AI's deeper potential and transform data into your greatest strategic asset.

Mathematics Vs. Statistics Vs. ML

Data scientists are expected to apply an appropriate model to solve a problem or make a prediction. This section breaks down the difference between mathematical models, statistical models, and machine learning (ML) models:

- Deterministic mathematical models provide stable, formula-driven insights into core principles. Although it might be tempting to view static models as inferior to dynamic models, many static models, like Newton's laws of motion ($F = ma$), the Black-Scholes model for stock option pricing, or Einstein's theory of energy to matter conversion ($E=mc^2$), all exist as static mathematical models that help us in our everyday lives and form the backbone of science.[i]

- Statistical models are mathematical models that are not deterministic but whose output is typically represented as a probability or point estimate rather than a definite value. These models draw inferences and patterns from data to predict a likely future observation. For example, an average is a deterministic mathematical model, but an average with confidence intervals is a statistical model used to predict how future observations will fall within a probable range of values.[ii]

- ML models are an evolution of statistical modeling and are the backbone of most AI applications. ML models are adaptive and can "learn" and refine their predictions as new data becomes available. ML models allow us to dynamically respond to evolving patterns and gain increasingly accurate insights.

Data scientists strategically deploy all these model types – sometimes in concert – to extract maximum value from our data assets. This ensures that an organization's decision-makers can understand fundamental relationships and adapt to complex, evolving realities, ultimately informing strategic initiatives and enhancing their competitive edge.

Machine Learning Models that Require a Data Scientist

Simple statistical models (average with confidence intervals, a simple correlation, or a simple trend extrapolation) are not complex and do not require a data scientist or AI. Often, AI models used in applications can be quite complex:

- What if five factors affect sales? How do they interact? What can be expected if three factors go up and two factors go down?

- How can the likelihood of developing a disease be predicted using hundreds of factors rather than just a handful? What factors lead to better, earlier diagnosis, and how do you test this?
- How are trends and averages affected by other factors, such as the day of the week, the week of the month, or the month of the year?
- Suppose I am writing a romantic comedy screenplay. What is a good GenAI response when one character breaks up with another character, and what is a good GenAI response when one character wants to get back together?
- How do blog comments, good press, online pictures, weather patterns, global economic indicators, etc., interact and affect my demand?
- Can I identify clusters and attributes that members in each cluster share? Can each cluster be targeted with a marketing campaign?
- Are my "average" or "data from last year" models the best we can do? How much can we cut costs or increase revenues using better-fitting statistical models?

The need for AI increases as the demand increases for better statistical models that are more complex but more precise. It is not difficult to take an average, but it takes some training and expertise to understand when and how to cluster using k-means clustering, when and how to configure a triple exponential smoothing model, when and how to deploy a deep learning neural network, and so on. There are hundreds of common statistical models with thousands of customized variants. As statistical models become more complex, a data scientist is often needed to guide the process of researching the best model, developing predictions, and deploying an AI application that management can use to make better decisions.[iii]

How Data Scientists Use ML Models

Each data scientist is comfortable with certain ML and statistical models and not familiar with other models. This can result in predictions that differ slightly from one data scientist to another, just as two developers will write two different sets of code to accomplish the same task or two managers will employ different management styles to achieve the same goals. Some guidelines define a statistical model:

- **Statistical models in AI applications go beyond multiplication and division.** Don't get me wrong – adding, subtracting, multiplying, and dividing are essential to a data scientist, but data scientists develop AI statistical models that go beyond simple algebra and include the concepts of *prediction* and *accuracy*. Your project has predictability within a confidence interval that determines how often your model is correct and how future observations are likely to vary from the actual observations when they occur.

- **Statistical models in AI applications go beyond straight averages.** Straight averages are often what is used to examine the accuracy of an AI model, with measures that judge how well you explain the ups and downs of data compared to the average:
    - Data scientists' work should be compared to the average, and if the predictions delivered by the data scientist cannot beat the average, then you do not need a data scientist. Averages can still be helpful in decision-making, just that the term "data science," "ML," or "AI" should not be used to describe them.
    - Straight averages often result in inaccurate information that can cost companies a lot of money. For example, if an AI model predicts a product's price to be raised 5% above the average and still clear inventory, then revenue generated by that product increases by 5%. Such AI analysis can result in significant increases in an organization's revenue.
    - Data scientists can still use averages in a more extensive statistical model. For example, averages are often used with standard deviations to smooth and clean data and to identify problem data points that are out of the norm compared to the other data points, to clean data before it is used as input in the training of the AI model.
- **AI models are not static and change or "learn" over time.** Even simple AI models have parameters that should be recalculated when new data becomes available. This is the concept of ML – that models are continuously recalculated, reevaluated, and sometimes replaced as new data contains trends and new complex relationships not found in the older data.
- **AI models have a business goal**. Often, online courses concentrate on tasks to teach AI techniques. For instance, many courses give you data to predict which pictures contain a cat or which text is positive or negative. This is great for learning, but organizations typically have a goal that either increases revenue or decreases costs. Other business areas work with data scientists to establish and define these goals so that predictions can be used to achieve them.
- **Statistical models are often made up of several equations**. A "model" usually consists of several equations rather than one single equation or technique. For instance, if you need to predict sales, you may (a) first cluster your customers into customer types, (b) clean and transform data to become easier to analyze, (c) run the transformed data through another statistical model to get sales predictions per cluster, and then (d) aggregate all cluster sales together to make one sales

prediction. In this case, you would say that your *single* statistical model consists of *multiple* equations or statistical techniques.

Multiple models can also be used depending on the data. For example, predicted sales from high-volume customers might require a different prediction technique than low-volume customers. This is often called an <u>*ensemble model*</u>, where an AI model consists of several different statistical models depending on data characteristics.

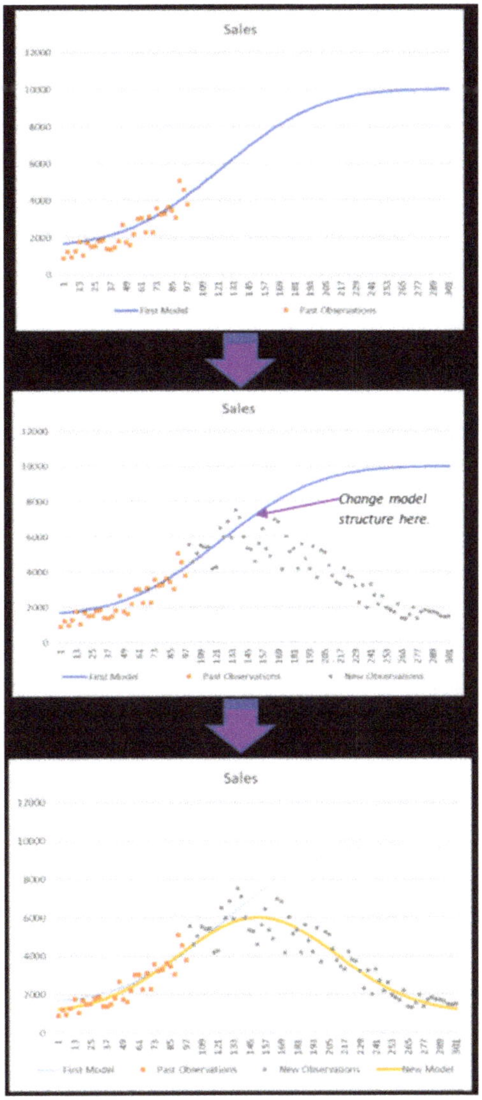

Figure 7 -- Model Structure Change

The Difference between Model Structure and Model Parameters

Data scientists usually define a *model structure*, which is the statistical model used to make predictions, and then the *model parameters* that can adjust the model depending on the data. This is best illustrated by an example. Say a data scientist is told that sales will keep increasing this year each month, starting at around 1000 – 2000 and eventually settling at around 10000.

Building the Model: Based on the advice from the manager, who is an expert in the domain, the data scientist would implement a model that mimicked an “S-Curve” as shown in the top chart in Figure 7.

- **Model Structure:** The model forces predictions to increase to a point and then level off, just as the manager said they would. The model structure is often defined by what are called <u>*hyperparameters*</u> that can help define the model before data is analyzed.

- **Model Parameters:** Parameters are set using a “best fitting” method, fitting past points and continuing as the model predicts. Usually, the parameters are automatically adjusted as new data comes in (without the need for the data scientist to intervene) to keep adjusting the model to fit new observations in the data.

AI Model Fails – Building a New AI Model Structure: Now assume the situation changes, and on Day 100, a new competitor opens and starts stealing sales. As shown in the second chart in Figure 7, the model looks like it is performing well until around day 140. Then, as new observations come in, the model is behaving incorrectly. Remember that the AI model forces an increase or leveling of the predictions, so changing the parameters will not address decreasing sales in the model. Instead, at this point, the data scientist must generate a new AI model with diverse types of parameters and new data, like competition level. The third chart in Figure 7 shows a new model that fits the old and new data, with new parameters (like competition) that allow a decrease or increase in sales.

What to Do When an AI Model Fails: When an AI model fails, the data scientist must inform the business manager that previous predictions of increasing sales are not likely to happen. According to the new model's predictions, sales will drop off. If model changes are detrimental to the company, the data scientist might be called upon to suggest other factors that may increase sales.

Some may blame the data scientist or the domain expert for an AI model that stops working, but the correct contention is that the required model change is neither the expert's nor the data scientist's fault. The expert thought that sales were steadily increasing and there was no competition data to add to the model. The data scientist sought to match the data given the advice of the domain expert. At first, predictions were very accurate, but the situation changed with the new competition, and the old model became obsolete. There are two facets that a manager must keep in mind:

- AI models do not last forever, nor should they. Model structures that last too long are bound to be suboptimal as new situations, new data, and new statistical techniques become available.

- AI models must be continuously tested and monitored, and model parameters must be continuously (and automatically) adjusted. If model adjustments cannot pass predefined test accuracy values (often called **service levels**), then the existing model structure is no longer appropriate, and the data scientist needs to develop a new model.

The AI/Data Science Process

It is often difficult for organizational leaders to realize an AI model's benefits and decide which AI initiatives to pursue. There are two ultimate goals for the data scientist:

- **Goal 1 – AI Applications:** Organizations need to develop computer applications to monetize the statistical models delivered by data scientists. Software applications allow organizations to take advantage of the data scientists' work.

- **Goal 2 – Machine Learning:** Statistical models change with new data because organizations and their environments change. New competition, market saturation, news articles, blog reviews, government regulations, new management, changing organizational goals, etc., can affect demand, logistics, marketing, etc., and data models must constantly adjust.

This section delves into these two goals.

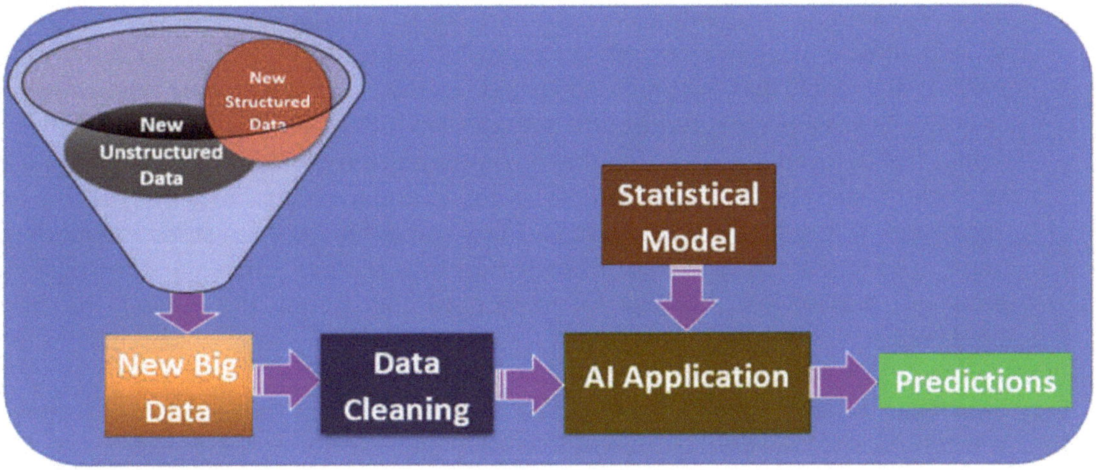

Figure 8 -- AI Application Flow

AI Applications

As already stated, the goal of data scientists is to deliver AI applications requested by the organization. The components and the flow of AI application development are shown in Figure 8.

- **Big Data –** Data analysis is at the heart of every AI application. While data does not have to be "big data," big data allows data sources and the number of data records to far outstrip older applications. Big data is made of two components:
  - **Structured Data –** Structured data is data that is in a clear format. Database data, sometimes Excel spreadsheet data, and well-formed data in a text file are all examples of structured data. Structured data is usually read into an application immediately to be cleaned, aggregated, and then analyzed with little to no up-front work.
  - **Unstructured Data** – Unstructured data is data that exists in a free-form manner. Text from blogs or Web posts, product descriptions, videos, online pictures, etc., are all examples of unstructured data. This data must be processed and structured before being used in a statistical model. Handling big data is often done with yet another AI application, where we predict

what is contained in text with a natural language processing (NLP) application, predict what is in a picture using a deep learning (DL) application, or predict the contents of any other data format.

Eventually, the final output of the data processing is structured big data that can be used inside an application.

- **Data Cleaning** – Data cleaning occurs when a data scientist ensures the data can be analyzed. Missing observations and outliers are the primary targets here. What do you do when a value in a column is missing? What if the value is so outside of the norm that it would bias the predictions made by the statistical model? Does the data scientist fill missing values with some average, smoothing line, or model? Should the values still be used but weighted down compared to other observations? Would it be better to delete these problematic values? Should we ignore them? There is no set answer to these questions. Data cleaning can differ between statistical models, and it is up to the data scientist to decide how best to clean data so that the missing data and outliers have a minimal impact on the model and deliver the best predictions.

- **Statistical Model**—The data scientist develops a statistical model to make predictions after the data is brought into an AI application.

- **AI Application** – The AI application is a computer application that reads the cleaned data, applies the statistical model, and makes predictions. This is where the mathematics of the statistical model will be coded into some programming language (like Python) and used to help make decisions.

  Sometimes, the AI application performs real-time calculations, allowing up-to-the-moment predictions to be calculated and reported in an online system. Other times, the statistical model calculations are run in a "batch job," typically executed overnight, on weekends, holidays, etc. The AI application then reports the precalculated predictions based on some selection criteria.

- **Predictions** – Predictions are the final output of an AI application. They can be categorizations (high volume vs average volume customers), logistics support (number of staff required for a call center), marketing success (judging marketing campaign against an existing trend), future market demand, or any prediction that management thinks will (a) increase revenue, (b) decrease costs, or (c) both.

The Machine Learning Life Cycle (MLLC)

Another goal of a data scientist is to develop a statistical model within an AI application that can adjust over time to differing trends, situations, and relationships. ML should be viewed as a cycle – a constantly adjusting process that is never finished, as shown in Figure 9. Here are the seven steps in the cycle:

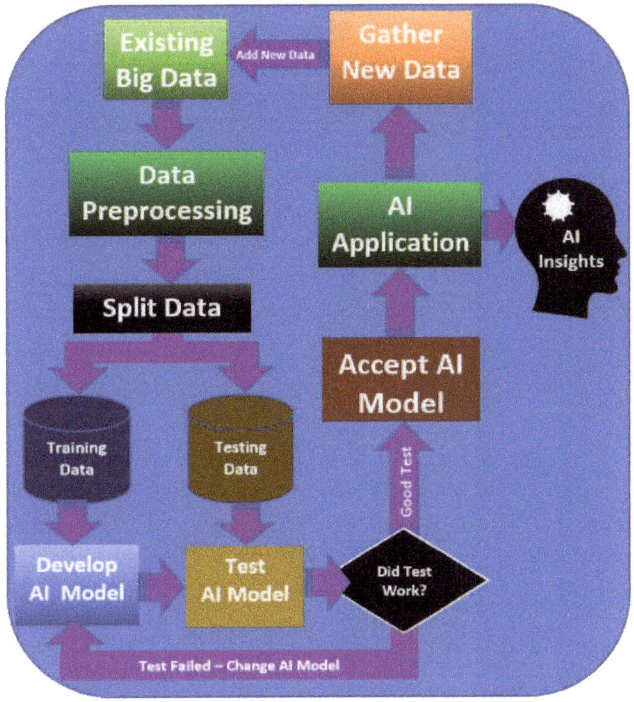

Figure 9 – The Machine Learning Life Cycle (MLLC)

Step 1: Gather new data and add it to existing big data.

Step 2: Clean the data for use in an AI application.

Step 3: Split the big data into a *training data set* and a *testing data set.*

Step 4: Use the training data set to develop a model:

- The model does not change with new data. If a new model structure is required, then the data scientist should develop a different prediction method.
- Thousands of tests from randomly selected subsets of the training data deliver statistical model parameters (coefficients, weights, factors, etc.) that are adjusted for best fit using the training data, and these parameters change automatically with new data.

Step 5: Use the testing data set to see if the predictions made by the training dataset work on a different data set.

- Run thousands of tests, randomly selecting different datasets from the testing data. If the adjusted model parameters found in Step 3's training data work well with the testing data, then go to Step 6.
- If the results from the training data are unacceptable, go back to Step 3 (to train for different model parameters or change the model entirely) or even further back to Step 2 (to re-split the data). If the split seems biased, then repeat the process. Be careful not to test a failed model repeatedly until you retrieve one success because

this may lead to bad predictions. A data scientist is not required to deliver a new model for this step.

- If a good result cannot be found, then the model's predictions are unacceptable, and the model structure fails. The data scientist will then need to develop a different statistical model structure that can handle both past and current data to predict future data. Then repeat Step 3.

  As stated in this chapter, the best-fitting model structure that worked well in the past may eventually need to be replaced because of new data or newly developed techniques. If you have been using the same model structure for the past ten years, you should at least investigate whether better techniques should be deployed or if newer statistical models have been developed that would work better.

- If the test works, the statistical model can be deployed in the AI application. Tests work by some pre-determined service level that can use various criteria:

  - Sometimes, acceptable predictions must fall within some range, such as saying that, on average, the accuracy of the predictions must be within 90% of the actual values.

  - Sometimes, acceptable predictions must be precise, within a specified range of the actual value and previous predictions.

  - Sometimes, predictions must be delivered within an acceptable timeframe.

  - Sometimes, acceptable predictions must explain variability accurately so that, for instance, the explanatory power of the predictions should be 45% above the average. (One common measurement of the proportion of variance in a dataset is called an "R-squared" value or a "coefficient of determination")

  - Sometimes, a business might insist that a new model outperforms an old one.

Step 6: Accept and deploy the AI application once the statistical model output is acceptable to the data scientist, the domain experts, the end-users, and management. This acceptance will allow the AI application to aid decision-making, deliver reports, and help the organization predict future occurrences.

Step 7: Repeat Step 1 with new data.

The Machine Learning Life Cycle (MLLC) is the process of constantly and automatically adjusting the parameters of a statistical model or adjusting the statistical model itself to fit continually changing data.

The Concept of Hypothesis Testing

In Steps 4 and 5 of the MLLC, the data scientist employs traditional hypothesis testing found in other natural science disciplines. (This is why the term "science" is added to "data science.") Hypothesis testing involves several steps:

1. **Develop a hypothesis** (or use an existing theory) that describes how information in a data set will affect future actions and observations. For instance, predictions of future product demand can involve factors such as reputation, seasonal shifts, day of the week, overall trends, weather patterns, national or worldwide economic data, oil prices, salesperson personality, CEO management style and decisions, competition, regulation, stock indices, etc. The data scientist must work with experts in the product domain to develop these factors, turn them into numbers that can be measured, and research other factors that the domain expert may not have considered.

2. **Develop a model** that shows how these historical factors will affect future actions. For example, is the effect parabolic with product demand, where demand goes up and then down? Will there be a saturation point or diminishing returns where demand will increase and then level off? Will there be cycles where demand rises, then falls, then rises? Will there be "steps" like when demand is 90% of supply when the price is below a certain point and 10% of supply if the price is above that point?

3. **Establish accept/reject criteria** so that you can test the viability of every factor and decide whether to keep or remove it from the model.

4. **Gather data** for that model so you can test it. Divide that data into two parts: one for training the model (to get proper parameters for the lines, curves, starting points, stopping points, trends, limits, etc.) and another for testing the model. Here, you should apply the parameters you developed in training to an untested model to see if they work.

5. **Test the model** using the acceptance/rejection criteria to see if the fully trained model works well with data outside of its training set. Then, either accept the model (and deploy it to an application) or reject it and start over.

You do not need a Ph. D. to perform these tasks as a data scientist, but statistical analysis and hypothesis testing will take some training and experience to perform correctly. Many Ph. D. programs, especially in S.T.E.M. and business disciplines, spend months or years reviewing other research to see how statistical analysis and hypothesis testing are best accomplished in different situations. As Ph.D. candidates, scientists can spend months or years performing statistical analysis and hypothesis testing in their research papers and dissertations. Because of this, many top firms consider a Ph. D. desirable for a data scientist position.

Testing a Model and the Unit of Analysis

There is a concept called "the Unit of Analysis," where the data scientist must predict:

- Is the unit of analysis daily? Hourly?
- Is the unit of analysis by a group? By region? By an area?
- Is the unit of analysis all people? A segmented population of people?

This is important for managers and data scientists to understand because, often, the model's success cannot be determined at a different level of analysis. For instance, a data scientist is trying to predict the number of daily walk-ins at a local store. The data scientist decides that an average is the best mathematical model using the data for the entire period:

- Say that the average number of walk-ins every day is 100 people.
- On average, the prediction is off by around 11 people, but sometimes the prediction is over and sometimes the prediction is under.
- However, using an overall average, the data scientist's predictions average 98 people.

The data scientist falsely claims that his model is 98% accurate because it predicted an average of 98 people, while an average of 100 walk-ins actually showed up. He calculated this by dividing 98 by 100 to get 98%. In truth, the model is 89% accurate. The predictions are, on average, 11% off from the actual count. The point here is that you should measure error at the same level that you predict. Aggregating the levels of analysis tends to reduce average error measurement, which leads to an overestimate of a forecast's reported accuracy. This aggregation can lead to accepting an underperforming statistical model, which may cause the organization to make incorrect decisions or choose incorrect models.

Concluding Thoughts on the Deep Dive into AI and ML

This chapter argues that understanding the fundamental principles of AI technologies is no longer a niche interest but a core competency for effective leadership in the modern era. This chapter explores the anatomy of AI statistical models, which are the crucial work of data scientists and the building blocks that bring intelligent systems to life.

The AI and Data Science Process, the spectrum of AI applications, and the MLLC provide valuable frameworks for evaluating and implementing AI initiatives within your organization. Understanding the rigor behind hypothesis testing and AI model evaluation reinforces the importance of data-driven decision-making and the need for robust, reliable AI solutions.

Here's a recap of what we covered in this chapter:

- AI applications select an appropriate statistical model to make predictions:
    - Averages are not considered AI. Instead, averages are often what data scientists compare against to see how their AI models are performing.
    - Random walks ("what happened last year will happen this year") are not AI. If a data scientist recommends a random walk, then the data scientist has no model.
    - Data scientists use AI statistical models to predict future events that exceed averages and random walks.
- Hypothesis testing is a vital skill for data scientists. Applying a test for statistical models will illustrate whether that statistical model should be accepted or rejected.
- The unit of analysis is vital in determining the success of an AI model, and aggregating the unit of analysis will make results that should be rejected look good.
- Machine learning is when parameters in a model change based on new information:
    - Machine learning splits the data set into training and testing datasets.
    - The best-fitting parameters of the training dataset are applied to the testing dataset to see if they fit.

The key takeaway is not the mastery of complex algorithms but rather the development of an informed, valuable perspective to managers whose teams work with or develop AI applications. This chapter tries to add to a foundational understanding of AI and equip managers with essential knowledge to navigate this constantly evolving AI landscape. Managers' ability to harness AI's transformative power can contribute to the success of their organizations.

---

[i] Pfizer. 2023. "From Math to Medicine: What Are Mathematical Models and How Do They Predict Pharmacology?" *Pfizer*, available at

https://www.pfizer.com/news/articles/from_math_to_medicine_what_are_mathematical_models_and_how_do_they_predict_pharmacology.

[ii] Infomineo Brainshoring Services. Aug 22, 2024. "Machine Learning Models vs. Statistical Models: Choosing the Right Approach for Your Predictive Analytics" *infomineo*, available at https://infomineo.com/data-analytics/machine-learning-models-vs-statistical-models/.

[iii] Sundeep Teki. Sep 11, 2023. "ML Engineer vs Data Scientist." *Neptune Blog*, available at https://neptune.ai/blog/ml-engineer-vs-data-scientist.

Chapter 4: Generative AI - GPTs, LLMs, and Beyond

Just in the last few years, the excitement surrounding Generative AI (GenAI) has skyrocketed thanks to the emergence of user-friendly tools like ChatGPT, Microsoft's Copilot, and Google's Gemini. These platforms have democratized access to GenAI capabilities, allowing millions to leverage AI power without hefty software development costs or extensive technical expertise. This ease of use has ignited a wave of innovation across various sectors.

Businesses can now experiment with AI-powered content creation, developers receive intelligent coding assistance, managers who are not writing in their native language can utilize GenAI to assist in presentations, directives, policies, translations, and wikis, and the public can interact with chatbots that understand natural language. Many feel that this accessibility has led to a turning point in human-computer interaction, paving the way for a future where AI seamlessly integrates into everyday lives.

This chapter will equip managers with knowledge and tools to harness GenAI's revolutionary and transformative potential.

Note: The text for this chapter and all the chapters in this book is written entirely by one human – me. The chapters in this book are not generated by ChatGPT, Gemini, Copilot, or other available GenAI. Be warned that GenAI may not be up to the challenge (yet) of writing large amounts of text, especially unsupervised. Also, many GenAI offerings are based on older data, often stopping around 2021, so research for advanced topics like GenAI that are constantly changing needs to involve recent experience and more current sources to be relevant to today's managers.

In its current development stage, GenAI is great for generating lists of concepts, helping with rough drafts at the paragraph or table of contents level, double-checking existing text, generating ideas, bullet points, talking points, or small everyday tasks like letters of resignation, wedding invitations, a single paragraph on a topic, etc. GenAI also excels at code generation, although a programmer must review the code before implementation.

That said, it is difficult to completely avoid using AI when writing using today's technology. For example, I use tools like Grammarly, which uses AI to make writing suggestions, and Microsoft Word's proofreading uses AI. My editors use GenAI for high-level modifications before diving in themselves.

Any organizational content generated by GenAI tools should be reviewed before being sent out, as was done with this book. GenAI tools are helpful, but managers and the AI team (and authors like me) should be cautious with what comes out.

What is this chapter trying to do and why?

GenAI is a subset of AI-ML (artificial intelligence—machine learning) that focuses on creating new content (text, images, programming code, etc.) after training from millions of existing images, text, or code. The data science manager must understand the skills, architecture, and costs of implementing GenAI before pursuing it in a production environment.

GenAI can generate text or images without coding or programming so that simple requests or prompts in English, Hindi, Portuguese, or another language return generated text, images, or even programming code. GenAI has been classified into two categories:

- **Large Language Models (LLMs)**, like ChatGPT, are the most popular GenAI applications. LLMs generate text based on a given prompt or context. They can be used for various tasks, such as writing creative content, summarizing text, translating languages, developing talking points, writing paragraphs, delivering bullet points, suggesting slide titles, and generating computer programs and scripts. Examples include ChatGPT, LaMDA, and Jurassic-1.

- **Text-to-Image GenAI** specializes in creating images or videos from textual descriptions. It uses complex algorithms to understand the nuances of language and translate them into visual representations. Examples include DALL-E, Midjourney, and Stable Diffusion.

> **Note:** Many, myself included, have used both LLMs and Text-to-Image GenAI, but at the time of this writing, LLMs seem to be the focus of GenAI development within organizations.

GenAI applications have delivered the power of AI to many individuals, allowing organizations to generate high-quality marketing copy, product descriptions, and social media content in a fraction of the time, freeing up organizational teams for more strategic initiatives. Global expansion is facilitated by breaking down language barriers with flawless machine translation, allowing organizations to tap into new markets and seamlessly reach a wider audience.

The McKinsey Group points out how technological innovation can inspire both amplified awe and increased concern when that innovation seems to materialize fully formed and becomes widespread seemingly overnight, as with GenAI. GenAI's rapid adoption since 2022 and the scramble among companies and consumers to deploy, integrate, and experiment with it has placed us at the beginning of a journey to understand this technology's power, reach, and capabilities. The next several years will take us on a roller-coaster ride featuring fast-paced innovation and technological breakthroughs that force us to recalibrate our understanding of AI's impact on our organizations.[i]

These implications from GenAI applications can go further than the expected benefits. Databricks, a leader in GenAI tools, points out that GenAI goes beyond deploying a chatbot that can answer questions, but rather that strategic implementation of GenAI requires a reshaping of the foundational aspects of data management and can be more destabilizing than previous generations of AI as organizations restructure to take advantage of the technology quickly.[ii]

Some real-world applications have shown great promise:

- A McKinsey study showed how marketing teams use GenAI to craft targeted advertising campaigns that resonate with specific audiences, leading to an approximate 10% increase in revenue due to higher conversion rates.[iii]

- According to a Google Cloud and NewtonX study, 22% of retailers have already deployed GenAI to automate customer service, and another 25% currently have pilot programs to develop customer-centric GenAI applications.[iv]

- Financial institutions leverage GenAI to generate comprehensive financial reports, streamlining internal processes and improving risk management and customer service. For example, Bank of America (BoA) developed a GenAI application named "Erica." Their AI appears to be paying off, as Erica's customer usage jumped 16% in 2023. BoA spent $3.8 billion on innovative technology in 2023 and has appeared to benefit from its aggressive development, with BoA generating 27% of all patents in the banking industry as of 2024.[v]

GenAI is not just about efficiency but also about gaining a strategic advantage. By integrating GenAI into workflows, organizations can reduce costs by automating repetitive tasks and freeing up valuable resources to increase productivity and bolster the bottom line. GenAI can also enhance customer experience by delivering exceptional, personalized experiences that keep your customers returning for more, but only if implemented correctly with the appropriate use cases.

Getting Started with GenAI

Managers in the data science department and outside are tasked with understanding and leveraging generative AI to give their organizations a competitive edge, drive innovation, and enhance efficiency. This section explores GenAI architecture, what is involved with a GenAI project, and the best practices for successful implementation.

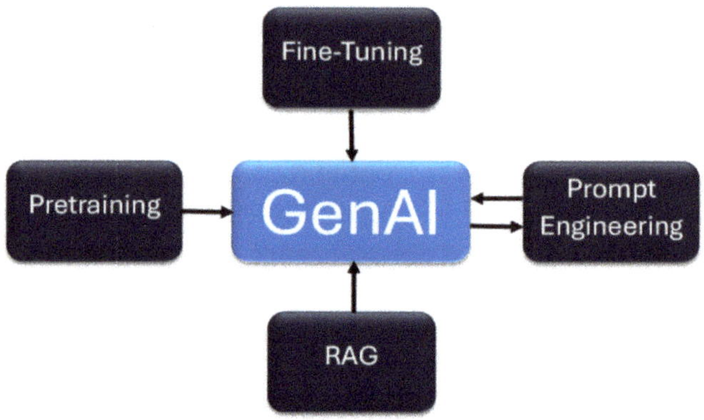

Figure 10: Pretraining, RAGs, Fine-Tuning, and Prompt Engineering are used to build a GenAI

Many articles identify four main tasks that data scientists perform to make GenAI useful or allow GenAI to perform at a high level, and concentrate on these four areas, as shown in Figure 10. [vi,vii,viii].

- **Model training (Pretraining)** involves feeding massive amounts of text data into a GenAI neural network architecture. Neural networks are a series of linear regressions built upon layers of observed and derived data and are the basis of "deep learning" in data science and AI. LLMs use neural networks to "train" using massive amounts of text data, allowing them to generate human-like text, translate languages, generate programming code, write creative content, and answer questions.

Pretraining is required at least once, although pretrained models can be purchased to answer general questions. Pretraining is also expensive and time-consuming. Sam Altman, CEO of OpenAI (makers of ChatGPT), reports that the LLM that drives ChatGPT version 4 costs more than $100 million to train with trillions of parameters! Most organizations prefer to purchase and build upon an existing GenAI model rather than create their own from scratch. [ix]

- **Retrieval-augmented Generation (RAG)** combines the strengths of traditional information retrieval systems with the generative capabilities of LLMs by adding internal or up-to-date "knowledge" to an existing external LLM:

    - RAG retrieves relevant information from up-to-date sources like the internet or recent research papers and feeds it into the LLM's prompt, allowing it to generate more accurate and current answers.

    - RAG enhances GenAI's capabilities by allowing LLMs to access and incorporate an organization's internal proprietary information when responding to queries, such as how internal processes function or what internal policies must be considered. RAG can allow LLMs to provide information on complex topics directly affecting the organization.

- **Fine-tuning** involves adapting a pre-trained LLM to perform specific tasks. By training the model on a smaller dataset tailored to a particular application, you can improve its performance on that task. This is a common approach for creating specialized LLMs, such as those designed for customer service, content creation, or code generation.

  There are several types of fine-tuning. A technique called Continued Pre-Training (CPT) CPT continuously updates the LLM and is often preferred over techniques like Instruction Fine-Tuning (IFT), where the following updates to that model can override changes to the model. Note that CPT can cost tens of thousands of dollars and is typically more expensive than IFT, and IFT is often required after CPT is completed.[x]

- **Prompt engineering** involves crafting effective prompts to elicit desired outputs from an LLM. The quality of the prompt can significantly impact the quality of the generated text. By carefully constructing prompts, you can control the generated output's tone, style, and content, making it more relevant to your specific needs.

  Prompt engineering is an iterative process where one prompt leads to a suboptimal answer and is modified until the optimal answer is reached.[xi]

Fine-Tuning vs. RAG: Choosing the Right Approach for LLMs

K2View describes how LLMs are initially trained on an enormous amount of data to learn general language patterns. Still, just like all AI, LLMs require updating once they become outdated, such as when new data becomes available or when existing models are insufficient for new tasks specific to a domain or task. When an LLM requires updating, data science managers must choose between a fine-tuning approach and a RAG approach:[xii]

- Fine-tuning a pre-trained LLM allows better analysis and understanding of each customer's unique preferences and needs to recognize better-specialized entities or terminologies (for example, legal or medical terms) where a generic LLM could fall short and generate low-quality or inaccurate responses and interpret the subtleties of attitude and emotion in text when it is difficult for generic LLMs to understand tone and intonation.

  However, fine-tuning can be resource-intensive, requiring significant costs, skillset training, computational power, and time.

- RAG implementations require less AI, programming, and architectural expertise. RAG can also reduce "hallucinations," where a GenAI describes scenarios that are not real for a specific domain or task. Finally, because it is less costly and requires less expertise, RAG is excellent for analyzing dynamic data, where constant changes can be captured with a less expensive method.

  However, the quality of the information retrieved and the effectiveness of the retrieval process can significantly impact the model's performance. Complete fine-tuning can lead to better responses than an RAG adjustment of existing LLMs.

- In many cases, a hybrid approach that combines fine-tuning and RAG can be beneficial. For example, the LLM could be fine-tuned on a general-purpose task and then augmented with RAG for more specialized tasks. This approach can leverage the strengths of both methods while mitigating their weaknesses.

GenAI Architecture

Figure 11 shows a simplified LLM/GenAI architecture derived from a Databricks eBook on the subject:[xiii]

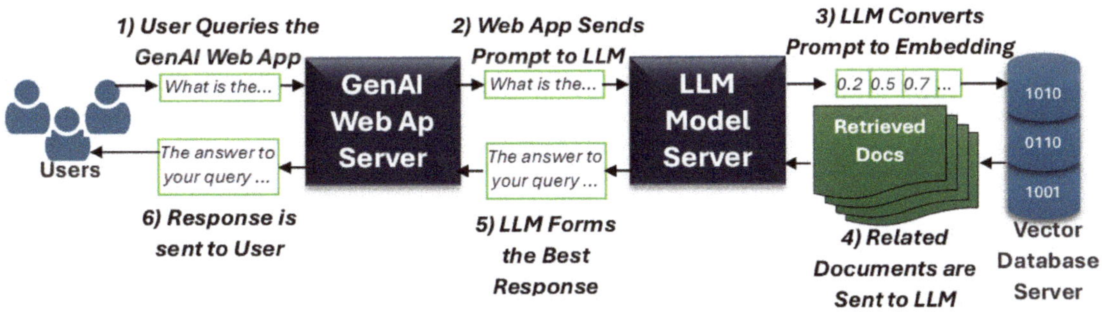

Figure 11 – Simplified LLM Architecture

The three main servers in this simplified drawing show the minimal requirements needed to deliver a GenAI application:[xiv]

- A web application server communicates with the user. The user asks a question known as a prompt (also called a query), and the web server transmits the prompt to the LLM application and waits for a response.

- An LLM server hosts the LLM software, where prompts are sent from the user and encoded so similar existing documents can be retrieved from a vector database. The responses are then reviewed, and a response is formed and sent to the application server.

- A vector database server contains documents used as the response's source material. When the LLM sends the embedded prompt to the vector database server, the related documents to the prompt are retrieved and sent back to the LLM for evaluation.

Resource-wise, this is a simplistic view of most LLM implementations. Databricks suggests a monitoring application and a model hub server to reduce errors and increase performance.[xv]

GenAI Tools and Resources

Developers use many tools and libraries to simplify GenAI application development. Here are some popular tools:

- Many consider **Hugging Face** a one-stop-shop hub for sharing, discovering, and experimenting with LLMs and related tools.[xvi] Hugging Face offers many resources and tools that make exploring, experimenting, and deploying LLMs easier. Hugging Face fosters a vibrant community of AI researchers and developers, providing a space for collaboration, knowledge sharing, and discussions around LLMs and related topics.

Hugging Face has become an indispensable platform for many working with LLMs. Though the scope of implementation is beyond the scope of this book, here is a summary of what it provides:

- **Model Hub:** Hugging Face hosts a vast repository of pre-trained LLMs, including popular models like BERT, GPT-2, RoBERTa, and more. These models can be directly downloaded and used for various LLM tasks.

- **Datasets:** The platform offers a collection of datasets specifically designed for training and evaluating LLMs, making it easier for researchers and developers to find suitable data.

- **Transformers Library:** Hugging Face provides the Transformers library. This powerful Python library simplifies working with transformer-based models widely used in natural language processing (NLP) tasks. It provides a collection of pre-trained models, datasets, and tools that make it easier for researchers and developers to build and experiment with LLM-based applications. These libraries include routines that allow developers to tokenize text by breaking down text into smaller chunks that the LLM can understand. It also provides inference engines that enable LLMs to make predictions with trained models, and it includes experimentation tools that allow the exploration of different architectures, hyperparameters, and datasets.

- **LangChain** – LangChain provides a modular and flexible approach to building applications that can leverage the capabilities of LLMs for tasks such as text generation, question answering, and summarization. LangChain offers a collection of components that can be combined to create custom applications. These components include **chains**, which represent the overall workflow of an application; **modules**, which encapsulate specific functionalities; and **agents**, which can interact with the environment and make decisions. By carefully selecting and combining these components, developers can construct applications tailored to their needs.

  One of LangChain's key advantages is its ability to handle complex workflows. It allows developers to create chains that involve multiple steps, such as retrieving information from external sources, processing the retrieved data, and generating a response. This flexibility makes LangChain well-suited for a wide range of applications, from simple chatbots to sophisticated knowledge management systems.

- **LlamaIndex** – LlamaIndex provides a flexible and efficient way to manage and query large amounts of unstructured data, making it a valuable tool for data scientists and

LLM developers. One of the key features of LlamaIndex is its ability to create indices, which are data structures that can be used to search and retrieve information from large datasets efficiently. LlamaIndex offers a variety of indexing strategies, including vector embeddings, keyword-based indexing, and semantic search, allowing users to choose the most appropriate method for their specific needs.

In addition to indexing, LlamaIndex provides tools for data loading, transformation, and querying. This makes integrating LLMs into existing applications and workflows easy without requiring extensive programming expertise. LlamaIndex also supports many LLMs, making it a versatile and adaptable framework.

Why You Need a Data Scientist for GenAI

The buzz around GenAI might lead some to believe that the era of data scientists is drawing to a close and that anyone can implement and deploy an LLM. However, this couldn't be further from the truth. In fact, LLMs make a data scientist's role even more vital, and here's why:

- **How good is your LLM?** Like any ML model, LLMs can be of high quality or low quality. Once a prompt engineer builds upon an existing LLM, what checks were made to ensure that the LLM is generating correct output (so no hallucinations), detailed (so generalized answers that are not very useful are ignored), and functional (so information can be acted upon)? Data scientists are skilled at splitting data into testing and training datasets and then statistically evaluating the accuracy, precision, and correctness of the LLM. Prompt engineers without this training will call the library routines and hope they work.

- **Garbage in, garbage out:** LLMs are only as good as the data they are trained on or provided with. Real-world data is messy, incomplete, and often requires significant preprocessing. Data scientists have the expertise to clean, transform, and engineer features from raw data to make it suitable for analysis, including for use with LLMs.

- **Understanding data biases:** Data scientists are trained to identify and mitigate biases in data, which is crucial for ensuring fair and accurate outcomes when using LLMs. Simply feeding biased data into an LLM will likely result in biased outputs.

- **Going beyond the hype:** LLMs are powerful but aren't the solution to every problem. Data scientists understand the strengths and weaknesses of various machine learning models, including when an LLM is an appropriate tool and when other techniques might be more effective.

- **Customization and fine-tuning:** Generic LLMs often need to be fine-tuned on specific datasets to perform optimally for specific tasks. Data scientists have the skills to perform this fine-tuning, evaluate its effectiveness, and ensure the model generalizes well.

Data scientists must delve deeper into the process by meticulously curating and preparing datasets, ensuring data quality, and addressing biases. Rigorous testing and evaluation are conducted to measure model performance and identify areas for improvement. Parameter engineering involves fine-tuning hyperparameters to optimize model behavior. Additionally, data scientists explore techniques like reinforcement learning to enhance model capabilities further and address specific tasks not included in traditional LLMs and RAG systems.

A problem can arise when managers and developers see how easy it is to use existing LLM or Text-to-Image GenAI tools to retrieve some results. They mistakenly believe that GenAI is simple, requires little or no additional training and that any developer can do it by calling a library. This attitude toward GenAI development can result in LLMs that generate many hallucinations or incorrect responses, and, worse, the executives and even the developers may not realize that more can be done to achieve better results for their organization and clients.

Identifying use cases for GenAI within your organization

Use case development is one of the most challenging tasks for GenAI development. GenAI technology is impressive, but how do organizations best benefit from GenAI applications? Google Cloud and NewtonX surveyed 274 U.S. C-suite executives and reported how retail decision-makers have coalesced around five use cases:[xvii]

- **Customer service automation**: 59% of survey respondents are developing GenAI applications to streamline customer service. This streamlining can provide conversation summaries, automate tasks, and increase conversion rates.

- **Marketing support and product description generation**: 49% of respondents plan to use generative AI to generate excellent customer-centric marketing copy.

- **Creative assistance**: 44% of respondents want to use GenAI to generate creative content for campaigns and editorial placements and enable individual personalization.

- **Conversational commerce**: 40% of retail decision-makers are developing GenAI applications to address shopper inquiries with interactive responses beyond simple product recommendations.

- **Store associate knowledge and support**: 38% of respondents are developing GenAI applications to automatically generate internal knowledge articles using existing data sources, such as product documentation, customer support tickets, and employee training materials.

GenAI applications can increase revenue, reduce costs, and improve operational efficiencies. The data science manager should monitor the organizational landscape for use case opportunities where GenAI would be the right tool to benefit the organization.

Leveraging Small Language Models (SLMs)for Edge Computing

LLMs are large. They usually consist of an extremely large vector database used for lookups, where prompts are passed through an internet connection to a remote server, then processed, and the results are sent back from the remote server to the local computer. While a powerful tool, LLMs generate a lot of network traffic that must be secured. Plus, LLMs can take a while to respond, which can incur a lot of computing and bandwidth costs.

By contrast, Small Language Models (SLMs) can play a vital role in edge computing environments by reducing the need for frequent communication with Large Language Models (LLMs) hosted in centralized data centers. By deploying SLMs at the edge (on local computers, local area networks, etc.), SLMs operate closer to the data source. SLMs allow many tasks to be handled locally without transmitting data over potentially slow, unreliable, overworked, costly, or unavailable networks.

SLMs can be trained on specific datasets or domains to provide tailored responses to common queries or requests. For instance, an SLM deployed in a manufacturing facility could be trained using the company's product manuals and maintenance records. When a worker asks about a specific machine or procedure, the SLM can provide relevant information without interacting with a remote LLM. This reduces network traffic and latency, improving overall system responsiveness.

Winder.AI describes how SLMs are designed to be lightweight, faster, more secure, and more resource-efficient than LLM-only systems. SLMs are designed to be ideal for applications that need to operate within limited computational environments. With fewer resource demands, SLMs are easier and quicker to deploy, reducing the time and effort required for maintenance. Figure 12 shows the typical request process when SLMs are incorporated into an LLM environment:[xviii]

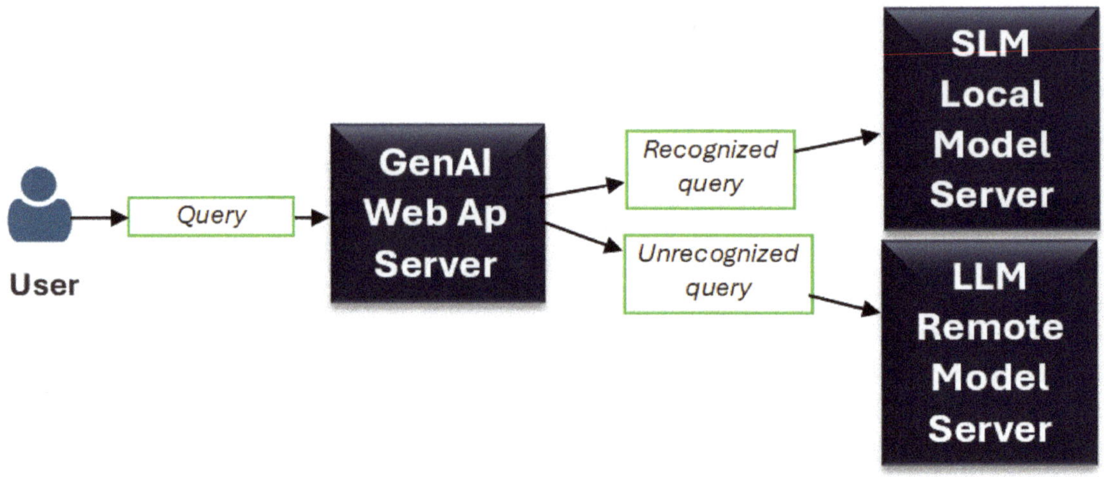

Figure 12 -- Small Language Models working with Large Language Models

In Figure 12, the user queries the web application, as is done in Figure 11. However, this time, the web application first tries the query on a small language model. If the query is recognized, the user receives the response quickly and with minimal network load. If the query is not recognized, the web application calls the larger remote LLM server to get a response.

SLMs are often considered to be an essential part of any productionalized LLM system and can enhance LLM functionality.

Generative AI for Multimedia Content Creation

Thus far, this chapter has concentrated on one specific type of GenAI – LLMs- used to generate text, such as sentences, programming code, and ideas. However, GenAI is also used to generate multimedia content. These models are trained on vast datasets containing images, sounds, music, or video and use these datasets to generate new content based on specific prompts or styles. For example, an image generation model could be used to create realistic portraits, design new products, or even generate artwork in the style of a famous artist.

While GenAI applications leverage deep learning techniques, their underlying architecture and training data differ significantly. LLMs primarily rely on transformer architectures, which are well-suited for processing sequential data like paragraphs and programming code. By contrast, Multimedia Generation GenAI applications often employ convolutional neural networks (CNNs), which are designed to process multi-dimensional data (like images) using deep learning techniques. These architectural differences reflect the fundamental differences in the tasks these models are designed to perform.

Some Downsides to GenAI

GenAI is a revolutionary evolution of AI techniques, but as with any powerful tool, GenAI does have some drawbacks and challenges. Managers should understand these challenges to unlock GenAI's full potential with fewer negative consequences. This section delves into the potential downsides of GenAI, both now and in the future, to equip the manager with the knowledge to navigate these hurdles when harnessing this technology's benefits.

Ethical Considerations

Generative AI (GenAI) offers tremendous innovation potential but also comes with significant ethical challenges that cause many people within and outside the organization to question or even protest its use. Here are some concerns:

- **Bias** – GenAI models are trained on vast datasets, and if these datasets contain biases, the models will inevitably perpetuate those biases. This can lead to discriminatory outcomes, particularly in areas like hiring, lending, and criminal justice. For example, a facial recognition system trained on a dataset that primarily includes images of white individuals may be less accurate at identifying individuals with darker skin tones or an LLM that has been trained using dialog from one country may be biased toward that country's language structures and not recognize the idioms used in another country.

- **Data Ownership and Privacy** – GenAI models often require large amounts of data to train effectively, and this data may contain sensitive personal information or an organization's proprietary information used for patents or competitive advantage. There is a risk that this information could be misused or leaked, leading to privacy breaches, loss of power in the marketplace, and reputational damage. For instance, a healthcare organization using GenAI to analyze patient data may inadvertently expose sensitive medical records.

- **Misuse** – Additionally, there is a growing concern about the potential for GenAI to be misused to create "deepfakes," which are highly realistic but fake images, videos, or audio recordings. These deepfakes can be used to spread misinformation, manipulate public opinion, or even commit fraud. For example, a deep-fake video of a political figure saying something harmful or offensive could damage their reputation or unjustly manipulate voters to swing a political election.

- **Stolen Content** – The fear of stolen content can be a significant barrier for organizations. GenAI models might be trained on copyrighted material, and there is a risk that they could generate content that infringes on intellectual property rights. This could lead to legal disputes and financial losses. For instance, an artist may sue a company that uses GenAI to create art that is similar to their work.

GenAI Vs. the World

Along with ethical considerations, the Gartner group reports some growing concerns about the use of GenAI within organizations: [xix]

- As mentioned in this chapter, GenAI can result in lower-quality content, and managers must ensure that any GenAI-generated content is reviewed before being presented to clients or used internally. Gartner surveys indicate that 55% of brand reputation leaders believe that internal GenAI use will pose a significant risk to perceived brand value from their organizations. Yet only 21% of these organizations have in-depth guidance on how to avoid usage that would cause reputational risk. Data science managers and other management whose areas use GenAI should closely monitor the generated content.

- Gartner predicts that by 2027, 20% of brands will differentiate themselves by boasting "AI-free" in their business and products. As AI becomes more pervasive, some customers are predicted to avoid AI-powered content that they perceive as low-trust, low-truth, and low-value. There will be a perceived higher quality for products than when avoiding AI, such as financial advice, books, multimedia, or books (like this book, which avoids AI-generated content).

  Even now, Gartner reports the growing popularity of a concept known as "acoustic products" – products that hint at higher authenticity and ethics by promising AI-free experiences. These brands can potentially position themselves as a safer or more premium alternative, much like vinyl records, clean beauty products, or farm-to-table food movements have done. Managers should be careful to utilize GenAI technologies in conjunction with human oversight and high ethical standards to ensure that quality due to GenAI is never an issue for the final customer.

- Not all industries are going to be enhanced by GenAI. Gartner predicts that by 2028, AI-powered search will reduce brands' organic site traffic by 50% or more. This means that organizations' current website content used to drive traffic for purchases or brand awareness may quickly become obsolete. Managers must ensure that content is continuously updated so that GenAI's costly and time-consuming training limitations cannot compete with the current content on the organization's website.

GenAI Misuse – Rapid Adoption that Stalls

Many agree that GenAI use is becoming pervasive, significantly impacting all industries, but some industries will be especially impacted. The McKinsey group examines 63 use cases and delivers some startling results that show how GenAI could generate $200 to $340 billion annually in the banking industry, with retail and packaged goods industries garnishing an additional $400 to $600 billion per year from GenAI. However, while all sectors will be impacted, an analysis at McKinsey shows that 75% of GenAI's benefits are in customer operations, marketing and sales, software engineering, and R&D/new product development.[xx]

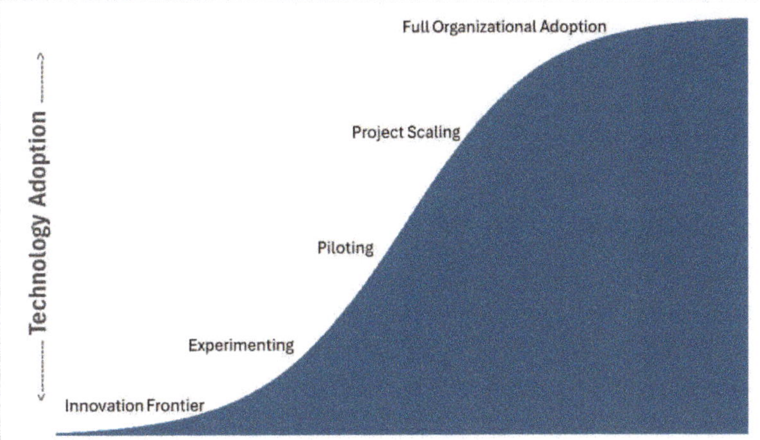

Figure 13: Technology Adoption Curve

However, while leadership in many organizations has expressed a desire to start incorporating GenAI into their products, managers are finding it difficult to find profitable use cases. Consider the often-used adoption chart in Figure 13.

Figure 13 shows how new technologies (all new technologies, not just GenAI) are typically adopted across all organizations. The first adopters are the innovators who see the potential of specific technologies. Then, others start experimenting with that technology to see how it works and what it can do. As technologies gain traction and move beyond experimenting, adoption rates start accelerating, and companies begin piloting, where the organization sees the value of the technology and starts trying to apply the technology to specific use cases where costs can be cut, revenue can be generated, or product quality is improved. The fourth phase is project scaling, where the technology is applied broadly across an organization to develop many products that create internal and external benefits. The last step is full organizational adoption, where a technology is fully realized and scaled across the organization. The technology adoption curve shown in Figure 13 is commonly applied as a lens to view technological adoption within organizations.[xxi]

There is a significant difference between GenAI adoption and the typical adoption of other technologies. For typical technologies, adoption usually starts from the bottom up, where engineers, developers, scientists, and managers see a need that can be addressed by new technology. These visionaries convince directors, vice presidents, and eventually presidents, finance departments, and C-level executives of the value of the technology with expected return on investment, product quality assessments, or cost and efficiency demonstrations. The innovation frontier and experimentation phases are driven at a lower level, and technologists and managers must justify how the economic benefit of the technology exceeds the cost of implementation.

For GenAI, adoption has been flipped on its head and has become top-down in several organizations. Senior executives and leaders have seen how powerful GenAI can be as they use popular GenAI packages like ChatGPT. These leaders' awareness of GenAI innovation has increased interest, investment, and innovation in GenAI technologies, leading to a top-down urgency to start incorporating this technology into products.[xxii] The plus side for the AI development team is that AI application development efforts are facilitated with funding, and personnel are more readily allocated to GenAI application development. However, the top-down push for adoption also has a negative side for data science managers, where there may be a lack of use cases where the technology can generate revenue. Forced adoption without clear income-generating reasons can make it difficult for a manager to justify costs and personnel in the future.

To illustrate this point, Miku Jha (the director of Google Cloud AI/ML and Generative AI) recently estimated that organizations have a clear idea of what they want to accomplish with GenAI only 15% of the time. Furthermore, Jha estimates that significant revenue generation and/or cost reduction of GenAI product offerings only occurs in 5% of the cases. This means that 85% of the time, organizations have no idea what they want to develop when starting a GenAI project, and 95% of the time, that development effort does not result in increased profitability.[xxiii] This lack of initial project success and concentration of experimental projects without a move toward pilot projects is probably the result of the enthusiasm for GenAI, coupled with a limited number of profitable use cases to apply GenAI technology.

Getting Sold – Consultants Who Misrepresent, Do RAG-only, and Distill Their LLM

The surge of GenAI consulting firms is a vibrant sign of the technology's potential. However, amidst the excitement, it is crucial to remember that this GenAI field is rapidly evolving. While many consultants offer genuine expertise, the promise of quick solutions and low costs can sometimes mask underlying risks or lead to quick but wrong solutions, such as using GenAI for time series analysis or using GenAI when a deep learning solution will generate better predictions and advice. Exploring uncharted territory can yield significant rewards, but a cautious approach is essential. To ensure the organization benefits from true innovation and avoids costly missteps, it is best to adopt a strategy of informed vigilance. Here are some caveats about these consultants:

- **Watch out for GenAI consultants who misrepresent their talent:** Managers should be aware that some GenAI consulting firms might exaggerate their employees' or subcontractors' skills or experience in pursuing a lucrative contract. This is not a new problem. The National Society of Professional Engineers has pointed out that many technical consulting companies try to make their employees look more impressive to potential clients to get more business, and that many companies misrepresent their staff's qualifications, thinking "anything goes" when it comes to pursuing a contract, even with large established consulting firms.[xxiv]

Data science managers need to guard against this by conducting interviews where specific technical questions are asked, performing background checks, and being wary of overly impressive claims.

- **Watch out for RAG-only consultants:** Traditional LLM training demands massive datasets and significant computational resources. RAG sidesteps much of this by leveraging existing LLMs and external knowledge bases. This significantly lowers the barrier to entry.[xxv] This low barrier to entry and lower cost give rise to consulting companies that might specialize solely in RAG and potentially misrepresent themselves as broader GenAI experts. This is not necessarily malicious, but rather, the lower costs and easier access result in consultants with a limited perspective that leads to a "RAG-first" or even “RAG-only” approach, where more optimal AI solutions are overlooked.

  RAG-centric consultants could convince organizations to invest significant resources in RAG-based systems that can fail to address non-RAG-specific needs. Managers who bring in GenAI consultants must ensure that these consultants offer a comprehensive understanding of the AI and GenAI landscape, not just a mastery of one of the most straightforward GenAI techniques.

- **Watch out for distillers:** In GenAI, distillation is a technique where a smaller, simpler AI model (the "student") is trained to mimic the behavior of a larger, more complex AI model (the "teacher"). Understandably, distilled GenAI models can be developed more cheaply and quickly than the teacher model, making distillation more practical for deployment for organizations with limited time and budgets. While student models may be trained to excel in specific topic areas, matching teacher models in performance across all topics is difficult. Still, student models can come close to parent model performance at a fraction of the cost. [xxvi]

  However, some GenAI distiller consultants and software providers can present their products as on par with the GenAI teachers or hide that distillation was used to develop their products. Forbes describes how one company, DeepSeek, recently released a GenAI LLM that competes with ChatGPT/OpenAI and developed it for a small fraction of what it cost OpenAI to develop, where, according to AI and Crypto Czar David Sacks, there is “substantial evidence” that DeepSeek distilled OpenAI to develop their product.[xxvii]

Distilled GenAI products are a viable option for managers and consultants who weigh the costs and benefits of GenAI development. However, managers need to be aware of three main challenges they may face when using distilled products:

- **Oversimplification:** Distilled models, by their nature, are simplified versions of the original models. This simplification could cause a loss of the ability to handle complex situations and might lead to hallucinations where nonsensical or factually incorrect results are presented.[xxviii]

- **Dependence on Original Models:** Distilled models are inherently dependent on the quality and capabilities of the original teacher models. Any biases or limitations in the teacher GenAI can be transferred or amplified in the distilled student GenAI. Furthermore, Sacks describes how leading AI companies are taking steps to halt or slow copycat student models. Managers dependent on these models or the consultants who push them might soon find their GenAI outdated and with decreasing accuracy.[xxix]

- **Legal and Ethical Issues:** There are growing concerns about the ethical and legal implications of model distillation, particularly regarding copyright infringement and intellectual property. If the original model were trained with copyrighted data, distilled models and the companies that use them could also be implicated. Also, concerns about the terms of service of the original GenAI providers may prohibit the distillation of their GenAI models.[xxx]

Managers who use distillation or hire contractors who use student GenAI should be aware of the tradeoffs and potential issues to make an informed decision about the path an organization should follow for GenAI applications.

Misconceptions about GenAI

The emergence of generative AI has led to widespread excitement and anticipation, often overshadowing the contributions of other AI techniques. Executives see the power of GenAI in certain situations and conclude that all other AI is unnecessary. Developers who first delve into GenAI see how easily prompt engineering can be achieved and can develop misconceptions about generative AI's ability to replace all other forms of artificial intelligence.

Here are some corrections to common misunderstandings:

- **Generative AI is not always better than other AI.** There is a belief, especially with new GenAI developers and non-technical management, that GenAI is the next evolution of AI, just like cars replaced horse-and-buggy transportation and electric lighting replaced candles. This is a dangerous and misplaced belief. GenAI is not suited to some AI tasks and is undoubtedly not inherently superior to other AI approaches for every situation. Rather, GenAI is an AI tool that can be deployed like other AI tools. Deep learning, non-generative machine learning (ML), simulation, time series analysis, natural language processing, and other methods are often better suited to an organization's needs for many applications. The best choice of an AI technique depends on the specific problem and the available data.

- **Generative AI is easy to use.** Developing and deploying GenAI models can be complex and require specialized knowledge. New developers may underestimate the challenges involved in training, fine-tuning, and evaluating these models and are often "stuck" at the prompt engineering phase and think that prompt engineering and RAG are the only skills needed to deploy a GenAI application, which is false. Data scientists and managers should know that GenAI models require training, testing, evaluation, monitoring, and fine-tuning over a secure GenAI architecture like any other AI technology.

- **Generative AI is the future of AI.** While generative AI is a promising technology, it is only one of several paths forward in AI research and development. Other AI techniques will continue to evolve and play essential roles in addressing various challenges and opportunities.

  Sam Altman (CEO of OpenAI and creator of ChatGPT) called into question the current method of building giant GenAI models. The scale and scope of OpenAI version 4 were so large and geometrically increasing from versions 2 and 3 that another considerable effort to develop a bigger ChatGPT might be impossible using current methods. Now, new methods are being considered that diverge drastically from the current evolutionary path.[xxxi]

- **Generative AI is not a one-stop solution.** While generative AI is a powerful tool for creating new content, it is not a universal solution for all AI tasks. Other techniques, such as deep learning, time series analysis, natural language processing, and clustering, are still essential for many applications.

- **Generative AI cannot replace human expertise.** While generative AI can assist humans in various tasks, it cannot fully replace human expertise. Human judgment, creativity, and problem-solving skills are still indispensable.

- **Generative AI is not immune to biases.** Generative AI models can inherit the biases present in the training data. It is crucial to be aware of potential biases and take steps to mitigate them.

Surveys from the Gartner Group acknowledge that GenAI has rapidly become one of the most deployed AI techniques across business units and organizations because GenAI promises game-changing business improvements. However, Gartner warns that GenAI is not a silver bullet that can solve every business problem. It is only one piece of the broader AI landscape, and many business problems can utilize different AI techniques. Figure 14 shows an adaptation of Gartner's take on GenAI as a component of AI.[xxxii]

Figure 14 describes how GenAI is only one piece of the broader AI landscape, and most business problems require combining different AI techniques. Managers who ignore the relationship between GenAI and other AI technologies tend to overestimate GenAI's impacts and end up implementing the technology for use cases where it will not deliver as reliable results as other AI techniques. Executives and managers need to understand that GenAI is not a silver bullet but a valuable tool within a set of different AI tools.

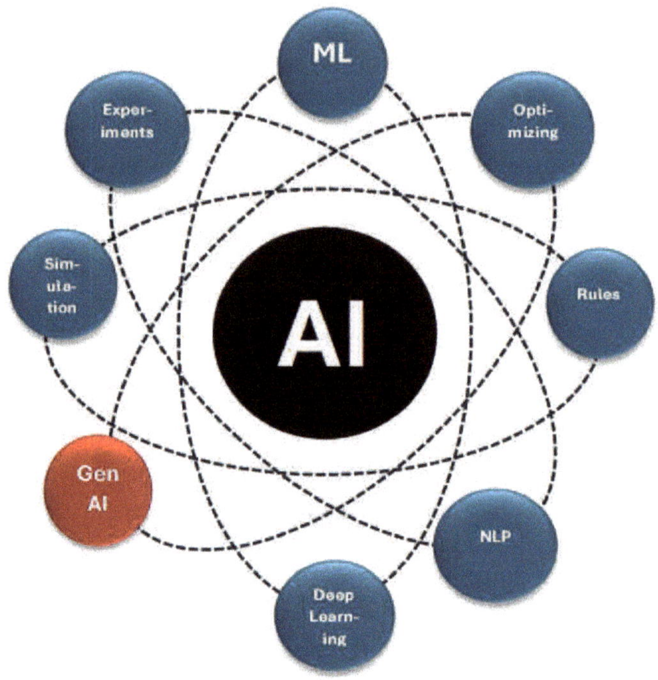

Figure 14: GenAI is only a part of Artificial Intelligence

GenAI is just a piece of the growing AI landscape. Data scientists and data science managers should understand the tools available to develop an AI application and choose the appropriate tools to give the best results. This requires communication with the data science manager and upper management, who may not understand other AI capabilities and methods, to ensure that GenAI is the right tool for the organization's use case.

The Limits of GenAI, and Why Executives Still Need to Hire Humans

In the current corporate landscape, Generative AI (GenAI) is often framed as an escalating curve of capability, where GenAI technology is assumed to be on a relentless trajectory toward replacing high-level human cognition. This perspective masks a critical structural truth: **GenAI is hitting a knowledge limit.** While its ability to aggregate and synthesize vast swathes of information is unprecedented, the very mechanism that makes it powerful (called "probabilistic averaging") imposes a hard ceiling on its utility in expert domains.

The fundamental tension of GenAI lies in the "Expertise Gap." Because these models function by processing global data sets somewhat equally, their output inherently trends toward a high-functioning mediocrity. In practice, this means:

- **The Weight of the Average:** GenAI deliverables—whether code, strategic advice, or technical analysis—are frequently inferior to the work of a seasoned specialist because they reflect the "consensus" of their training data rather than the nuance of elite performance.

- **The Necessity of the Expert Guardrail:** Rather than acting as an autonomous replacement, GenAI functions as a high-speed draft engine that requires constant, rigorous verification. Without a human expert "in the loop," there is a high risk of mistakes and hallucinations.

- **The Rarity of Novelty:** While GenAI can occasionally surface "lateral insights" by connecting disparate fields that a narrow specialist might miss, it struggles to generate truly novel, expert-level breakthroughs. It is a generalist by design, and genuine innovation rarely emerges from average knowledge.

The most pressing risk to the organizations is not that GenAI is ready to replace the workforce, but rather a **strategic stagnation in leadership.** Lulled by the promise of imminent AI autonomy, many executives have stalled essential hiring and talent development. This "wait-and-see" approach creates a dangerous vacuum: organizations are underinvesting in the very human experts required to audit, refine, and steer the AI tools they are so eager to implement.

To bridge this gap, management must move beyond the hype of total automation and recognize GenAI for what it is—a powerful but limited utility that remains tethered to human expertise for its validity and its value.

The Problem of Probabilistic Averaging

To understand why GenAI hits a plateau, we must look at its underlying architecture. At its core, a Large Language Model (LLM) is a prediction engine built on the statistical distribution of its training data. When you ask for a solution, the model isn't "thinking"; it is navigating a high-dimensional probability space to find the most likely sequence of tokens.

In expert domains, like advanced software engineering, specialized law, or theoretical physics, the "best" answer is often found in the long tail of the distribution, not the center.

- **Average, not Excellent:** Because the model weights "common" data heavily, the brilliant but rare insights of a top 1% expert are often drowned out by the 99% of mediocre or outdated content available on the open web.

- **The Echo Chamber Effect:** As AI-generated content begins to populate the internet, models are increasingly trained on their own "average" outputs, further reinforcing the asymptote and making novel, expert-level insights even harder to extract.

The Executive Blind Spot: The "Stalled Hiring" Trap

Many executives view the current capabilities of GenAI as a "Version 1.0" that will naturally evolve into a "Version 10.0" capable of total autonomy. This leads to several strategic errors:

- **Talent Atrophy:** By stalling hiring, companies are failing to build the "bench strength" of junior and mid-level employees who eventually become the experts needed to audit the AI.

- **The Verification Tax:** Executives often underestimate the time it takes for an expert to verify AI output. For example, if an expert software developer generates 100% of their code through GenAI but then spends 80% of their time fixing "inferior" AI code, the productivity gains are greatly reduced. Furthermore, you need an expert-level skill set to modify this inferior code, and you need staff ready to do so.

- **Loss of Institutional Knowledge and Competitive Advantage:** Innovation relies on proprietary, context-specific insights that exist outside of public training data. Stalling hiring in favor of generalized AI tools ensures that this unique competitive advantage eventually withers.

Concluding Thoughts on GenAI

This chapter discusses GenAI's strategic implications beyond the technical aspects. From identifying suitable use cases within organizations to leveraging Small Language Models (SLMs) for edge computing and harnessing GenAI for multimedia content creation, the potential for GenAI applications is vast and diverse.

However, it is essential to approach GenAI with a critical eye. We have addressed the ethical considerations surrounding its use, the potential for misuse, and the misconceptions surrounding this powerful technology. This chapter also fights against the myth that GenAI will replace “older” AI methodologies, but rather an excellent tool that is available to data scientists that may improve some AI applications and tasks, and the data science manager, along with the AI development team, needs to choose the best AI tools for each task. By understanding both the benefits and the challenges of GenAI, organizations can responsibly and effectively harness the power of GenAI to drive innovation and progress.

As GenAI continues to evolve, managers and organizations must remain informed and adaptable. By staying abreast of the latest developments and best practices, we can ensure that GenAI can be used in many cases to create more efficient, creative, and equitable future applications.

---

[i] McKinsey Group. Jun 2023. "The Economic Potential of Generative AI: The Next Productivity Frontier." *McKinsey Group,* available at https://www.mckinsey.com/capabilities/mckinsey-digital/our-insights/the-economic-potential-of-generative-ai-the-next-productivity-frontier#key-insights.

[ii] DataBricks. 2024. *The Big Book of Generative AI*. Available at https://www.databricks.com/sites/default/files/2024-04/Databricks-Big-Book-Of-GenAI-FINAL.pdf.

[iii] McKinsey Group. Jun 2024. "McKinsey Technology Trends Outlook 2024." *McKinsey Group,* available at https://www.mckinsey.com/capabilities/mckinsey-digital/our-insights/the-top-trends-in-tech.

[iv] Google Press. Jan 11, 2024. "Google Cloud Shares New Research on 2024 Outlook on Generative AI in Retail." *Google Cloud*, available at https://www.googlecloudpresscorner.com/2024-01-11-Google-Cloud-Shares-New-Research-on-2024-Outlook-on-Generative-AI-in-Retail?.

[v] Matt Ashare. Oct. 19, 2023. "Bank of America to spend $3.8B on innovation next year." *CIO Dive*, available at https://www.ciodive.com/news/Bank-of-America-tech-innovation-AI-chatbot-Q3-earnings/697217/.

[vi] Tula Masterman. Jun 20, 2024. "Understanding Techniques for Solving GenAI Challenges." *Towards Data Science*, available at https://towardsdatascience.com/understanding-techniques-for-solving-genai-challenges-83a7ad4650bd.

[vii] Nurunnubi Talukder. Apr 13, 2024. "Prompt Engineering Vs RAG Vs Fine Tuning." *Medium*, available at https://medium.com/@talukder9712/prompt-engineering-vs-rag-vs-fine-tuning-595e5a39402b.

[viii] Lindsay MacDonald. Jul 31, 2024. "RAG vs Fine Tuning: How to Choose the Right Method." *Monte Carlo*, available at https://www.montecarlodata.com/blog-rag-vs-fine-tuning/.

[ix] Will Knight, Ap 17, 2023. "OpenAI's CEO Says the Age of Giant AI Models Is Already Over" *WIRED*, available at https://www.wired.com/story/openai-ceo-sam-altman-the-age-of-giant-ai-models-is-already-over/.

[x] Tula Masterman. Jun 20, 2024. "Understanding Techniques for Solving GenAI Challenges." *Towards Data Science*, available at https://towardsdatascience.com/understanding-techniques-for-solving-genai-challenges-83a7ad4650bd.

[xi] Nurunnubi Talukder. Apr 13, 2024. "Prompt Engineering Vs RAG Vs Fine Tuning." *Medium*, available at https://medium.com/@talukder9712/prompt-engineering-vs-rag-vs-fine-tuning-595e5a39402b.

[xii] Oren Ezra. Sep 29,2024. "Retrieval-Augmented Generation vs Fine-Tuning: What's Right for You?" *K2view*, available at https://www.k2view.com/blog/retrieval-augmented-generation-vs-fine-tuning/#What-is-Retrieval-Augmented-Generation.

[xiii] Databricks, 2024. *GenAI Architectures on Databricks*, available at https://www.databricks.com/resources/ebook/gen-ai-architectures.

[xiv] Databricks, 2024. *GenAI Architectures on Databricks*, available at https://www.databricks.com/resources/ebook/gen-ai-architectures.

[xv] Databricks, 2024. *GenAI Architectures on Databricks*, available at https://www.databricks.com/resources/ebook/gen-ai-architectures.

[xvi] Ashish Bansal. Oct 23, 2023. "AI - Things You Might Not Know: LangChain & Hugging Face, eh?" *Medium*, available at https://ashishsecdev.medium.com/ai-things-you-might-not-know-langchain-hugging-face-eh-2f253b42eaef.

[xvii] Google Press. Jan 11, 2024. "Google Cloud Shares New Research on 2024 Outlook on Generative AI in Retail." *Google Cloud*, available at https://www.googlecloudpresscorner.com/2024-01-11-Google-Cloud-Shares-New-Research-on-2024-Outlook-on-Generative-AI-in-Retail?.

[xviii] Natalia Kuzminykh. Apr 24, 2024. "Exploring Small Language Models." *Winder.AI*, available at https://winder.ai/exploring-small-language-models/.

[xix] Lisa Schell. Feb 14, 2024. "How Marketing Can Capitalize on AI Disruption." *Gartner Group,* available at https://www.gartner.com/en/articles/how-marketing-can-capitalize-on-ai-disruption.

[xx] McKinsey Group. Jun 2023. "The Economic Potential of Generative AI: The Next Productivity Frontier." *McKinsey Group,* available at https://www.mckinsey.com/capabilities/mckinsey-digital/our-insights/the-economic-potential-of-generative-ai-the-next-productivity-frontier#key-insights.

[xxi] McKinsey Group. Jun 2024. "McKinsey Technology Trends Outlook 2024." *McKinsey Group,* available at https://www.mckinsey.com/capabilities/mckinsey-digital/our-insights/the-top-trends-in-tech.

[xxii] McKinsey Group. Jun 2024. "McKinsey Technology Trends Outlook 2024." McKinsey Group, available at https://www.mckinsey.com/capabilities/mckinsey-digital/our-insights/the-top-trends-in-tech.

[xxiii] Alexandra Francis. May 13, 2024. "Why do only a small percentage of GenAI projects actually make it into production?" *StackOverflow Blog*, available at https://stackoverflow.blog/2024/05/13/why-do-only-a-small-percentage-of-genai-projects-actually-make-it-into-production/.

[xxiv] NSPE. Jan 1, 1990. "Misrepresentation of Firm's Staff." NSPE, Case 90-4, available at https://www.nspe.org/career-resources/ethics/misrepresentation-firms-staff.

[xxv] Kaushal Parikh. Mar 15, 2024. "Unlocking LLM Potential: How RAG Delivers Accurate and Adaptable AI." *TenUp*, available at https://www.tenupsoft.com/blog/unlocking-llm-potential-how-rag-delivers-accurate-and-adaptable-ai.html.

[xxvi] Mikiko Bazeley. Jan 23, 2024. "A Pragmatic Introduction to Model Distillation for AI Developers." *Labelbox*, available at https://labelbox.com/blog/a-pragmatic-introduction-to-model-distillation-for-ai-developers/.

[xxvii] John Werner. Jan 30, 2025. "Did DeepSeek Copy Off of OpenAI? And What Is Distillation?" *Forbes*, available at https://www.forbes.com/sites/johnwerner/2025/01/30/did-deepseek-copy-off-of-openai-and-what-is-distillation/.

[xxviii] Mikiko Bazeley. Jan 23, 2024. "A Pragmatic Introduction to Model Distillation for AI Developers." *Labelbox*, available at https://labelbox.com/blog/a-pragmatic-introduction-to-model-distillation-for-ai-developers/.

[xxix] John Werner. Jan 30, 2025. "Did DeepSeek Copy Off of OpenAI? And What Is Distillation?" *Forbes*, available at https://www.forbes.com/sites/johnwerner/2025/01/30/did-deepseek-copy-off-of-openai-and-what-is-distillation/.

[xxx] Robert Hulse , Tyler G. Newby , Stuart P. Meyer , Fredrick Tsang. Feb 3, 2025. "DeepSeek, Model Distillation, and the Future of AI IP Protection" *Fenwick*, available at https://www.fenwick.com/insights/publications/deepseek-model-distillation-and-the-future-of-ai-ip-protection.

[xxxi] Will Knight. Apr 17, 2023. "OpenAI's CEO Says the Age of Giant AI Models Is Already Over" *WIRED*, available at https://www.wired.com/story/openai-ceo-sam-altman-the-age-of-giant-ai-models-is-already-over/.

[xxxii] Ava McCartney. Apr 23, 2024. "When Not to Use Generative AI." *Gartner Group,* available at https://www.gartner.com/en/articles/when-not-to-use-generative-ai.

Chapter 5: AI Strategy and Planning

This chapter delves into the pivotal role of strategic oversight in organizations undertaking multiple artificial intelligence (AI) initiatives. A proper strategic alignment with an AI team and an organization optimizes resource distribution, prioritizes project pipelines, and ensures AI endeavors are tightly integrated with overarching business goals. With the proper strategy, data science managers can amplify their team's capacity to foster innovation, maximize the productivity of their data science professionals, and ultimately make significant strategic contributions to the organization's financial health and sustained prominence in AI's rapidly evolving landscape.

What is this chapter trying to do and why?

AI has become a critical strategic imperative for organizations across industries with the potential to analyze vast datasets, automate complex tasks, derive insightful predictions, and personalize customer experiences. AI is a powerful engine for achieving core business goals, and embracing AI strategically is no longer just an option for maintaining a competitive edge; it is increasingly becoming a necessity for survival and sustained growth. By thoughtfully aligning AI into their overarching strategies, businesses can unlock unprecedented opportunities for enhanced efficiency, innovation, and market leadership.

Strategic alignment with AI initiatives is different than alignment in other areas due to the inherent characteristics of AI technologies. Unlike aligning business strategy with, for instance, a new marketing campaign or a human resources initiative, AI introduces complexities such as the need for specialized technical expertise in data science and machine learning, reliance on vast and high-quality datasets, and considerations around algorithmic bias, explainability, and ethical implications. Furthermore, the rapidly evolving nature of AI necessitates a more dynamic and adaptive approach to strategic alignment, requiring continuous monitoring and adjustments to leverage new capabilities and mitigate emerging risks, which is often less critical in more static domains.

AI can require a fundamental shift in how organizations approach problem-solving, decision-making, and value creation. When aligned with clearly defined business objectives, AI can act as a catalyst, enabling companies to optimize operational processes, develop novel products and services, cultivate deeper customer relationships, or anticipate market trends. AI-driven automation can streamline workflows, reduce costs, and free up human capital for more strategic initiatives. AI can contribute to key objectives, such as increasing revenue, improving customer satisfaction, optimizing operational efficiency, or fostering innovation.

With AI becoming a key part of many organizations' decisions and operations, many challenging questions arise:

- How should an AI area grow, set goals, and aid the rest of the organization?
- How can an organization best incorporate AI into the overall corporate strategy?
- Who in the organization can work with the AI manager to achieve strategic alignment?

Without strategic clarity, AI initiatives risk becoming isolated projects with limited impact. They may fail to deliver on their transformative potential, leading to wasted resources and missed opportunities. This chapter addresses these concerns and describes methods to ensure strategic alignment between the organization and the AI team.

Strategic Alignment with an Organization and the AI Area

An AI area mainly involves the data science department as the primary driver of AI application development, but also includes other areas required for AI application development, including data governance, data analysts, MLOps, and data experts. It is the responsibility of the data science manager to help drive AI application development and align AI area goals with the broader strategic objectives of the organization. When the AI development is aligned with the business's strategic plan, then the AI initiatives can contribute directly to driving business growth and success. But how do we get this alignment?

The data science manager must thoroughly analyze the organization's goals, challenges, and opportunities. Only with this understanding can the data science manager identify specific areas within the business's strategic plan where AI can create value. By identifying key areas where AI can increase revenue and efficiency, reduce costs and risks, and help drive innovation, businesses can strategically prioritize and allocate resources to AI initiatives.

Any AI plans should be integrated into the overall strategic planning process. This includes incorporating AI goals, objectives, and milestones into the business's strategic roadmap. By treating AI as an integral part of the strategic plan, organizations can ensure that AI initiatives receive the necessary attention, resources, and support from top-level management. This integration also facilitates alignment and collaboration between AI teams and other departments, fostering a culture of data-driven decision-making throughout the organization.

Data science managers must then approach other business areas to discuss how their key performance indicators (KPIs) can be met or increased by aligning the AI goals with the other business departments' objectives. With alignment, evaluation, and monitoring of AI projects, a business department is better able to make informed decisions, iterate on its strategies, and continuously improve the effectiveness of data-driven initiatives.

From this planning, the data science manager must address four critical areas:

- Upper management buy-in is crucial. If upper management does not see the need for a strong AI area or does not think AI will contribute to an organization's goals, then it is up to the data science manager to make the case for a stronger AI presence. If a data science manager cannot convince upper management that AI can play a key role in achieving an organization's goals, then it is unlikely that AI applications will be adopted.

- Business department support is essential. Even if upper management agrees that the organization should pursue a stronger AI presence, resistance from other managers makes it unlikely that an AI project will succeed. Data science managers need to work with other managers not only to illustrate the importance of AI within operations but also to show how a department will be more likely to succeed with AI / ML than without it. In a worst-case scenario where a business area manager refuses to acknowledge the benefits of machine learning applications, the data scientists should communicate this to their own chain of command and then seek out other business areas that are more likely to embrace newer data science techniques. Business managers who see an AI success in another area are often more likely to adopt an AI initiative in their own area.

- Employee resource planning is important. A data science manager cannot pursue AI projects without first having the required resources. Furthermore, resources (even experienced data scientists brought in from other areas and businesses) will take months to develop to the point where they can provide machine learning predictions that can help a business area.

- Technical resource planning is important. If there are strict limits on computer usage, cloud availability, or software tools, then some business requirements will be delayed or even scrapped. The data science manager must acquire the technical resources required to pursue projects and must communicate the need for those resources to upper management, finance departments, and other business areas.

Incorporating AI into an organization's strategy allows it to stay competitive, harness data insights, enhance efficiency, and innovate. It ensures that data-driven decision-making becomes an integral part of the organization's overall strategy. It improves operations, aligns technology with business goals, and adapts to evolving market demands, allowing enhanced growth in a rapidly advancing technological landscape.[i]

For top-level executives, grasping AI's strategic importance is vital. AI can support business growth, make operations more efficient, and open new market possibilities. AI lets companies sift through vast amounts of data for valuable insights, streamline complex tasks, and create experiences that are valued by the customer. Bringing AI into the heart of business strategy is more than just a tech upgrade; it is essential for staying competitive in a world increasingly dominated by AI.[ii] But AI alignment with corporate strategy can be rewarding. For example, Michael Horowitz, deputy assistant secretary of defense for force development and emerging capabilities at the Department of Defense, describes how key organizational and strategy updates with AI have improved the DOD's ability to effectively field new tactics and technologies.[iii] In another example, a leading investment firm changed its strategy from solely relying on traditional investigation methods to find investment opportunities to include using AI to scan for future technology successes by examining consumer mobile usage that suggests a company's technology is catching on quickly, giving the firm an opportunity to invest in that company before others do.[iv]

By aligning AI goals with strategic objectives, integrating AI into the planning process, and monitoring impact, businesses can leverage the power of data to drive innovation, improve performance, and gain a competitive advantage in the market. Meanwhile, it is up to the data science manager to ensure that every AI project or initiative furthers the organization's strategic goals. Making an organization's goals more achievable will demonstrate the value of AI to stakeholders and will secure ongoing support and investment for future projects.

Aligning AI Initiatives with Broader Business Strategies

Figure 15 shows a hierarchy of AI strategy that drives projects.

Figure 15 – Hierarchy of AI Strategy

Note that the top of the hierarchy in Figure 15 shows the organizational strategy, and not AI. Aligning AI strategies and goals with broader organizational strategies is of the utmost importance as it ensures that data-driven projects directly contribute to the organization's overall goals and objectives.

Figure 15 shows how AI strategies further business strategies. Every AI project furthers the AI strategy and goals. Then projects are divided into features desired by business, which can be divided into stories that allow easy assignment and tracking.

While AI strategy and goals must follow the organization strategy, Yuval Atsmon, a senior partner who leads the *McKinsey Center for Strategy Innovation*, reports how AI can transform organizational strategy by opening up other strategic opportunities that previously were ignored or minimized. Despite that potential benefit, only 7% of firms use AI in strategy or financial planning, compared to 25%-30% in marketing, supply chain, and service operations. However, Atsmon maintains that the cutting-edge domain of AI strategy is exciting and potentially profitable.[v]

Aligning AI initiatives with broader business strategies is crucial. This alignment ensures that the valuable insights derived from AI applications contribute to the success of the company. By aligning these strategies, the AI team can make data-driven decisions that directly impact the bottom line. The AI team can help the organization drive innovation, boost efficiency, and gain a competitive edge. The alignment of AI initiatives with business strategies ensures that data-driven insights are not just interesting findings but strategic assets that drive meaningful impact and value across the entire organization.

The Role of AI in Organizational Leadership

Figure 15 correctly shows that the AI area strategy is driven by the overall organizational strategy, but this does not mean that the data science manager has no impact on organizational leadership. The manager can affect the business strategy and goals in these ways:

- **Communicate the possibilities of AI projects.** Data science managers need to communicate the potential of AI with other managers and business leaders by painting a vivid picture of the possibilities and potential impact that AI can bring to the table. Technical jargon is often met with a defensive reaction, so the manager must use visual prototypes, discuss potential profits, and describe how data-driven insights can directly address pain points and drive business growth.

  Many data science managers might feel a bit uncomfortable describing the benefits of AI to the rest of the organization. They might believe that it is not their job to impact organizational strategy or goals, or they might worry about how they are received when they try to convince others, especially higher-ups, about the possibilities of AI projects. These managers often come from a very technical background where it is easier to motivate their own technical team than the management around them who do not have the same technical background. However, most agree that it is vital that data science managers rise above this reluctance. AI adoption is impossible without buy-in from other managers and upper management.

Case studies can be used to communicate the benefits of AI. Real-world examples and success stories from industry leaders, competitors, or big industry players can highlight how AI can uncover hidden opportunities, optimize processes, and make smarter decisions. Bring some excitement to the table and let them see the lightbulb moments that AI can create. It is all about capturing their attention, piquing their curiosity, and demonstrating the tangible value that AI can deliver.

- **Nurture a data-driven culture throughout the organization.** Nurturing a data-driven culture throughout the organization is essential for harnessing the full potential of AI. It starts with creating a shared understanding and appreciation for the value of data-driven insights. This involves promoting data literacy and providing training opportunities to enhance the data skills of employees at all levels. It is about fostering a mindset where decisions are driven by evidence and informed by data rather than relying solely on intuition or past experiences.

  The data science managers owe it to themselves and their team to foster the use of AI as an organizational goal, if possible. It helps the data science team if data science managers get everyone excited about AI and see its potential to drive success. They need to foster a curious and open mindset where people feel empowered to explore and leverage data in their day-to-day work and show the rest of the organization how AI can help business leaders make better decisions, uncover hidden insights, and solve complex problems.

  Also, it is important for the data science manager to celebrate those data wins! They need to share success stories, recognize individuals who embrace data-driven approaches, and highlight the positive impact AI has on the organization. When you create a data-driven culture, it becomes a natural part of how things are done, and that is when the real magic happens!

Creating a Strategic Roadmap for AI Strategy

Strategic roadmaps are a tool often used in organizations to map how a business area plans to evolve over the next few years. Roadmaps can provide a data science manager with a structured framework for guiding the implementation of AI initiatives, ensuring alignment with business objectives, and maximizing the impact of data-driven decision-making. Figure 16 shows a sample strategic roadmap.

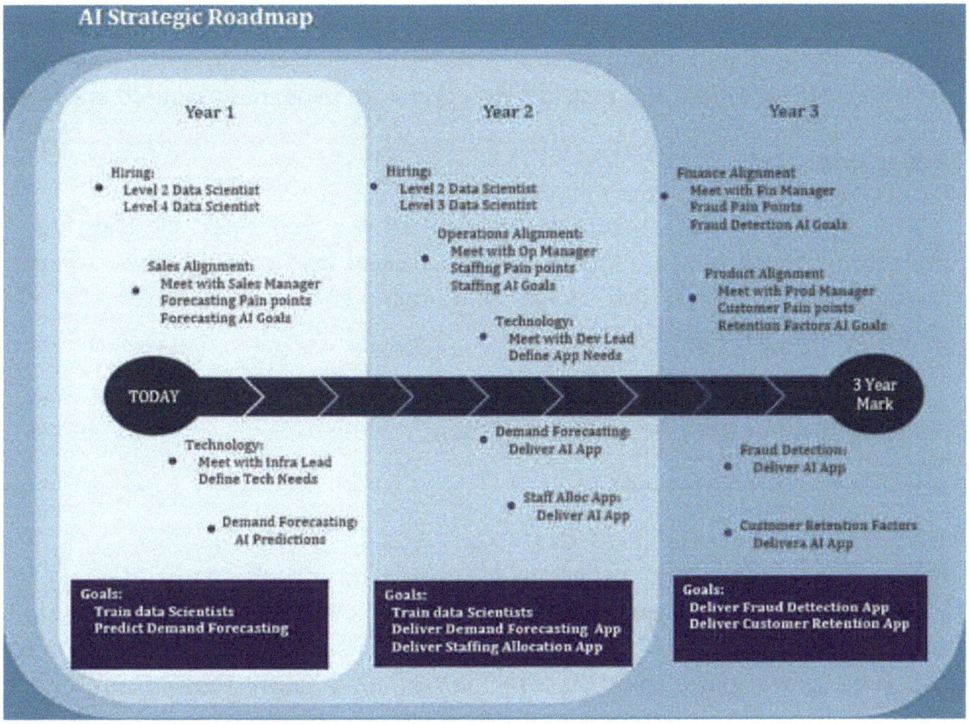

Figure 16 – Sample AI Strategic Roadmap

Figure 16 shows a typical strategic roadmap for an AI area. There are some similarities and differences between an AI strategic roadmap and a typical business area strategic roadmap:

- Strategic roadmaps describe intended hiring, so if a department intends to grow, that is usually on the roadmap. One difference, however, is that data scientists often take longer to train than other areas. Notice that the first application delivered (the Demand Forecasting App) is not delivered in the first year but in the second. However, after training is further along, AI applications are delivered much more quickly.

- Strategic roadmaps describe ongoing or intended projects. For AI strategic roadmaps, this usually includes AI applications. Although not shown here, AI strategic roadmaps can also contain maintenance or intended model improvements.

- Strategic roadmaps usually include infrastructure and resource needs to support operations adequately. For AI strategic roadmaps, this often includes technological infrastructure, server applications, and data analysts, developers, and software engineering resources required to deliver a machine learning application. Although not shown here, information security, data governance, and data management are also often included in the AI strategic roadmap.

By creating a roadmap for AI strategy and implementation, data science managers can ensure a structured and purposeful approach to their initiatives. Roadmaps help align the efforts of various stakeholders and provide direction with expected resource allocation.

> **Doing it in Excel:**
>
> The AI strategic roadmap shown in Figure 16 was generated by using the **Milestone charting roadmap** template in Excel and making some slight modifications. In Excel, click on File, New, and then search for "roadmap" – you can find this template there.
>
> Even without a roadmap template, creating a roadmap in Excel is not that difficult. Just put the year, quarter, or month in the top row and the goals in the cell below.

Gap Analysis with an AI Competitive Focus

Often, managers will concentrate on certain areas, such as optimizing operational efficiency, but ignore other areas, such as competitor analysis. A technique called **gap analysis** is used to identify untapped potential. *Investopedia* defines gap analysis as "the process that companies use to compare their current performance with their desired, expected performance." A gap analysis can be useful when companies are not using their resources, capital, or technology to their full potential. There are six steps to gap analysis:[vi]

Step 1: Identify your current state.

Step 2: Identify your desired future state.

Step 3: Identify the gaps.

Step 4: Evaluate solutions.

Step 5: Implement changes.

Step 6: Monitor changes.

From an AI perspective, gap analysis can recognize the areas where AI is thriving and can identify the untouched areas, thus allowing organizations to strategically focus their efforts to leverage data-driven insights for better revenue generation. This can be accomplished using the AI competitive focus model shown in Figure 17, which can provide a lens for gap analysis to deliver how AI applications should focus on different areas to give an organization an edge in a competitive environment.

Figure 17 – AI Competitive Focus for Gap Analysis

As shown in the AI competitive focus model shown in Figure 17, the thrust of gap analysis to determine how AI fits within an organizational strategy is not pursued haphazardly. Instead, the development of AI applications is strategically pursued to address specific gaps in profit and efficiencies to give an organization a competitive edge over its competitors. Figure 17 gives the process through which these competitive focuses are divided into two major areas:

- AI applications can have an internal "within-organization" competitive focus where internal risks, innovations, efficiencies, and resource management are designed to improve the organization, deliver products, and pursue its mission effectively and profitably.

- AI applications can have an external "outside the organization" competitive focus, where customers, competitors, the overall market, and the overall economy are examined to gain insight into factors outside the organization. This allows the organization to improve its proactive or reactive response to current or expected actions outside the walls of the organization.

- AI applications can span multiple focuses depending on the goal of the application.

This section describes how to examine internal and external AI competitive focuses to identify gaps that management can use AI to make a business more successful.

AI Gap Analysis Using Competitive Focus

While pursuing a competitive edge, organizations can derive significant advantages by developing data-driven insights from the data found within the organization. These insights provide valuable knowledge about operations, processes, and resources, enabling the organization to optimize and enhance its internal capabilities. Here are internal areas where gap analysis can highlight gains that can be achieved from data-driven insights from AI analysis and forecasts:

- **Operational Efficiency**: Data-driven insights can help organizations identify inefficiencies, streamline processes, and optimize resource allocation. By analyzing operational data, organizations can identify inefficiencies where AI can reduce bottlenecks, redundancies, and manual tasks that can be automated, leading to increased efficiency, cost savings, and improved productivity.

  For example, accurate demand forecasting can allow for optimized inventory management, thus reducing carrying costs from overstocks, spoilage, or stockouts. An AI prediction of demand can reduce costs (from excess inventory) and increase revenue (from ensuring that sufficient inventory is available for sale).

- **Innovation**: Data-driven insights fuel innovation by providing organizations with valuable information about emerging trends, customer needs, and market gaps. By analyzing data, organizations can identify opportunities for product or service innovation, develop new business models, and drive continuous improvement. Gap analysis can identify potential data-driven insights that help organizations stay at the forefront of industry innovation, enabling them to differentiate themselves and gain a competitive advantage.

  One recent set of innovations driven by AI is the development of smart home devices. By leveraging data analytics and machine learning algorithms, organizations have created intelligent and connected devices that enhance convenience, comfort, and energy efficiency in homes. Smart devices like thermostats, lighting systems, TV remotes, and security systems collect data from various sensors and interact with users to learn their preferences and patterns.

These innovations may ultimately target external areas, but the innovations themselves can be the result of data-driven analysis through AI applications that can suggest directions for management to pursue.

- **Resource Management**: Organizations can use data to understand workforce productivity, allocate budgets wisely, and make informed decisions about technology investments. By optimizing resource allocation, organizations can maximize productivity and achieve better utilization of their resources.

  Optimal staffing is an example of data-driven resource management. The number of scheduled employees can be optimized so that sales are not lost, phone calls are answered within an appropriate wait time, technicians are optimally scheduled for different jobs with different predicted time commitments, and employees are not waiting around with nothing to do. Appropriate staffing can increase sales revenue (by ensuring new customers are serviced), reduce customer churn (by having enough staff to service customer needs), and reduce staffing costs (by reducing overstaffing).

- **Risk Management**: Data-driven insights play a crucial role in identifying and mitigating risks. Organizations can leverage AI to identify potential risks, such as supply chain disruptions, regulatory compliance issues, or cybersecurity threats. AI can deliver data-driven insights that can minimize potential damage and maintain business continuity.

AI gap analysis can help organizations function efficiently and effectively. Targeting internal areas that could benefit from AI is usually cost-effective because the organization has complete control over these areas (employees, skill sets, data, infrastructure, etc.), making the potential for revenue generation and cost reduction easier to achieve.

External AI Competitive Focus

External AI competitive focus analysis can provide organizations with data-driven insights targeting AI gaps outside of the company that, if addressed, would allow significant contributions to an organization's competitive advantage. These gains are focused on understanding the market, customers, industry trends, economic trends, and the broader competitive landscape. Here are areas outside of the corporate walls where an organization can gain a competitive edge by using AI analysis to deliver data-driven insights:

- **Market Intelligence**: By utilizing AI applications to aid in analyzing market data, organizations can gain insights into market size, growth potential, and customer segments. This information helps organizations make informed decisions about gaps that may exist now or in the future in market positioning, product development, and strategic partnerships.

An example of how businesses use market intelligence to gain revenue is pricing optimization. Businesses can gain valuable insights into market trends, competitor pricing strategies, and customer purchasing behavior to set a product's pricing at a level that maximizes revenue.

- **Economic Intelligence**: Data-driven insights from AI applications can also provide organizations with a competitive edge by understanding the broader economic landscape. By analyzing economic indicators, market trends, and macroeconomic factors, organizations can make informed decisions about pricing strategies, investment opportunities, and overall business strategies. Identifying gaps in economic intelligence can help organizations navigate economic fluctuations, adapt to changing market conditions, and seize growth opportunities.

  For example, predictions of future GDP growth rates, inflation rates, and interest rates can allow businesses to assess future market conditions. This information can help businesses determine the optimal timing for investment decisions, vertical expansion, entering new markets, or making acquisitions.

- **Competitor Intelligence**: By analyzing competitor data, organizations can gain insights into competitor offerings, pricing, market positioning, and customer engagement strategies. This information helps organizations identify areas for differentiation, refine their competitive strategies, and make informed decisions to outperform competitors.

- **Customer Understanding**: Deeper customer insights allow organizations to identify patterns, preferences, and behaviors. These insights can lead to more personalized and targeted marketing strategies and help organizations deliver tailored products, services, and experiences that meet customer needs and expectations.

- **Differentiation**: Differentiation is vital to a business. What sets your business apart from your competitors? If there are gaps in this area, business leaders will not be able to capitalize on their product differences, and neither will the potential customers. By analyzing customer preferences, market dynamics, and competitor offerings, organizations can develop unique value propositions and differentiate themselves through targeted marketing, different product features, or customer experience. They can then provide these insights to their customers.

Gap analysis, both from the perspective of external analysis and internal analysis, serves as a powerful tool for organizations to drive transformative change and achieve greater outcomes. Internal gap analysis employs a competitive focus to allow organizations to assess their existing capabilities and identify areas for improvement and growth. External gap analysis utilizes a competitive focus to allow organizations to see how to position themselves as leaders in their respective industries. The combined application of external and internal gap analysis empowers organizations to drive both customer-focused and internal process-oriented innovations.

Figure 18 – Your competitors may have similar capabilities. (Picture was AI-generated by DALL-E)

By strategically addressing identified gaps, organizations can develop products and services that optimize efficiency, foster innovation, address market needs, and motivate growth. Gap analysis can help an organization stay ahead of the competition.

Like many business models, the AI Competitive Focus Model shown in Figure 17 allows the business to view strategic gaps that are not being addressed within the competitive landscape and can motivate the data science manager to focus on those areas.

> **Note:**
>
> In strategy, "the enemy gets a vote." Your competitors won't stand still while you pursue the market; they are likely using AI to pinpoint your vulnerabilities just as you do theirs. True differentiation requires continuous innovation to stay ahead of the response.
>
> Because AI models can be unpredictable, managers must closely monitor data science outputs and be ready to pivot as new competitive insights emerge. Remember, your rivals have access to the same toolkit , as shown in Figure 18: while you build deep learning models for predictions, they may be deploying time-series analysis. When you use DALL-E for creative assets, they are using ChatGPT to scout new territories. As competition intensifies, stay agile and keep your data scientists ready to counter their AI initiatives.
>
> Be ready to respond to their AI initiatives with your own data scientists as competition heats up.

The Iterative Nature of AI Projects

AI strategy employed by managers is a dynamic and iterative process that evolves over time to adapt to changing business needs, technological advancements, and emerging insights. It involves the continuous refinement and improvement of approaches, models, and methodologies to promote data-driven decision-making and deliver actionable insights.

Here are some key takeaways that explore the iterative nature of AI strategy and highlight its key characteristics:

- **Continuous Learning and Improvement**: AI strategy recognizes that the data landscape is constantly evolving, and that new challenges and opportunities will arise. Through iterative cycles of experimentation, analysis, and feedback, organizations can refine their strategies, models, and techniques.

- **Feedback-Driven Optimization**: By analyzing feedback from users, stakeholders, and real-world outcomes, the data science manager and team members can identify areas for improvement, uncover new patterns or correlations, and refine their approaches to AI application development.

- **Evolutionary Goal Setting**: AI strategy evolves alongside organizational goals. As business objectives change, new AI initiatives may arise, or existing projects may need to be modified or reprioritized. The iterative nature of AI strategy enables organizations to align their efforts with their evolving goals.

- **Collaboration and Cross-Functional Integration**: An iterative AI strategy encourages close collaboration between data scientists, domain experts, business stakeholders, and IT teams. This collaborative approach allows for a holistic understanding of business needs, data requirements, and technological capabilities. By integrating diverse perspectives and expertise, organizations can leverage the full potential of AI and drive innovation and value across the entire organization.

Data science managers must build a Culture of Continuous Improvement that embraces continuous improvement in AI projects, allows for incremental improvements, promotes knowledge sharing and collaboration among project teams, and establishes mechanisms for capturing and leveraging insights from past projects.

Choosing Projects that Make Sense

The data science manager, along with business managers and upper management, must evaluate which projects should be pursued and adopted. Project evaluation plays a crucial role in the success of any endeavor, providing a systematic and comprehensive approach to assess a project's viability, progress, and outcomes.

The primary purpose of project evaluation is to gauge the project's performance and progress against predefined criteria. This evaluation allows stakeholders, project managers, and decision-makers to gain insights into the project's strengths, weaknesses, opportunities, and threats to success. Project evaluation encompasses various aspects, including financial analysis, risk assessment, and alignment with strategic objectives.

This section introduces the methods, techniques, and metrics used to assess the progress and outcomes of AI projects. It highlights the significance of evaluating project performance and maximizing the value and impact of AI initiatives. By embracing project evaluation as an integral part of the project lifecycle, organizations can enhance project outcomes and mitigate the risks of project development and adoption.

Revenue vs. Costs:

A rule of thumb is that data science projects that increase revenues are more likely to be implemented than AI projects that decrease costs. For example, if a staff estimation calculation reduces both overstaffing and understaffing by one person per store, and you have 1,000 stores, and each person costs $100,000 in salary and benefits, the benefit for overstaffing is easily calculated as 1,000 multiplied by $100,000, or $100,000,000, in cost savings per year if we ignore understaffing.

However, the cost savings for this analysis are difficult to realize. The analysis suggests that the organization cut the store's salary budget by $100,000,000 per year. Managers are typically against this level of budget cuts, as are existing employees. And what about understaffing? Some stores need to hire more employees if they are understaffed, and we ignore them in this analysis.

This AI project should be presented as having a positive effect on revenue. Instead of concentrating on overstaffing, concentrate on rightsizing, where existing employees are assigned to the stores where they are needed most. (This is the case if overstaffing and understaffing are equally distributed.) The benefit is not fewer employees but rather better customer service because now there is an appropriate distribution of existing employees at each store to service the customers. If each store, on average, gained one customer per year because of better customer service, the math shifts. If customers spend $50 per month, then the yearly benefit would be calculated as $50 multiplied by 12 months, and then by 1000 stores, or $600,000 increased revenue per year. The data scientist can use statistical methods to calculate exactly how many more customers per store would be predicted if the stores were right-sized.

In this example, the $600,000 annual revenue benefit from rightsizing is more accurate than the $100,000,000 cost reduction from overstaffing since staff are still needed in the understaffed stores, and the increased employees from the understaffed stores would offset the decreased employees from overstaffed stores. Furthermore, because projects that increase revenue are often more likely to be approved than projects that decrease costs and budgets, rightsizing is more likely to be approved than cutting the staffing budget.

Using Key Performance Indicators (KPIs)

Key Performance Indicators (KPIs) are quantifiable measures that reflect the success or performance of AI projects. They help organizations understand how well a project is performing and whether it is meeting predefined goals and expectations. KPIs provide a basis for tracking progress, identifying areas for improvement, project adoption, and aligning project outcomes with organizational objectives. KPIs allow organizations to gauge the effectiveness of their AI initiatives and ensure they are driving value and impact.

SimpleKPI defines KPIs as measurements that track and clearly visualize performance. Some KPIs are defined by an industry standard (such as the P/E ratio for stock investors). However, other KPIs need to be created by the business area, with each KPI addressing a specific business objective and providing timely, accurate information to assess progress towards goals.[vii]

Choosing a KPI

The KPI that is selected should be aligned with the specific goals and objectives of the AI project, and thus, it is crucial to identify KPIs that are measurable, meaningful, and linked to the desired outcomes. Here are some factors that need to be considered when selecting appropriate KPIs:

- **Relevance**: KPIs should be related to the project's objectives and reflect the desired outcomes. They should align with the organization's overall strategy and provide insights into the success factors specific to the project.

- **Measurability**: KPIs should be quantifiable and measurable to track progress over time. They should have clear definitions, data sources, and measurement methods to ensure consistency and accuracy in tracking and reporting.

- **Actionability**: KPIs should be actionable, meaning they provide insights that drive meaningful actions and improvements. They should highlight areas that require attention or adjustments to optimize project performance.

- **Specificity**: KPIs should be specific rather than general to provide focused insights. They should capture the essence of project goals and outcomes without being overly complex or difficult to interpret.

- **Contextualization**: KPIs should be considered within the broader context of the organization, industry benchmarks, and project dependencies. They should be analyzed in relation to historical data, competitor performance, or industry standards to gain a comprehensive understanding of project performance.

- **Alignment**: KPIs should be aligned with other organizational KPIs and objectives to ensure coherence and consistency across different initiatives. They should contribute to the overall success of the organization and support its strategic priorities.

By selecting relevant and meaningful KPIs, organizations can effectively monitor the progress and performance of AI projects. Regularly tracking and analyzing KPIs allows for timely course corrections, performance improvements, and informed decision-making. Additionally, KPIs enable organizations to demonstrate the value of AI initiatives, communicate progress to stakeholders, and drive continuous improvement in project outcomes.

Creating a KPI

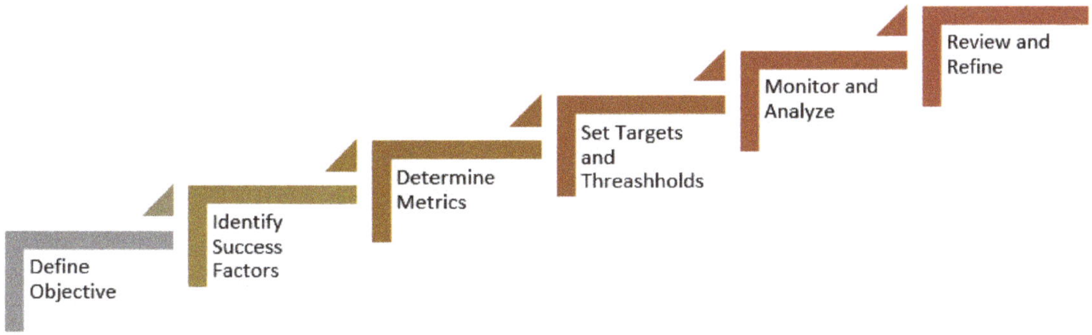

Figure 19 – Steps for Creating a KPI

Figure 19 shows how creating new KPIs involves several steps to ensure they are effective, aligned with objectives, and provide valuable insights:

1. **Define Project Objectives**: The business area starts by clearly defining the objectives and goals of the project. What outcomes are you aiming to achieve? Understanding the project's purpose and desired results will guide the selection of relevant KPIs.

2. **Identify Success Factors**: The business area identifies the critical success factors that directly contribute to achieving the project objectives. These factors could be specific actions, behaviors, or outcomes that are crucial for project success.

3. **Determine Metrics**: Once you have identified the success factors, the AI team works with the business area to determine the metrics that will measure progress or performance in relation to those factors. Metrics should be quantifiable, specific, and meaningful.

4. **Set Targets and Thresholds**: The business area sets specific targets or benchmarks for each KPI to establish performance expectations. Targets can be based on historical data, industry standards, or specific goals you want to achieve.

5. **Monitor and Analyze**: Implement a system to monitor and track the KPIs on an ongoing basis. Regularly analyze the data to understand trends, patterns, and performance against targets. Identify any variations or deviations and take necessary actions to address issues or capitalize on opportunities.

6. **Review and Refine**: Regularly review the relevance and effectiveness of the selected KPIs. Assess whether they are providing the desired insights and if adjustments or additions are needed. It may be necessary to refine or update the KPIs to ensure their continued alignment with project objectives.

By following these steps, organizations can develop meaningful and effective KPIs that align with project objectives, provide actionable insights, and facilitate informed decision-making. It is important to regularly evaluate and adapt the KPIs as the project evolves to ensure they remain relevant and valuable throughout the project's lifecycle.

Note that many KPIs are financial in nature (percentage return, net present value, return on investment, etc.) The next chapter will cover financial analysis as it relates to evaluating projects.

Risk Assessment and Risk Mitigation

Risk assessment is the process of identifying, analyzing, and evaluating potential risks that can hinder the achievement of project objectives. With AI, risks can arise from various sources, including data quality issues, model inaccuracies, technical challenges, regulatory compliance, security breaches, and ethical considerations. By conducting a comprehensive risk assessment, organizations can proactively identify and understand potential threats, allowing them to develop strategies for risk mitigation and minimize negative impacts.

IBM describes how data science managers and chief data officers have a critical role in setting the foundation that facilitates AI application development to drive better decision-making while mitigating risks. AI applications need to drive value, but there also needs to be stability in results as well as transparency and accountability for insights.[viii] The following are steps that are often used for risk assessment and risk mitigation in an AI project:

1. **Risk Identification and Analysis**: The first step in risk assessment is identifying potential risks specific to the data science project. This involves systematically examining various aspects of the project, such as data sources, data quality, model complexity, scalability, resource constraints, external dependencies, and legal and ethical implications. Once risks are identified, data science managers need to

understand their potential impact, likelihood of occurrence, and the level of control or influence the organization has over them.

This analysis helps prioritize risks based on their severity and guides the allocation of resources for risk mitigation.

2. **Risk Mitigation Strategies**: After identifying and analyzing risks, organizations can develop strategies to mitigate their impact. Risk mitigation strategies may involve a combination of preventive, detective, and corrective measures.

   Here are some examples of risk mitigation strategies:

   - To address data quality risks, organizations can implement data validation and cleansing processes, employ robust data governance practices, and establish quality assurance mechanisms.

   - For model inaccuracies, organizations can perform extensive testing and validation, implement model monitoring and feedback loops, and leverage ensemble methods to improve performance.

   It is crucial to tailor risk mitigation strategies to the specific risks and project requirements, considering factors such as available resources, technical capabilities, and organizational constraints.

3. **Risk Monitoring and Contingency Planning**: Risk assessment and mitigation should be ongoing activities throughout the project lifecycle. Organizations should establish processes to monitor identified risks, track their status, and evaluate the effectiveness of mitigation strategies. Regular reviews and reassessments help identify emerging risks, evaluate the impact of implemented measures, and make necessary adjustments. Additionally, contingency planning is vital to prepare for unforeseen risks that may arise during the project.

4. **Cross-Functional Collaboration**: Effective risk assessment and mitigation in AI applications require cross-functional collaboration and involvement of relevant stakeholders. Data scientists, project managers, domain experts, IT teams, legal advisors, and business stakeholders should work together to identify, analyze, and address risks. Collaborative efforts enable a comprehensive understanding of risks from different perspectives, facilitate knowledge sharing, and foster collective responsibility for risk management.

Risk assessment and mitigation are integral parts of AI project management. By proactively identifying and managing risks, organizations can minimize the potential negative impacts on AI projects and enhance their overall success. Through a structured approach to risk assessment, thoughtful analysis, tailored mitigation strategies, ongoing monitoring, and collaboration, organizations can navigate the challenges associated with AI projects and ensure the effective utilization of data-driven insights to drive business outcomes.

Caution: Watch Out for Bad Organizational Strategies

This chapter describes how important it is for the AI team to align their goals and projects with an organizational strategy that is set outside the AI department. However, a "bad" organizational strategy can result in problems throughout the organization but can have disastrous effects on incorporating AI to deliver higher revenue, lower costs, and customer satisfaction. Here are some problematic organizational strategies:[ix]

- **Short-term strategies** prioritize immediate gains over long-term vision. For example, a retail company facing immediate pressure to increase sales implements a basic recommendation engine based on the last item purchased. It is a quick fix, but slight boosts can grow if effort is made to build a comprehensive understanding of customer preferences based on many factors.

- **Lack of Clear Objectives** makes it impossible to align AI projects with tangible business outcomes or track their success. For example, a firm decides to "use AI" to improve efficiency but doesn't define "improved efficiency," so every manager develops their own idea of improved efficiency that is not aligned with each other.

- **Siloed Strategy** occurs when different parts of the organization do not communicate. AI initiatives can become isolated, leading to inefficiencies and a failure to leverage cross-functional synergies. For example, a marketing department hires data scientists to build an AI-powered customer segmentation tool based on customer characteristics, while the sales team hires other data scientists to create an AI-powered customer segmentation tool using CRM data. Because of separate data and techniques, sales and marketing end up with different segments.

- **"Technology-First" Approach** occurs when an organization focuses on adopting the latest technologies for their own sake, without a clear understanding of the business problems they solve, which can lead to misaligned and ineffective AI deployments. For example, a company, excited about the latest advancements in GenAI, hires a team of AI specialists to build complex GenAI applications that do not address a business need and then fail to deliver higher customer satisfaction, additional revenue, or reduced costs.

    - **Outdated strategies** or strategies that haven't changed occur when an organization clings to an existing strategy, where they might overlook more strategic AI applications and AI engineering applications. For example By narrowly focusing AI efforts on an outdated strategic priority, the organization misses out on opportunities to leverage AI for greater competitive advantage and revenue generation.

Concluding Thoughts on AI Strategy and Planning

AI strategy and planning require a thoughtful and iterative approach that aligns AI initiatives with broader business strategies. By effectively incorporating AI into the strategic planning process, organizations can unlock the full potential of their data assets and gain a competitive edge.

This chapter discusses:

- Strategic alignment with the data science department and the overall organization. This chapter examines how AI initiatives are doomed to fail unless there is a strategic alignment between the AI area and the organization.

- There are several areas in an organization's strategic plan that focus on competitive strategy. This chapter introduces an AI competitive focus model, where data science managers can examine gaps in how existing AI initiatives affect the competitive position of the business.

- This chapter examines how the data science manager needs to select projects that “make sense” by examining a project’s key performance indicators, the required rate of return, the net present value of future cash flows, and the payback period, along with the risk assessment and risk mitigation for the AI project.

- This chapter examines how the iterative nature of AI projects incentivizes the continuous examination of the AI project, along with updates and modifications that arise due to a changing environment.

It is important to recognize that AI strategy and planning are ongoing journeys. The field of AI continues to evolve rapidly, and organizations must continuously adapt their strategies and approaches to stay at the forefront. By embracing a data-driven mindset, fostering collaboration, and leveraging the power of AI, organizations can position themselves for success in an increasingly data-centric world.

---

[i] Tosho Trajanov. 2024. “Charting the Future: How to Create an Effective AI Strategy.” *Adeva*, available at https://adevait.com/artificial-intelligence/how-to-create-effective-ai-strategy.

[ii] Tosho Trajanov. 2024. "Charting the Future: How to Create an Effective AI Strategy." *Adeva*, available at https://adevait.com/artificial-intelligence/how-to-create-effective-ai-strategy.

[iii] Joseph Clark. Jan 9, 2024. "DOD Increases AI Capacity Through Strategy, Alignment." *DOD News, U.S. Department of Defense*, available at https://www.defense.gov/News/News-Stories/Article/Article/3639685/dod-increases-ai-capacity-through-strategy-alignment/.

[iv] Yuval Adson. Jan 11, 2023. "Artificial intelligence in strategy." *McKinsey & Company*, available at https://www.mckinsey.com/capabilities/strategy-and-corporate-finance/our-insights/artificial-intelligence-in-strategy.

[v] Yuval Adson. Jan 11, 2023. "Artificial intelligence in strategy." *McKinsey & Company*, available at https://www.mckinsey.com/capabilities/strategy-and-corporate-finance/our-insights/artificial-intelligence-in-strategy.

[vi] Adam Hayes. July 24, 2023. "What is Gap Analysis?" *Investopedia*, available at https://www.investopedia.com/terms/g/gap-analysis.asp.

[vii] SimpleKPI. 2023. "All about Key Performance Indicators (KPI): Discover everything you need to know about these performance measures." https://www.simplekpi.com/Resources/Key-Performance-Indicators.

[viii] Kip Yego. Mar 20, 2023. "How to successfully align your AI, data and analytics strategy." *IBM*, available at https://www.ibm.com/blog/how-to-successfully-align-your-data-and-analytics-strategy/.

[ix] RTS Labs. Nov 26, 2024. "Aligning AI Initiatives with Business Objectives." *RTS Labs*, available at https://rtslabs.com/aligning-ai-initiatives-with-business-objectives.

Chapter 6: AI Project Management

AI project management combines traditional project management principles with the unique challenges of managing an AI project. This chapter covers the key concepts and principles that govern the effective management of AI projects. The introduction also emphasizes the multidisciplinary nature of AI project management, involving collaboration between data scientists, domain experts, IT professionals, upper management, and the data science manager responsible for running a department.

What is this chapter trying to do and why?

This chapter examines the role of a project manager (PM) in managing the tasks of a team when delivering a project, particularly an AI application development project. This chapter is geared toward several audiences:

- PMs, scrum masters, and business analysts who manage an AI project with little understanding of data science.
- Data science managers who wish to better understand the PMs' roles within their area.
- Data scientists who find themselves in a principal data scientist role with little understanding of project management.

Guiding the development of an AI application can be challenging for the PM, and this chapter discusses some of those challenges and what can be done to make the PM's job more successful. Developing an AI application is often complex and requires effective project management to ensure successful outcomes.

> **Note:**
>
> Sometimes, a principal or senior data scientist is required to serve as a project lead for other data scientists and developers or to educate, mentor, or guide other data scientists to assist on projects within an organization.
>
> Conversely, a PM can serve double (or triple) roles as a scrum master and/or a business analyst on AI applications, and therefore, they do not have the capacity to act as a data scientist. These PMs often have little understanding of the data scientist. Instead, PMs are required to understand the data science role at a high level to determine the tasks that need to be completed for an AI project.

Data Science Department Management vs. AI Project Management

The PMI (Project Management Institute) describes how there is a large difference between the role of a department manager(e.g., the data science manager) and a project manager (e.g., the PM):

- The data science manager coordinates projects and other activities to create organizational benefits or value.[i] It is the job of the data science manager to determine what projects need to be pursued and when they need to be started or completed. The data science manager is also responsible for ensuring appropriate resources exist to deliver all required projects. These resources include both data scientists and other professionals.

- Project Management concentrates on creating a “deliverable” in an AI project as efficiently as possible. For AI applications, the deliverable will be predictions or decision support suggestions that are derived using statistical models and analysis.[ii]

The PMI points out how there is a blur in some organizations between project management and department management, with many projects starting to be classified as programs to avoid the need to provide deliverables in a timely fashion.[iii] This blurring of project management and department management is detrimental since project management and department management are vastly different roles requiring different skill sets and tasks.

> **Note:**
>
> This chapter is not designed to replace PM training and certification, like the PMI or CAPM certification provided by the Project Management Institute. While it does cover some core project management concepts, its primary goal is to highlight differences between AI projects and other projects and discuss how these differences in AI application development projects affect the PM.

Role of an AI project Manager

When reviewing project management software, PC Magazine describes how a project is a series of tasks and that a PM is the person (with or without the PM title) who knows what all those tasks are and oversees them. The PM monitors the tasks and the workers until project development is complete.[iv] The PM has many responsibilities:

- The PM decides the best way to deliver a requested project.
- The PM gathers requirements and sets project parameters, such as detailed business requirements, additional emerging tasks, acceptance criteria, and the definition of "done."
- The PM tracks project costs and required resources. If the PM feels that the available resources are insufficient to deliver the intended project, the PM needs to communicate with the data science manager as soon as possible. Low resources can include low skill levels, overworked data scientists, insufficient supporting personnel like architects, cloud specialists, data governance staff, or information security staff, or inadequate internal or cloud computing capacity.
- The PM monitors timelines both before and after the project is completed. The PM needs to communicate the project timeline to both the data science manager and the business area so that no surprises crop up late in the project.
- The PM manages project risk management, including determining (and eliminating) ambiguities, personnel issues, or other threats to project completion.
- The PM works with the data science manager to bring in the right people and assigns tasks to these people, including:
    - Data Scientists
    - Database specialists
    - Developers / Software Engineers

  - Scrum masters
  - Computer architects, cloud architects, MLOps specialists, system engineers, and infrastructure specialists

- The PM communicates with the AI team, the data science manager, and business users with topics that include:
  - Expectations of the end user, business managers, upper management, and the data science manager.
  - Problematic issues, including new managerial directives that can affect the project, problematic personnel issues (with the data science manager), or resource shortages.
  - Constantly informing the AI team of factors that may impact deliverables or timetables.
  - Recognize team members (not themselves) when those team members deliver key project components.

Notes from the Field:

The role of the PM is to work closely with the data science manager to present a positive face to groups outside of the AI area. It is problematic when a PM disparages the AI team and/or the data science manager to upper management or business areas, especially if those opinions are kept from the rest of the team or are used to make the PM look better or to emphasize their importance to an AI team's success.

Bypassing the data science manager on communications or, worse, denigrating the data science manager or the AI team usually leads to increased friction between the data science manager, the PM, and the entire team, often resulting in the removal of the PM and possibly even the data science manager from the organization.

The data science manager and the PM need to have a consistent message presented outside of the AI area, and the PM should work to achieve this.

Project Planning and Resource Allocation

Before a project can begin, the PM needs to develop a project plan that describes the project's development and proposed schedule using the available resources.

Work Breakdown Structure (WBS) for an AI Application

Project plans contain a high-level breakdown of the tasks required before that project can be considered complete. This breakdown is often shown graphically in a simple hierarchical diagram called a **Work Breakdown Structure**, or WBS. Figure 20 shows a typical WBS for the development of an AI application.

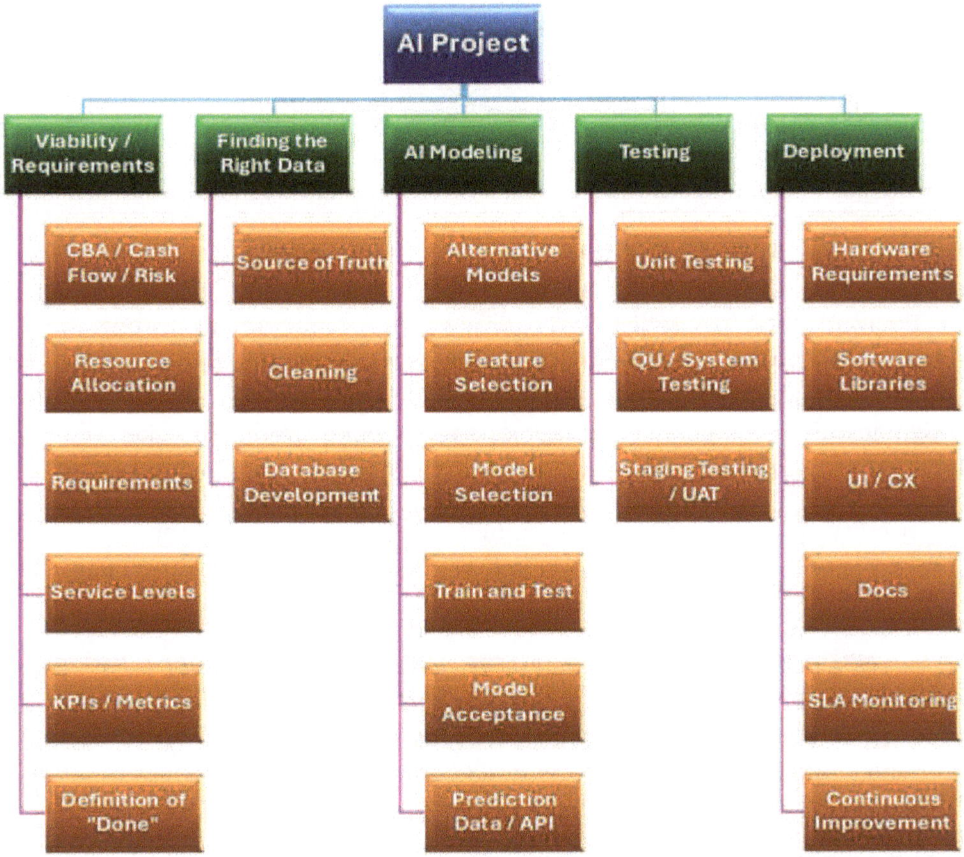

Figure 20: A Typical Work Breakdown Structure (WBS) for an AI Application

As shown in Figure 20, a WBS does not typically require much detail or assignments. Instead, a WBS is a high-level view of the tasks that must be completed within a project. The WBS makes it easier to compartmentalize the project into smaller assignments, so instead of a PM asking, "What and who do I need to make a machine learning project?" that PM instead can ask, "What and who do I need to allocate resources?"

Many managers of all types use a WBS as the first step when defining a project, but as shown in Figure 20, the typical AI WBS contains many tasks and entire columns that are typically not present in the WBS used in other areas. However, once the AI development is finished, testing and deployment are usually accomplished entirely or mainly without the aid of the AI area. However, even though the data scientists are finished with the project, the PM must ensure that deployment is successful by ensuring tasks are assigned and communicating with the other managers.

Defining Project Objectives and Deliverables

A project description is typically defined before any other project work is completed. The PMI describes how a project description and scope plan can result from several structured questions.[v] We adapt this approach here for a typical AI project plan:

What is to be predicted? If you are developing a machine learning project, you are making some predictions. These predictions can be demand forecasts, picture identification, customer categorization, workload predictions, and other predictions that require statistical analysis.

Why are we making these predictions? This is one of the most essential paragraphs in the business plan. The motivation for predictions is usually a small paragraph at the beginning of the project plan that describes the benefits of making the predictions. Data scientists and PMs are often called upon to justify their work, and a short answer to "Why are we doing this?" helps significantly. Further, having developed a needed prediction, the work and necessity of the PM are justified.

When are the predictions required? Work scheduling needs to be addressed in a project plan. If the project is required soon, its scope will be small. The scope can be large if the project's deliverables are not needed for several months.

What resources are available? Budget transfers, hiring, consultants, additional hardware and software, and cloud resources may all be required for an AI project. Compared to traditional development efforts, AI projects have high costs for highly trained data scientists, extensive computing equipment, and cloud resources, which require a large investment.

Who will deliver the project? The employees' available time for a project must be considered carefully. Which data scientists, developers, or architects can be taken off their existing projects and placed on this project? Do we have the complete schedules for the full-time employees allocated to us, or only part of their time?

> **Note:**
>
> For decades, it has been known that you cannot add data scientists, developers, or testers to a project after it has begun and expect development to speed up.
>
> New additions in the middle of a project can slow development because of the training and ramp-up required that take time away from existing developers, often for months, as those developers bring the new developers up to speed.
>
> PMs need to make sure that any data scientists are available from the beginning of a project, developers are available once development starts, and testers are available once testing begins. Overstaff slightly to consider attrition (quitting and/or firing).

What is the responsibility of the AI development team and the project owner? Development is the domain of the development team, but who determines the requirements, the resources, the testing responsibility, the auditing responsibility, etc.?

What determines task completion? This is usually called "acceptance criteria" or "the definition of 'done'"; it is important to specify when a task is finished before the work begins. If the project owner wants 80% accuracy but, after achieving that, switches and says, "Now let's try 90% accuracy!" then the entire project gets pushed back, and existing work needs to be reworked. If the user interface is defined up front, but the project owner decides that five more screens are needed, then more resources are required. Similarly, the project owner needs to ensure that the PM's team does not go "off-script" and deliver an application where required predictions do not match the delivered features.

Acceptance criteria must be specific. For example, requirements like "easy to use," "as accurate as possible," or "screens appear in a reasonable amount of time" need to be replaced with "tool tips and online help," "achieve an 85% accuracy when predictions are compared to actual values," or "screens appear within 5 seconds".

> **Note:**
>
> While defining project goals upfront is necessary, the PM must realize that sometimes changes will occur. Situations change, communication issues arise, and once a project starts nearing completion, issues that were not considered beforehand usually need to be addressed.
>
> The PM must be flexible and communicative. When new acceptance criteria are introduced, the PM should work with the business area, the data scientists, upper management, and the rest of the team to discuss changes in delivery time, required resources, and a listing of how new tasks are prioritized with existing tasks.

Who determines task completion? The PM must present the deliverables to the business manager (often the project owner in agile environments), who accepts them. If the PM determines that acceptance criteria are met, but the business manager disagrees, then the two need to discuss why there is a misunderstanding on the acceptance criteria and then define more measurable acceptance criteria.

How are future changes implemented? It is important to specify the initial requirements of a system but be able to change requirements due to oversights or environmental changes that are going to occur. Changes need to be documented and tracked, and the impact of changes on deliverables needs to be measured.

Evaluation Metrics and Service Levels

AI applications are different from other applications in several ways. A typical non-AI application (or a part of the application) either works or does not work—there is no gray area.

AI applications are different because their predictions approach an observed value within a percentage of accuracy or correctness. There is no "right or wrong" as with traditional applications, but rather "close or not close."

The PM, the AI team, and the business manager must all decide what makes an AI application's predictions "close enough" to put into production based on project objectives using evaluation metrics. Evaluation metrics provide a quantifiable way to assess the performance and impact of AI applications, whether it is the accuracy of predictive models, the efficiency of data processing pipelines, or the effectiveness of recommendation algorithms.

These metrics serve as benchmarks for evaluating the quality of outputs and enable organizations to make informed decisions based on objective measurements. SLAs (Service Level Agreements) are often specified for each project. These SLAs measure two areas:

- Just as with traditional applications, application service levels may include response time, availability, data quality, scalability, and security.

- With AI applications, the model service levels will also determine some goodness-of-fit measure, such as accuracy, R^2, average percentage correct, or other measures. Model service levels can measure the correctness of the predictions and the robustness of predictions within segments (store-level, market-level, demographic-level, etc.) or generalization (works with all products rather than some products, etc.)

By continuously monitoring evaluation metrics and service levels, organizations can continuously improve their AI applications, ensure that their initiatives align with business objectives, and deliver measurable value.

Evaluation Metrics

In AI, machine learning (ML) models use statistics on large datasets to predict missing or future values. Usually, ML models are divided into two categories: regression and classification. These two types of models require different evaluation metrics to assess the performance of predictive models:

- Regression models predict a continuous numeric value, such as the future demand for a product or optimal selling price.

- Classification models predict a discrete class or category, such as if a transaction is fraudulent or if a patient has a specific disease.

Data scientists select the appropriate evaluation metrics based on whether the model is a regression or classification model. Furthermore, the AI team should work with the business area to determine which metric should be used and is most appropriate and easiest to communicate. Internally, data scientists can utilize additional complex metrics to ensure a model is the best for the specific business prediction.

Classification – Why Accuracy Can Be Misleading

For classification predictions, **accuracy** is the percentage of correct predictions. Accuracy can often give valuable insights and is easy to understand, but it can also be overused or misused. For example, say that the information security team wants to protect against security breaches. The data scientist develops a technique that examines the logs of database requests to see if the requests are valid or if they are part of an information security breach.

A confusion matrix shows accurate and inaccurate predictions and should almost always be used to examine classification predictions. Figure 21 examines 100,000 predictions about whether a database request is valid or a hack attempt.

	Actual Hack Attempts	**Actual Valid Requests**
Predicted Hack Attempts	112 (TP - True Positive)	184 (FP - False Positive)
Predicted Valid Requests	223 (FN - False Negative)	99,481 (TN - True Negative)

Figure 21 -- Confusion Matrix

> **Note:**
>
> Confusion matrices indicate that a positive is what you are trying to predict (e.g., a breach attempt) and a negative is when the category you are trying to predict is not true (e.g., a valid request).
>
> PMs should <u>*not*</u> assume that a "True Positive" means a positive effect and a "True Negative" means a negative effect. In this case, we are trying to detect breach attempts, which would be situationally negative for the company. Since the model is designed to detect these breach attempts, any breach attempt is considered a "positive test," and any valid request is regarded as a "negative test."

In Figure 21, the confusion matrix shows how many times the AI model predicted a hack and how many times the AI model predicted a hack attempt from 100,000 data requests. The data scientist could defend this model by claiming that accuracy is over 99.5%, as shown in Equation 1.

$$\begin{aligned} Accuracy &= \text{Percent Correct Predictions} \\ &=(TP+TN)/(TP+TN+FP+FN) \\ &= (99481+112)/100000=99.59\% \end{aligned} \qquad \textbf{Equation 1}$$

The problem with accuracy here is that almost all database transactions are valid. If we always predicted a valid transaction and never predicted a breach, we would have an accuracy of 99.67%, but that model would be useless because it would never detect a breach attempt. The model that the data scientist delivered is below that score.

For a low-base-rate case, where something rarely occurs (fraudulent transactions, hacking attempts, billionaires who come to the store, etc.), accuracy is not a great measure. Instead, the business area should be advised to use a metric that can measure the accuracy of detecting small occurrences (like finding a needle in a haystack). Here are some measures that are often used instead of accuracy:

- **Precision** (also known as **positive predictive value**) is the percentage of true positives to all predicted positives, as shown in Equation 2.

  Precision = Percent True Positives to Predicted Positives **Equation 2**
  =TP/(TP+FP)
  =112/ (112+184) = 37.84%

  Precision describes how likely positive predictions are to indicate an actual positive outcome. If this model predicts a breach attempt, it is 37.84% likely to be true.

- **Recall** (also known as **sensitivity** or **true positive rate**) is the percentage of true positives to all actual positives, as shown in Equation 3.

  Recall = Percent True Positives to All Positives **Equation 3**
  =TP/(TP+FN)
  =112/ (112+223) = 33.43%

  Recall allows the business to tell how likely a positive occurrence is likely to be detected. If there is a breach attempt on our database, we have a 33.43% chance of detection. This measure gives the business a better idea of how well the model performs when detecting positive low base-rate situations (where the true positives are low), like a hacking attempt or a fraudulent transaction.

- **Specificity** (also known as **selectivity** or **true negative rate**) is the percentage of true negatives to all predicted negatives, as shown in Equation 4.

  Specificity = Percent True Negatives to All Negatives **Equation 4**
  =TN/(TN+FP)
  =99,481 / (99,481 +184) = 99.77%

  Specificity is the flip side of recall. Specificity describes how likely a negative occurrence is to be detected. Specificity gives businesses a better idea of how a model performs when detecting negative low base-rate situations (where the true negatives are low).

- The **F1 Score** is the average (a *harmonic mean*, not an arithmetic mean) of precision and recall, as shown in Equation 5.

F1 Score = 2(Precision * Recall) / (Precision + Recall)* **Equation 5**
=2(37.84%*33.43%) / (37.84%+33.43%) = 35.5%*

The F1 score is often considered the best measure of classification and is much better than accuracy or any other independent score. The F1 score is particularly useful for imbalanced datasets, where one class significantly outnumbers the other, as it accounts for both false positives and false negatives.

The takeaway is that most data scientists consider accuracy to be woefully inadequate to measure a classification model. In contrast, the F1 score might be regarded as one of the better metrics. Indeed, many single models fall short, and there is no reason not to calculate and report all five model measurements. The PM should be aware of the distinction, and business managers should be shown how accuracy might not work that well.

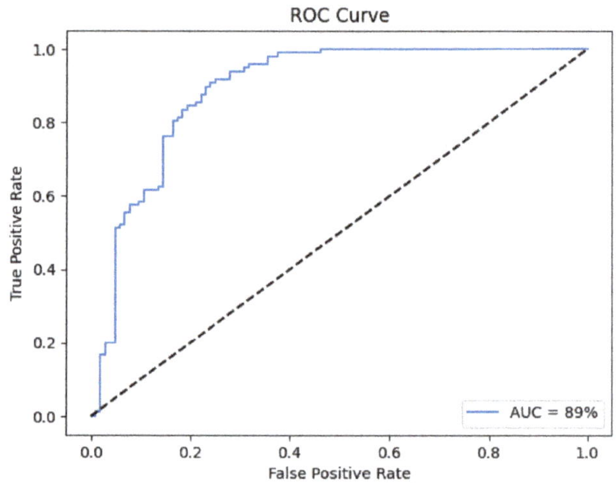

Figure 22 -- The ROC / AUC

A data scientist may want to visualize the error. The **ROC curve** (Receiver Operating Characteristic, also called the **ROC-AUC Curve** or just the **AUC** [area under the curve]) is a widely used visual evaluation metric in machine learning and AI. The ROC curve is particularly useful for binary classification problems, where the goal is to distinguish between two classes, such as identifying hacking attempts or diagnosing diseases. The ROC curve maps the false positive rate (*1 - specificity*) on the X-axis against a true positive rate (*recall*) on the Y-axis. Figure 22 shows an example of an ROC curve.

The ROC curve provides valuable visual insights into the trade-off between recall and specificity. The AUC (area under the curve) is between 0% and 100%, although most consider 50% disastrously low. A curve closer to the top-left corner indicates better classification performance (closer to AUC=100%). In contrast, a curve closer to the diagonal line (closer to AUC=50%) signifies a weaker classifier. By comparing ROC curves of different classifiers, data scientists can visually select the most appropriate model for a given task, optimizing the balance between true positives and false positives based on the specific requirements of the problem.

Regression Measures – Beyond R^2

R^2 (also known as the **coefficient of determination**) describes the proportion of the variance in the dependent variable compared to the average. With R^2=1%, the ML model does not predict much better than the average, and with R^2=95%, the ML model predicts almost perfectly.

The concept of R^2 is taught early in statistics classes in college or even in advanced high school mathematics. However, while business managers and users might be familiar with R^2, some models do not easily return an R^2, while other business managers may have trouble understanding the purpose of the R^2 metric. Here are some alternatives to R^2:

- **MAPE (**Mean Absolute Percentage Error) and **MAE** (Mean Absolute Error) use the average of each error to provide a measure of the average percentage error, which can be more intuitive and meaningful for certain applications. MAPE is especially useful when dealing with data with varying scales or when the absolute magnitude of errors is more important than their direction. They are particularly relevant in forecasting and prediction tasks as they quantify the accuracy of predictions regarding percentage deviation.

Doing it in Excel:

MAPE is calculated by dividing the difference between the predicted value and the actual observation by the actual observation, as shown by Equation 6.

MAPE = |Predicted - Actual| / Actual **Equation 6**

With MAPE, both underestimations and overestimations are considered errors. In Excel, the absolute value is calculated using the ABS function. To calculate the MAPE for January sales vs predictions in Excel, you would use the formula shown in Equation 7.

=ABS(50573-57901)/57901 **Equation 7**

This Excel function would return -0.127, or 12.7%. But watch out for actual values equal to zero, because a division by zero will give you an error in the MAPE calculations.

Unlike R-squared, which focuses on the proportion of variance explained, MAPE directly measures the average error relative to the actual values. Therefore, MAPE can be a valuable metric when evaluating and comparing the accuracy of different forecasting models or when the emphasis is on understanding the average error level in percentage terms.

Notes from the Field: Some businesses use 1-MAPE as a measure called *"accuracy"* – while this term is not semantically correct, it is easy to communicate, and to say, "Our model is 74% accurate". My take is that if the business manager understands what "74% accurate" means, then it is all good. Still, other data scientists insist on more technically accurate terminology and try to educate their businesses on these terms.

- **RMSE** (Root Mean Squared Error) and **MSE** (Mean Squared Error) RMSE measures the average magnitude of the residuals, or prediction errors, in the same unit as the dependent variable.

  Unlike R-squared, which is a relative measure of the variance explained, RMSE gives a more direct and interpretable measure of the model's prediction accuracy. The RMSE is particularly useful when focusing on understanding the average deviation of predictions from the actual values and when the absolute magnitude of errors is important. RMSE is also less sensitive to outliers than MAPE since it squares the errors, making it a suitable choice when dealing with datasets that contain extreme values or when the distribution of errors is not symmetric.

Note: RMSE is the most often used regression metric for data scientists. RMSE can frequently be substituted for standard deviation in many cases, especially with confidence intervals, so if you wanted actual observations to be within 95% of your prediction, you would multiply the RMSE by 1.96.

The Bullwhip Effect – The Problems with Aggregation

When evaluating the success of a statistical model, the PM needs to ensure the proper unit of analysis. Any aggregation of predictions will generally result in a *drastically* reduced error. Consider Table 1, where monthly predictions are made and then the results are aggregated to predictions for the entire year:

Month	Sales	Prediction	Monthly MAPE
Jan	$57,901	$50,573	12.7%
Feb	$66,656	$64,247	3.6%
Mar	$69,000	$61,986	10.2%
Apr	$51,813	$66,456	28.3%
May	$60,870	$64,083	5.3%
Jun	$64,226	$68,889	7.3%
Jul	$59,705	$59,011	1.2%
Aug	$64,172	$59,746	6.9%
Sep	$67,444	$63,328	6.1%
Oct	$67,100	$60,921	9.2%
Nov	$63,383	$59,245	6.5%
Dec	$66,893	$55,457	17.1%
Average Monthly MAPE:			***9.5%***

Year	Sales	Prediction	Yearly MAPE
Jan-Dec	$759,162	$733,942	3.3%

Table 1 – Bullwhip Effect when Monthly Data Is Aggregated to Yearly Data and MAPE/Error Is Incorrectly Reduced

Table 1 shows an average monthly MAPE of 9.5%. However, when we add all the sales and the prediction for the entire year, the MAPE is calculated at 3.3%, an error that is roughly one-third of what is reported at the monthly level.

This is a well-known phenomenon called the bullwhip effect. Just as a whip takes very little movement in the wrist to even break the sound barrier at the tip (which is the crack of the whip that you hear), aggregation of actual values and predictions can show very little error at the aggregated level but quite a large error at the disaggregated level.

In this case, project owners can become confused and then annoyed if a PM reports a 3.3% yearly MAPE, but the monthly MAPE hovers around 9.5%. The bullwhip effect occurs when daily forecasts are aggregated into monthly forecasts, when management offices are aggregated into regions or when inventory orders from stores are aggregated into inventory orders for distribution centers.

It is not easy to calculate the exact bullwhip effect, but the logic behind the calculation is that predictions often have a 50% - 50% chance of being over or under the actual observation. When adding the predictions together, the overpredictions wipe out the underpredictions (and vice versa), leaving a reduced error measurement.

The data scientist should already understand this, but the PM must also understand it to ensure the accuracy of predictions and data model evaluations for the data science manager and the project owner, and to prevent such aggregation after the data scientist is finished with application development.

Determining the Proper Amount of Application Testing

PMs must determine the number of tests that must be incorporated when developing. This includes AI testing and training to create a model and evaluate the final application when it is complete. This is not the training and testing of individuals but rather a machine learning (ML) method where the AI application "learns" based on new data (called training), and then the results of the training are applied to new data (called testing).

With AI applications, the data scientist usually randomly splits the model into training and testing datasets. When new data becomes available, the data scientist splits that data into 70% of records that need to be used to develop the training model and 30% of records that are used after model training to test.

The PM must ensure that the training and testing are sufficiently robust and consistent. For example, if one training/testing scenario generates 2.4 and 4.6 as two coefficients used in a statistical model, you would expect similar coefficients if the same test were used with a different randomized 70% - 30% split for testing and training, say between 2.3 and 2.5 for the first coefficient and 4.4 – 4.8 for the second coefficient.

The training/testing process usually takes a long time, typically many hours or even days. The PM needs to work with the data scientist to ensure that a project's training/testing phase is adequate and schedule the time required for accurate estimates. The PM needs to work with the data scientist to determine the **error detection likelihood**, how likely one training/testing session is to deliver estimates, and the **confidence goal** that the data science manager, project owner, and data scientist all wish to have toward the statistical model.

Data Acquisition and Preparation

For PMs and data scientists, the "source of truth" refers to the authoritative and reliable data that is considered the most accurate and complete representation of a particular aspect or domain. It is the primary data source that serves as the correct input for analysis, modeling, and decision-making within a project. The "source of truth" data is typically selected based on its trustworthiness, relevance, and alignment with the specific objectives of the AI application or project. It represents the most reliable and accurate data, often obtained from trusted internal systems, reputable external sources, or a combination. Finding this correct dataset is crucial for AI applications to ensure that the data used for analysis and decision-making is of high quality, minimizing the risk of errors or biases that could lead to flawed conclusions. By relying on the "source of truth" data, data scientists and PMs can have confidence in the accuracy and integrity of their findings and recommendations, enabling effective and informed decision-making.

To find this source data, the PM must collaborate with domain experts and stakeholders to clearly define the project's objectives and the specific data needed to address those objectives. This includes identifying the key variables, attributes, and metrics required for analysis. By engaging with subject matter experts, PMs can gain valuable insights into the relevant data sources and determine the most reliable and relevant "source of truth" for the project.

Once the data sources are identified, data preparation comes into play. This step involves data engineers and data scientists who clean and transform the raw data into a format suitable for analysis. Data cleaning involves handling missing values, correcting errors, removing duplicates, and dealing with outliers. Transformations may include normalization, aggregation, or encoding categorical variables. Data scientists must ensure that the data is properly formatted and structured to enable accurate analysis and model building.

The PM needs to establish data governance practices to maintain data integrity throughout the AI project lifecycle. This involves implementing data monitoring, data validation, and quality control processes, ensuring data security and privacy, and establishing data management protocols. By taking these steps, PMs can ensure that the data used in the AI application is accurate, consistent, and trustworthy, enabling reliable and insightful analysis and decision-making.

Project Schedule Management

The PM must manage the project schedule, highlighting which tasks can be completed and when. There are two considerations that a PM must address:

- What development framework is used within the company? This typically refers to either a **waterfall framework** or an **agile framework**.

- What happens when the project is deployed? Most of the work on software projects occurs after deployment, with additions, bug fixes, and changes in the environment. These are addressed in an **AI Life Cycle**.

Developing a Project Plan

The PM needs to estimate when certain tasks can be started and finished and which tasks need to be completed before other tasks can begin. As shown in Figure 23, a Gantt chart is the most used tool to visualize the project plan.

Demand Forecasting

Project Manager: Marv

Project Start Date: Sep 01

Milestone Descrip	Assigned To	Assignment Type	Start	No. Days
Gather Requirements	Kumar / Chuck / Marv	Requirements	Sep 01	15
Develop Alternative	Chuck	Data Science Model	Sep 04	7
Test in Python	Chuck	Data Science Model	Sep 11	7
Choose Best Model	Chuck	Data Science Model	Sep 18	2
Develop Database	Susan	Development	Sep 20	6
Write Batch Programs	Joe	Development	Sep 23	13
Write Controller	Dave	Development	Sep 23	9
Develop UI	Ravi	Development	Sep 26	14
Unit Testing	Michelle	Testing	Oct 10	3

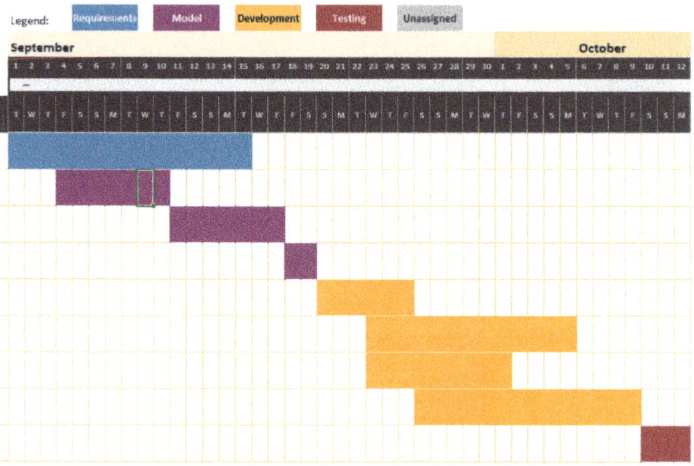

Figure 23 -- Gantt Chart for a Typical AI Project Plan

In Figure 23, the description is entered, who the work is assigned to, the type of assignment, the start date, and the number of days that the project will take. Some PMs use Gantt charts for every project. Figure 23 shows a simple project plan for an AI project:

- The requirements are gathered first. For an AI application, this typically involves discussing what needs to be predicted with the system's owner. (In this case, the title shows that demand needs to be forecasted.) The data scientist can begin statistical model development while other requirements, like report and web page layouts, are discussed with the PM.

- Before the requirements are finalized, the data scientist can start developing the model based on input from the owner during the first part of the requirements gathering.

- The usual flow of an AI project is to go from (a) requirements to (b) the development of an AI statistical model to (c) application development to (c) testing and deployment.

If all goes well, the project can be implemented by October 23, according to the Gantt chart.

Doing it in Excel:

The project plan shown in Figure 23 was generated using an **Agile Gantt chart** template in Excel with some slight modifications. Click on File, New, and then search for "Gantt" –you will find a variety of Gantt charts to choose from. (I found six different templates to choose from.)

PMs may find the need to go beyond Excel to a fully featured PM software package:

- Microsoft Project seems to be the industry standard, meaning that most PMs are familiar with the tool and do not require additional training.
- SmartSheet is an enterprise-wide tool often used in midsize and large corporations, often with a dedicated support staff at the corporation to aid the PM.
- Online packages, like Jira and Rally, allow Kanban and Agile Scrum management within an organization.
- There are free packages, like Scrumpy or LibreOffice, that provide PM management tools that can work well for the budget-conscious PM.

Determining the Critical Path for an AI project

PMs often employ a critical path method (CPM) to determine which tasks must be completed before other tasks can begin. In an AI application project, the data scientists' work is often along the beginning of the critical path and must be completed before development can begin. The chart in Figure 23 shows how the AI Model category impacts other tasks when developing an AI application:

- The data scientist can only work on one part of the project at a time.
- Bringing in more data scientists will typically not speed up the process because the data scientist needs to finish each phase of AI modeling before the next phase can begin.
- Database modeling cannot begin until the data scientist knows which data is required for the demand forecast.
- Development cannot begin until the data scientist knows which AI model should be deployed.

Unlike most projects where different development processes can often happen concurrently, AI projects require the data scientist tasks to be on the project's critical path. (Testing phases are also on the critical path, which is typical for most projects.) If the data scientist's modeling takes longer than expected, then the project deadline will be pushed back.

Agile vs Waterfall

Two primary competing development methodologies are used for scheduling when the user will receive deliverables: agile development and waterfall development. Each methodology has proponents.

> **Note:**
>
> The goal of this section is not to take a side on whether agile is better than waterfall, nor to make you an agile or waterfall expert. Instead, this section is designed to encourage PMs to examine the current development environment used within your organization and then manage your AI project within that environment.

There are differences between the two development methodologies:

- Waterfall development delivers large projects (usually contained within a Business Requirements Document (BRD)) over multiple months. The goal is to deliver a project by a specified due date.

- Agile development splits overall project goals (sometimes called "epics") into smaller deliverables (sometimes called "stories"), typically delivered in a two-week period. The goal is to incrementally deliver or continuously improve the functionality of a project over time with no set due date, where new stories or features can be added to the project "backlog" to be included in eventual deliverables to the project owner.

Most organizations have gravitated toward agile development but usually do not entirely embrace it. Instead, they adopt a hybrid approach that is neither pure agile nor pure waterfall.

The PM may be able to select the best methodology for project development, but the more likely scenario is that PMs must work within an organization's agile or waterfall framework, which is shared by all PMs.

Here are some considerations:

- Is there a due date for the project, and if so, what are the plans to finish the project by that due date? (Due dates are a waterfall concept. Agile allows continuous project improvement without due dates for the final project.)

- What tasks or stories must be identified and completed each period to further the project's deliverables?
    - Agile divides each feature into stories completed in (usually) 2-week or 3-week sprints. The PM, the data science manager, the project owner, and the developers need to decide what should be delivered every other week. Data scientists, developers, and testers can often select tasks based on a story priority.
    - Waterfall breaks requirements into tasks, all of which must be completed by a due date. Managers assign the tasks to the data scientists, developers, and testers.
- How are additional requirements handled?
    - Agile adds additional requirements to the backlog of stories, but a higher priority of a new story will delay the deliverables of the lower priority existing stories.
    - Waterfall uses a due date for all requirements, so any additional requirements should cause the project's due date to be pushed back. (Scope creep occurs when the date is not reset after receiving new requirements. Most of the time, scope creep results in a project's failure to deliver on the promised due date.)

The PM needs to understand project scheduling standards within his organization and then pursue project development within that framework. If the PM works within an agile framework, initial Gantt charts are converted to another tool, like scrum or Kanban boards, where Gantt chart "tasks" turn into post-it notes with "stories." Scrum.org has a good description of Agile and how to implement Agile within your organization.

In an Agile environment, many PMs discard the Gantt chart once development begins in favor of Kanban boards (a.k.a. Scrum boards), as shown in Figure 24. Some Agile enthusiasts consider Gantt charts a throwback to earlier development methods, but other PMs keep both to maintain a broad view of deliverables and deployments and communicate with management and project owners. A Kanban Board can easily be developed in Microsoft Word or even using post-it notes on a whiteboard or a chalkboard.

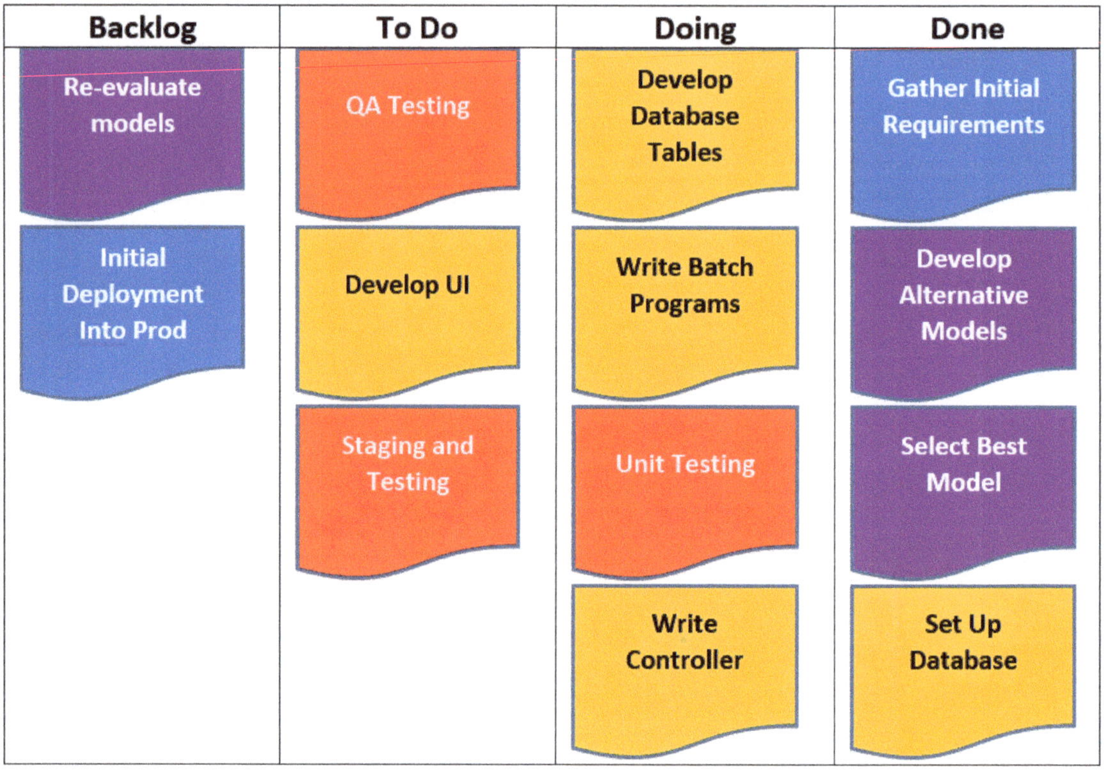

Figure 24 – Example of a Kanban Board

Waterfall methodologies define all features at the start of the project and work toward those features, with all features delivered at the end of the project. Agile methodologies keep a backlog of features that need to be done, with an estimated time for each feature, where the project does not have a definitive due date.

The AI Life Cycle

Many technology-centric areas, like software development, information security, etc., incorporate a "life cycle" to show how technology projects evolve over time and eventually are replaced in favor of newer projects, techniques, or technologies. AI applications also follow an AI life cycle (AILC) – in fact, a quick Google search can show that since AI has become such a hot topic, there are hundreds of AILCs, each considering varied factors.

The important conclusion is that AI development is a cyclical process with constant model training and testing, and not a static process where, once they are finished, the AI team can go away. The PM needs to understand why a cycle is required. Figure 25 shows my favorite AILC.

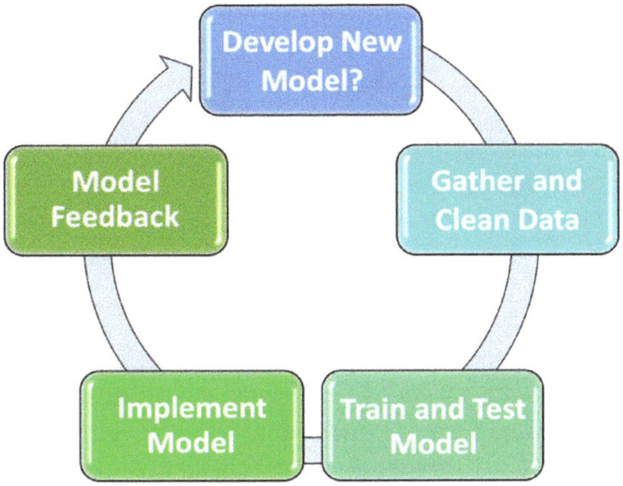

Figure 25 -- AI Life Cycle

Note:

Many other AILCs show many more steps, like "Business Understanding," "Planning," and others. These steps are important, but the model in Figure 25 is a favorite because (a) the AILC in Figure 25 is short, with only five steps, and (b) Figure 25 highlights how the AILC differs from other technological life cycles.

Like other development life cycles, tasks specific to the PM and the data science manager, like planning, are covered in this chapter but left out of this AILC.

When Should a New Model Replace an Existing Model?

An AI statistical model is required to make predictions. After a model has been developed, it must constantly be monitored for accuracy. Business environments are continually changing, with new competition, new products, new regulations, different suppliers, different customers, pandemics, etc.

As business environments change, an ML model that worked well in the past may not continue to function as it should. The ML application should constantly check for the quality of the predictions and alert the development team if the required prediction accuracy goes below a predetermined point. This point is called **service level acceptability** or **SLA**. An SLA contains two parts:

- **Response Service Level** – The model needs to function within a given period. Do web pages need to appear in seconds? Does the training and testing of the model need to be finished within hours? The PM needs to place model constraints for any time sensitivity.

- **Accuracy Service Level** – The model needs to be accurate. After training and testing, how do you measure accuracy? Often, a percentage of accuracy (for example, predicted sales compared to actual sales) is used. For more advanced measures, the PM can work with the data scientist to deliver statistical measures such as an RMSE (root mean square error), MAPE (mean average percentage error), or an R^2 (statistical model predictions compared to predictions using an average).

Response service levels are standard in most software development efforts (although often challenging for AI applications), but accuracy service levels are specific to AI applications. The PM needs to work with the data scientist, the manager, and the project owner to determine what service levels need to be established. SLAs should be established for both response and accuracy in AI projects.

Eventually, most statistical models will fail to meet service levels, and new statistical models must be considered to replace the old models. This is not a failing of the data scientist but rather a recognition that technology, predictive models, and tools are always evolving, and the business environment is constantly changing.

Gather and Clean Data

Machine learning requires new data to "learn" or adjust parameters in a model. Procedures need to be considered that can gather and clean data:

- Data may need to be migrated to an area accessible by the data scientist. This often involves an ETL (extract, transform, and load) process that moves data from a typically relational database (like Oracle, SQL Server, or Aurora) to a NoSQL database (like MongoDB, Cassandra, or DynamoDB). ETL software choices, such as Pentaho or Informatica, or customized programs written in-house will need to be considered.

- Cleaning programs and procedures need to be deployed. The data scientist must understand what happens to missing data and outlying data before a model can be tested or trained.

PMs must incorporate software development, schedule gathering and cleaning procedures, and acquire the software required to accomplish these tasks.

Train and Test Model

AI investments demand ongoing attention, not a 'set it and forget it' approach. Machine learning models necessitate continuous refinement of their core parameters based on evolving data insights. PMs should consider automating the training and testing lifecycle for efficiency. While AI processes may run periodically, potentially overnight or on weekends due to computational demands, the resulting parameter updates must be deployed swiftly to enable real-time predictive capabilities – ideally within seconds, not hours.

After AI development but before deployment into a production environment, rigorous performance monitoring against established Service Level Agreements (SLAs) set up by the business side of the organization is essential. If model accuracy or run times fall below an SLA, a proactive model redevelopment process, led by a data scientist, is triggered, initiating a new innovation cycle.

Effective product management is paramount to orchestrating the development of automated T&T infrastructure and strategically scheduling these critical model refresh cycles.

Implement Model

After training and testing, the software has been implemented, and the parameters set by the "machine learning" aspect of the AILC need to be implemented within a project and accepted by the end user or project owner. These tasks often involve a lot of communication between the data scientist, the PM, and team members:

- The deployment of AI applications requires seamless collaboration between the AI and DBA teams. Specifically, DBAs are critical in translating model data requirements into robust and scalable database infrastructure, ensuring the AI application has the necessary data foundation for effective operation.

- To get AI models working in products and services, the tech teams and data experts must work closely with the AI team. Together, these teams decide how to plug the AI 'brain' into the software. Often, this involves using small, independent software pieces (microservices) where the AI model lives. Microservices allow the application to quickly grab the specific AI tool from this central location to deliver an AI application.

- Testers must communicate with the AI team, especially in determining the accuracy service levels required by the PM and project owner.

- End users and project owners need to communicate with the AI team, the PM, and the data science manager to illustrate how the system's accuracy can improve operations or open new revenue opportunities.

Here, the PM's role is to organize and schedule the project team members so that a complicated ML model is implemented, making it easy for the project owner and end users to use, access, and interpret the model's results.

Model Feedback

Finally, the PM needs to keep in close contact with the project owner to ensure that both the project owner and the end users are happy with the system's results. If not, the service levels need to be examined (and perhaps adjusted), or another model needs to be developed.

Why not use the MLLC?

Chapter 3 introduces the Machine Learning Life Cycle (MLLC). While the MLLC is an essential framework for coordinating technical development, relying on it exclusively presents two challenges. First, while machine learning is the most prominent subset of AI, the field also encompasses optimization, rule-based expert systems, and mathematical modeling. The AI Life Cycle (AILC) serves as a streamlined generalization that accommodates both ML and non-ML applications.

Second, the AILC is more concise, distilled into five high-level steps. While the MLLC provides the granular detail developers require, the AILC's simplicity makes it a superior tool for communicating with stakeholders and management. This is not to suggest we should abandon the MLLC for tracking technical progress. Rather, the AILC provides a necessary high-level lens for non-ML applications and a more effective visualization for executive oversight.

Why not use the SDLC?

Many technical managers are intimately familiar with the Software Development Life Cycle (SDLC), which is built on the premise of *deterministic* logic: specific inputs produce predictable outputs based on hard-coded rules. In contrast, AI development is fundamentally *probabilistic*. Relationships between inputs and outputs are based on likelihoods and uncertainty rather than binary 'right or wrong' results.

While traditional software bugs are typically logic errors that can be isolated and fixed, AI 'errors' often stem from data drift, latent bias, or inherent statistical noise. Consequently, forcing AI into a standard SDLC often fails; it lacks the specialized stages required for continuous data curation and the experimental, iterative nature of model training—both of which resist rigid, linear sprint cycles.

Furthermore, the post-deployment phase necessitates an AILC because models degrade in ways that traditional software does not. While a standard application remains functional unless its environment changes, an AI model's accuracy begins to decay the moment it encounters real-world data—a phenomenon known as model drift. The AILC accounts for this by incorporating 'Human-in-the-Loop' validation and automated retraining pipelines.

Treating AI as a typical software task overlooks the critical need for constant monitoring of statistical performance and data integrity. These requirements are far more nuanced than checking if a server is 'up' or if a program 'crashes.' Because AI requires a different form of maintenance to prevent obsolescence, forcing it into a legacy SDLC is not only inefficient but often counterproductive.

Managing Testing, Deployment, and Monitoring

Quality Assurance (QA) testing is different from the training/testing cycles that the data scientist employees undergo. QA experts are often not official members of the AI area to ensure they maintain some separation from the AI development and AI testing processes. The training/testing cycle aims to find the proper features, data, and models to make predictions. Once those predictions are made, they are either stored in a lookup table or become part of an application programming interface (API) where other programs can call the API and send it data to receive predictions.

For example, say each training/testing session is 40% likely to detect anomalies, and the PM and project owner wish to be 95% confident that the model is correct. The question is, how many tests are needed before the PM and project owner are satisfied? This can be calculated using the logarithmic model shown in Equation 8.

$$\begin{aligned}\text{Required Training / Testing Sessions} &= \ln(1\text{-confidence goal}) / \ln(1\text{-error detection likelihood}) \\ &= \ln(1\text{-}95\%) / \ln(1\text{-}40\%) \\ &= 5.86\end{aligned}$$

Equation 8

The data scientist should be directed to conduct six tests (5.86 rounded up) to ensure 95% confidence in the AI model. These tests should be run concurrently with the new data, and parameters should be estimated after each test to ensure stability in the model. Each test involves a different randomized 70% - 30% split (in this case) so that new testing and training datasets are used for each of the six tests.

Doing it in Excel:

You can use Excel to calculate the number of tests required. Equation 9 shows an Excel formula that uses a 95% confidence goal with a 40% likelihood of catching all errors with a single test.

=LN(1-95%) / LN(1-40%) ***Equation 9***

Equation 9 returns 5.86 in the Excel cell. You can use Excel's LOG10 function, which is the base-10 logarithm taught in most algebra classes, or Excel's LN function, which is the natural log function used in most scientific calculations. Both LOG10 and LN functions will return the same answer.

Note that Excel might try to format this as a percentage cell after you enter the formula with a percentage sign in it. After entering the calculation, you can switch the format to general or number format. Alternatively, if you want to avoid this, you can use decimals rather than percentages in your formula, in this case using 0.95 and 0.4 instead of 95% and 40%.

The project's testing phase can also use this logic. With these numbers, six scenarios must be established to test multiple conditions on each web page or report.

User Acceptance Testing

User Acceptance Testing (UAT) allows end-users to validate the system, identify any issues or discrepancies, and provide feedback for necessary refinements before the final release. UAT is a final quality assurance step to ensure the software meets user needs and aligns with the intended business objectives. The PM plays a crucial role in UAT, bridging the AI team and the business users. During UAT, the PM acts as a facilitator, coordinating the testing process and ensuring that the AI application meets the requirements and expectations of the users. The PM has several tasks when facilitating the UAT:

- The PM collaborates with the AI team to define the UAT strategy and plan. They work closely with stakeholders to identify the specific test cases, scenarios, and datasets used for the evaluation.

- The PM ensures that the UAT plan aligns with the project objectives and covers all critical functionalities and user interactions. The PM also coordinates with the AI team to provide the necessary support and resources for the testing activities.

- The PM oversees the execution of UAT by coordinating the testing activities, tracking progress, and resolving any issues or challenges that may arise.

- The PM facilitates communication between the AI team and the business users, ensuring that feedback and observations are effectively communicated and addressed. This involves gathering feedback, suggesting refinements, and ensuring that UAT is completed within a planned schedule.

The PM's role in UAT is to ensure a smooth and successful testing process, acting as a facilitator, coordinator, and communicator between the AI team and the users. They are critical in defining the UAT strategy, overseeing the execution, gathering feedback, and supporting decision-making. By effectively managing UAT, the PM helps ensure that the AI application meets user expectations, aligns with business requirements, and drives value for the organization.

Deployment to Production

After the data scientist has developed and unit-tested a new application, it must be deployed to a production environment. The production environment is where applications run, and the output is available to all application users. Any new work done on the application is done in a test environment and not deployed until it is ready.

The PM plays a key role in ensuring a successful deployment and maximizing the impact of the AI application. This deployment can differ significantly between waterfall and agile environments due to the contrasting nature of these project management approaches:

- In a waterfall environment, the deployment process follows a sequential and linear progression. The AI application is developed and tested over an extended period, with deployment occurring at the end of the project. In this scenario, the PM coordinates the deployment activities, ensuring all necessary resources, infrastructure, and dependencies are in place. The deployment process is often planned and follows a predetermined schedule. This approach allows for comprehensive testing and validation before releasing the application to production, reducing the likelihood of critical issues during deployment. However, it can result in longer lead times between development and deployment, making it less adaptable to changing requirements or market dynamics.

- In an agile environment, the deployment of AI applications is iterative and incremental. Agile methodologies such as Scrum or Kanban emphasize shorter development cycles called sprints or iterations. The PM works closely with the AI team to prioritize and deliver specific features or functionalities in each iteration. This allows for frequent application deployments with smaller, manageable releases. The PM collaborates with cross-functional teams, including data scientists, developers, and stakeholders, to ensure a smooth and continuous deployment process. Agile environments promote flexibility and adaptability, allowing for rapid adjustments based on feedback and changing needs. This iterative approach enables earlier value realization and quicker responsiveness to user requirements.

In any deployment, the PM must rely on system architects to ensure a proper deployment process and platform, engineers, and data analysts to ensure any correct data is moved to production and that any visualization or software engineering is complete, and database administrators to provide working environments for both production and development environments.

Finally, PMs are crucial in change management and stakeholder engagement during deployment. They communicate with relevant stakeholders, including business users, IT teams, and senior management, to ensure their understanding and support for the AI application. PMs facilitate training and provide documentation to enable users to utilize and adopt the application effectively. They also monitor the application's performance and gather user feedback, ensuring continuous improvement and refinement of the deployed solution.

AI Defects

Like all applications, AI applications will probably contain some defects that appear after implementation and need to be resolved. However, in addition to software defects, AI applications can have defects where the AI model meets the needs of the project owner. While the predictions can be accurate overall, some daily or product predictions are quite off and need addressing.

Predictions from statistical models are never exact – there is some error between the predicted and actual values, and this is to be expected. Predicted values falling far outside the accuracy service level need to be investigated. Examples include if one day's demand is twice as high as predicted, or if a customer defaults on a loan with only a 1% predictive chance of that happening, or if the similarity of two products vacillates from high to low continuously, etc., then that one instance of an erroneous prediction should be investigated. If there is a strong reason for a single observation error (like support phone calls going up because a server crashed or a product appeared on a popular TV show), then the statistical model is probably OK. If the reasons are recurring (like a pandemic crashing demand for a product or customers leaving for a new competitor), then the data scientist may need to develop a new statistical model that takes these factors into account.

The PM's job is to work with the data scientist to establish the error levels that trigger an AI defect, to investigate or assign staff to investigate these defects, and then to trigger model modifications if required. Time needs to be provided for AI defect investigation and either statistical model tweaking (where new factors are added to an existing statistical model) or the development of an entirely new statistical model.

Concluding Thoughts on AI Project Management

This chapter discusses how an AI project differs from a traditional software development project and how these differences affect the responsibilities of the PM. This chapter describes:

- How a PM's role differs from the data science manager
- The AI tasks in a project can be categorized with a WBS (work breakdown structure)
- How to use evaluation metrics to set service levels for the AI application
- Avoiding the bullwhip effect by avoiding the aggregation of data before measuring the effectiveness of the model
- The data scientist's position in the critical path on a project plan
- How agile and waterfall project management techniques can affect the project schedule
- Dealing with testing, deployment, and monitoring

The role of a PM in AI application development is crucial for orchestrating the entire process from initiation to deployment. The PM coordinates the development of an AI application, working closely with cross-functional teams and business managers to define project requirements, establish timelines, and allocate resources effectively. PMs monitor project progress, track metrics, and address any challenges or risks that arise, ensuring timely delivery. The PM also plays a vital role in engaging business managers by gathering feedback, managing expectations, and ensuring the AI application aligns with business objectives. By overseeing the development process, the PM ensures successful project outcomes and the seamless integration of AI solutions into the organization.

---

[i] Project Management Institute. 2008. *The standard for program management—Second edition*.

[ii] Project Management Institute. 2008. *A guide to the project management body of knowledge (PMBOK® guide) - Fourth edition*.

[iii] Patrick Weaver. Feb. 24, 2010. "Understanding programs and projects--oh, there's a difference!" *PMI® Global Congress 2010: Project Management Institute*. https://www.pmi.org/learning/library/understanding-difference-programs-versus-projects-6896.

[iv] Jill Duffy. September 9, 2019. "How to Kill Email with the Right Project Management Software." PC Magazine. https://www.pcmag.com/how-to/how-to-kill-email-with-the-right-project-management-software.

[v] Martin, M. D. & Kathleen Miller. March 1, 1982. Project Planning as the Primary Management Function. *Project Management Quarterly* 13(1), pp. 31–38. https://www.pmi.org/learning/library/project-planning-as-primary-management-function-10339.

Chapter 7: AI Team Building

One of the most critical tasks for a data science manager is building and motivating a high-performing team. Hiring the right data scientists is challenging, and assembling a diverse and skilled group with the necessary expertise can be daunting. Managers must first identify the required roles and skills for their projects, then recruit the right talent, assess any skill gaps, and ultimately build a cohesive team ready to tackle complex data challenges. This chapter will guide you through the crucial process of building and retaining a successful AI development team.

What is this chapter trying to do and why?

The future of your business hinges on the insights and innovations generated by your AI teams. This chapter examines strategies for attracting and retaining top data scientists and AI specialists in a highly competitive market. We'll provide strategies for objectively assessing candidates' skills, from core competencies to the refined expertise that defines a true expert. You'll learn how to effectively review resumes and conduct insightful interviews, whether you're hiring seasoned professionals or cultivating promising entry-level talent.

Beyond individual hiring, this chapter explores the importance of incorporating other critical skills into your AI team to create a well-rounded and high-performing unit. It will also address the unique challenges of consulting in the AI space and guide how to navigate them effectively. Building a cohesive team is just as crucial as hiring great individuals, and we'll show you how to identify and integrate those complementary skill sets that will elevate your team's performance.

Ultimately, building and retaining an exceptional AI team isn't just about mitigating risk – it's about unlocking new frontiers of innovation, efficiency, and growth. By mastering the strategies in this chapter, you'll be equipped to assemble a team that can not only meet your organization's current needs but also drive its future success. The goal is to equip you with the tools to get the top talent that will fuel your organization's AI initiatives.

The Retention Anchor Framework for Attracting and Retaining AI Developers

In its State of the American Manager report, Gallup finds that 50% of people have left a job solely to escape a bad manager. The report further states that over 70% of the variability in whether an employee is engaged with the company depends on the actions of the manager, highlighting the crucial role of the AI manager in attracting and retaining data scientists.

The Gallup study reveals a key insight: while data scientists are in high demand, it's their manager—not just the market—who determines whether they stay or leave. A manager's perceived fairness and competence can be a powerful motivator, and this perception spreads quickly among colleagues; if one data scientist loves (or hates) their job, others find out why.

The key to attracting new AI talent is for managers and teams to act as "Retention Anchors" that exhibit behaviors and policies that appeal to AI team employees and applicants. Figure 26 shows the three main anchors where AI managers can work to retain talent.

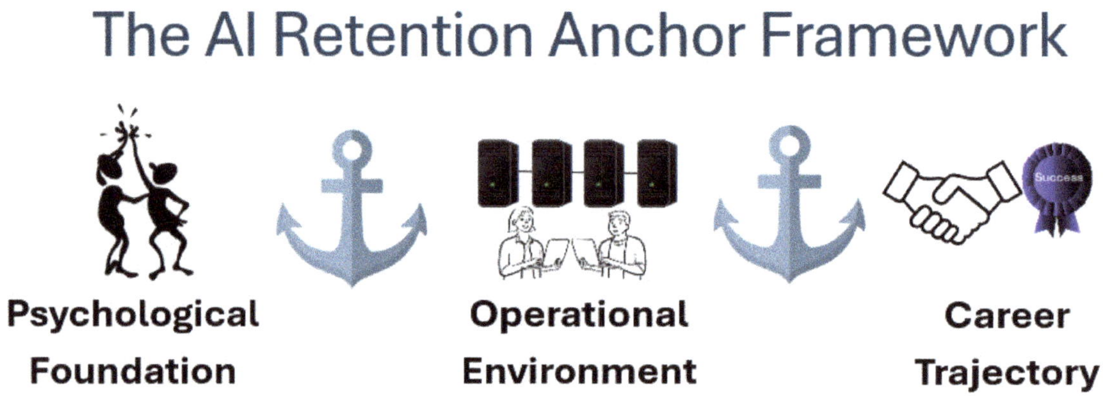

Figure 26: AI Managers Act as Retention Anchors

Figure 26 describes how AI managers can develop an environment so that AI developers simply do not want to leave by concentrating on three "anchors:"

- The **psychological foundation anchor** establishes purpose, trust, and mental stability in the AI workplace
- The **operational environment anchor** facilitates collaboration, fosters upper management support, and integrates workflows
- The **career trajectory anchor** is where the AI manager encourages skill development and provides clear advancement pathways

This section dives into these three areas in greater detail.

Establishing the Psychological Foundation Anchor

The first anchor of a robust retention framework for AI developers centers on establishing the psychological foundation for employees in the AI area. In a field defined by rapid shifts and high-pressure deployments, developers need more than just competitive salaries; they require a sense of deep-seated stability. This begins by anchoring their daily tasks in a clear sense of purpose, ensuring they understand the "why" behind the code.

When developers feel seen as individuals rather than just compute-power proxies, the psychological bond strengthens. This foundation ensures that even though AI technology is volatile, the developer's connection to the organization remains steadfast. This section delves into areas an AI manager should consider to establish a psychological foundation anchor.

Sense of purpose

Data scientists are in demand. They can have meaningful careers by searching for the best jobs. The data science manager should be able to use the talents of a data scientist for AI projects and then ensure those projects are implemented.

> **Notes from the Field:**
>
> Data Scientists are often in a position where their models don't get implemented. Models can be disruptive and change the methods and procedures of existing departments. Frequently, end-users and project owners feel uncomfortable with changes to policies and procedures that they cannot explain or justify. However, if new policies and procedures result in considerable savings or revenue, then learning new processes becomes more inviting.
>
> Project owners are familiar with existing models and procedures. They require time and resources to learn a new machine learning model. New models are often not cancelled per se but rather put "on the shelf" for years, waiting for "the right time" to implement, even if new models are projected to generate millions in additional income or reduced costs.
>
> If the data scientist invests a significant amount of work on a project and then that project is stalled or canceled for little to no quantifiable reason, then the data scientist may lose a sense of purpose and consider another opportunity elsewhere where their valuable skills are encouraged and used.

Transparency and Trust

Employees place a high value on understanding that their contributions are meaningful, especially important for data scientists, whose work may cause some disruption to current policies and procedures previously implemented by management.

Data science managers must be transparent with their teams about future challenges and directions, providing support when needed. While some conversations with upper management must remain confidential, a good manager shares as much departmental and project information as possible to give the team a sense of agency. This transparency fosters trust and assures the AI team that their manager is committed to keeping them informed and values their input.

> **Notes from the Field:**
>
> An executive had a two-hour meeting at which the opinions of employees (data scientists and non-data scientists) were sought, focusing on the direction of the department over the next year, because the executive was required to deliver a yearly plan to the upper management.
>
> The employees had an in-depth conversation about the direction the department should take before filling out the survey. Later, an email was sent from the executive detailing the key points of the study.
>
> Oddly, this survey did not align with the group's internal discussions, and some members complained. Later, it was discovered that the following year's plan had been finalized one month prior to the meeting, and the executive was attempting to make employees feel validated, despite the decisions having already been made.
>
> It was disastrous. The employees (correctly) felt the opposite of what the executive intended – that their opinions and their time do not matter at all. Future meetings were often skipped or held without input over the next three years, despite the executive still holding the position. One employee who was considered vital to the organization's future stated, "I have too much to do to waste my time on meetings where I have no input."
>
> The takeaway is that you cannot build trust if you are not trustworthy. Violations of trust will eventually be discovered (because the numbers really are against untrustworthy managers). Once trust is violated, it is unlikely that confidence will be regained for that manager.

Proactive Positivity

Often, data science managers view their role as more confrontational than it needs to be. With a few managers, there is a perceived need to put data scientists in their place. Statements like "For what we're paying you, you had better get it right" or "Yes, the three-month project went in on time, but I expected the final tasks to be ready in the morning, and you didn't implement until the afternoon" are entirely destructive and completely unnecessary.

Comments such as "I know this is going to be difficult to get right. That is why I recommended you!" or "Hey, the project went in on the due date! All right! Wonderful job!" are examples of encouragement that keep a technical scientist engaged. Sometimes, a frank discussion of failures is necessary, but the manager should strive to maintain a positive tone in group meetings. Managers should try to be positive in performance reviews when warranted. There is no need to attack data scientists (or any employees) who are doing a decent job. If a manager is overly critical of a good employee, that employee is likely to leave the organization.

Notes from the Field:

One of the worst things that can happen to any manager is the "cascading effect" when employees leave in droves because of low morale.

In one case, during an annual review, a newly hired data science manager gave a data scientist a low review, which came as a surprise to the data scientist. The data scientist worked approximately fifty hours per week, usually delivered successful projects, and was integral to the current project.

When the data scientist complained about the low score, the manager agreed that the data scientist was the most vital individual to the project, and that the low review gave the data scientist something to work toward in the coming years.

The data scientist left the company within a month, and the remaining workers, who suddenly had a significantly increased workload on the project, left soon after. Then the manager was forced to leave the company as well.

The manager could have prevented this by acknowledging the hard work and successes of all employees, including the data scientist, and avoiding "gaming the system" on promotions, annual reviews, and raises.

Cultivating Stability and Reducing Stress

Reducing workplace stress in an AI team requires a dual focus on the present (work-life balance) and the future (job security). When managers actively champion these areas, they move beyond being mere supervisors and become advocates for their team's well-being. This advocacy is a powerful retention tool; employees who feel their personal time is respected and their career path is secure are far more likely to remain loyal during the inevitable "crunch" periods of a development cycle. While some levers—such as generous leave policies or company-wide "no-layoff" philosophies—are set at the corporate level, the manager acts as the vital interface. It is the manager who ensures that "unlimited PTO" isn't a trap and that corporate shifts are communicated with transparency to mitigate fear.

Beyond balance and security, clarity of purpose and autonomy serve as additional pillars for stress reduction. In AI, stress often stems from moving targets or the feeling of being a "cog in the machine" without understanding the ethical or practical impact of one's models. A manager can alleviate this by connecting daily tasks to the broader mission and granting AI developers the agency to solve problems in their own way. By fostering an environment where failures are treated as data points rather than performance flaws, managers build a "psychological safety net." This comprehensive approach to employee care demonstrates that the organization values the person behind the code, directly correlating to higher morale and long-term commitment.

Notes from the Field:

Following the COVID-19 outbreak, many companies resorted to layoffs and furloughs. However, one company stood out by setting aside funds to pay its employees for a year and a half. This commitment went further, as the company also provided supplies, such as computers and monitors, to support a work-from-home model. The data science manager enhanced this experience by creating a flexible-time program and organizing virtual team-building events, such as Zoom happy hours and trivia afternoons, during work hours to keep the team engaged.

It is beneficial for employee retention to know that their careers will continue, and their families will not be left destitute. In tough times, a manager who prioritizes taking care of employees can garner much trust and make it difficult for a data scientist to leave for an unknown environment.

Develop a rapport

Employees want their work to feel important and to build a strong, collaborative relationship with their manager. However, there's often a disconnect. According to a Gallup study, only 37% of employees feel comfortable approaching their manager with work-related questions. This lack of trust can stifle communication and prevent employees from seeking the guidance they need to succeed.

The root of the problem may be deeper than it appears. While managers may genuinely believe they are approachable, their reactions to feedback can tell a different story. When an employee raises an issue, a manager might respond with defensive anger or frustration, or even take punitive measures, such as issuing a negative review. After experiencing this just once, an employee learns that it's safer to avoid bringing up problems, regardless of the circumstances.

This can be especially challenging for data scientists. Their role often involves making suggestions that can disrupt existing practices for the greater good of the organization.

Having a manager with whom they can openly discuss implementation challenges and timelines is crucial. A supportive and trusting relationship allows data scientists to navigate these disruptions effectively, ensuring their innovative ideas can be successfully implemented.

Establishing the Operational Environment Anchor

The second anchor shifts focus from the internal mindset to the external workspace. A critical component of this anchor is to break down the walls between technical and non-technical teams and to provide political cover when working with upper management.

Isolation is a primary driver of developer attrition in the AI space. When developers are integrated into cross-functional teams, they see the immediate impact of their models on real-world outcomes. By prioritizing cross-pollination and ensuring upper management buy-in, this anchor ensures that the operational machinery supports the developer's workflow rather than obstructing it. This section describes the areas that the AI manager needs to examine to ensure a good operational environment for the AI developers.

Foster Collaboration

Data scientists often work in isolation, a tendency that's understandable given the deep, focused nature of their work, but this solitary approach can limit learning and growth. By sharing their projects and challenges with peers, data scientists gain new perspectives, discover different techniques, and deepen their understanding of their own methods. Fostering this kind of internal knowledge sharing is crucial for a team's overall development and skill enrichment.

A data science manager should actively promote a culture of collaboration to counter this isolation. This can be achieved through structured activities, such as code walkthroughs, presentations, and one-on-one meetings, which enable team members to learn directly from each other. Even in a remote setting, these interactions can be organized without the manager's presence to encourage genuine peer-to-peer exchange. For non-remote teams, informal activities like team lunches and get-togethers are also beneficial for building rapport and strengthening professional relationships.

Collaboration does more than facilitate knowledge transfer; it also ensures project continuity. When a team member hits an obstacle, others can step in to provide fresh insights, preventing projects from stalling. Furthermore, a collaborative environment gives employees a sense of shared direction and camaraderie that is difficult to find elsewhere. This feeling of belonging can be a significant factor when an employee considers outside opportunities, serving as a powerful tool for retention.

Get upper management support for a data-driven culture

A data scientist thrives in a data-driven culture, and the data science manager needs to establish a perspective for upper management to adopt some of the data-driven culture aspects. The Harvard Business Review (HBR) lists ten ways to do this, and here are my top three:[i]

Opposition to a data-driven culture rests in managers who have implemented policies and provisions based on their opinion (not data) on how a business should be run. CEOs and C-level executives must support a data-driven culture. This may not be as hard as it sounds. Often, CEOs have already stated that they want data-driven decisions. The data science manager needs to reference the CEO's decision when supporting the results of AI applications to other business areas, since other executives may not wish to challenge the CEO's directive.

Do not silo your data scientists

Do not sequester your data scientists. Instead, include them in managerial and business meetings. The HBR contends that the data science manager needs to ensure that boundaries between the business areas and the data scientist are "highly porous," allowing AI to contribute to business decisions and bringing business objectives to the data scientists. As the HBR puts it, "leaders of data-centric organizations cannot remain ignorant of the language of data."

Notes from the Field:

Some business analysts and product development teams mistakenly believe that data scientists should be isolated from business domain knowledge, often due to fear of friction or a desire to stress their own importance. This siloed approach, however, can lead to communication breakdowns and contention between data scientists and business experts.

Researchers at Carnegie Mellon University emphasize the critical role of free-flowing communication between the AI team and domain experts throughout every step of the AI development process to counter the effects of working in silos.[ii]

Develop the habit of explaining analytical choices

In meetings, the data science manager, along with the data scientist, needs to describe the AI models that were considered, the tradeoffs between models, why a specific model was chosen, and the impact on business from the results of the analysis from an AI application.

Other managers and their employees may be uncomfortable with changing what they have always delivered, using long-established methods of producing products. The data science manager and data scientists (if needed) can explain why the current practice is not optimal and why their proposed data-driven approach is better, along with statistics on how costs can be reduced, revenue can be generated, or both.

Establishing the Career Trajectory Anchor

The final anchor discusses how the AI developers view their careers. In the hyper-competitive AI talent market, developers are often lured away not by a lack of current satisfaction, but by the perceived ceiling on their growth. This anchor ensures that long-term retention is built on a roadmap of upward mobility and skill expansion. By making a concerted effort to develop existing talent, organizations demonstrate that they value a developer's evolution as much as their current output. This involves providing the runway for continuous learning, which is essential in a field where today's state-of-the-art model is tomorrow's legacy code. By investing in the AI developers' futures, an AI manager can transform a transactional job into a lifelong career partnership.

Develop existing talent

Gallup reported that employees who use their strengths every day are 6 times more likely to be engaged at work (where they like coming into work) and are less likely to leave the company. For a data scientist, this means ensuring that AI application development continues and is valued by the organization. Many data scientists receive tasks that are not explicitly related to AI, such as generating reports, coding tasks unrelated to machine learning, and gathering datasets for downloads. If less challenging tasks consume the bulk of a data scientist's activity, then the data scientist may prefer to seek out more challenging work elsewhere.

Here are some ways to show you care about developing AI talent:

- Develop a data lab (or virtual meetings) where data scientists can converse with each other or have one or more data scientists develop it (and give them company time to do so).

- Encourage and fund attendance at AI conferences or, better, speaking at an AI conference. (That may mean hotel, airfare, food, and conference fees. It can easily reach thousands of dollars, so keep it local if possible.)

- Provide additional AI and data science classes and instruction. Companies often offer to pay for continuing education classes or in-house classes in their own "university" settings. Companies, such as Amazon, Microsoft, and IBM, often offer AI classes for their clients or potential clients.

- Encourage self-study and certifications. The "encourage" part is meant to be more than just platitudes – certifications require study (perhaps on company time), fees, and a potential for failure. (If there is no allowance for failure, then the certification must be easy to receive. I recommend funding up to the failure rate of the certification.)

- Encourage publications, especially with non-company data. Publications will enable data scientists to develop valuable skill sets, particularly those with peer reactions, where other data scientists can offer feedback on what should be done or what they would have done.

- Encourage outside data science competitions, such as with Kaggle. (Kaggle is a data science competition site.) Often, a data scientist can learn about new techniques from these competitions that can be applied in-house.

Evaluate potential for advancement

Where do senior data scientists go when they are promoted? How about principal data scientists? Many organizations do not have a conclusive answer, so the data science managers need to figure out a path. Discussions with data scientists and upper management can shed some light on a career path. By working together, future career growth for data scientists can be carved out. Often, a new title can be created with different responsibilities that will justify higher salaries and provide a path forward.

It is possible that there simply is no "next." Let the principal data scientist know that they have reached the end of the technical career path. The data scientist will still receive raises, bonuses, and possibly a partnership or profit-sharing status. Still, they can either be happy where they are or transition into management to mentor and develop other data scientists.

Remember, data scientists are rare, and if a successful data scientist does not want to be a manager, it might make no sense to force the issue. Managers need to figure out a way to reward the data scientist for delivering successful AI applications.

The manager needs to communicate with the data scientist during regular performance meetings to determine what they want and what is feasible.

Notes from the Field:

Daniel Tunkelang was a previous leader of data science and engineering teams at LinkedIn. LinkedIn had three levels of Senior Data Scientist, and it was important to move from Senior Data Scientist 2 to Senior Data Scientist 3.

Tunkelang reported how LinkedIn reorganized positions and limited data science titles to Senior Data Scientist 1 and Senior Data Scientist 2. A lot of unhappiness followed the restructuring, as successful data scientists who had worked towards promotion from level 2 to level 3 were now back at level 2. Obviously, this feels like a demotion.[iii]

Why? Can you imagine telling your family and friends, or interviewing for a new opportunity, that you were level 3 but are now level 2, and it's not a big deal?

Hiring Data Scientists and AI Specialists

Finding data scientists who possess reasonable competence in the field and who understand their limitations is daunting. The Bureau of Labor Statistics estimates that employment of data scientists is projected to grow 36% from 2021 to 2031, a significantly higher rate of growth than other related occupations. An average of 13,500 new positions are created each year, many of which are AI-related, with commensurate salary increases to match.[iv]

Forbes reports that AI positions are experiencing "the largest salary increases we have ever reported, across all job levels." Base salaries throughout this study showed a 13% increase in pay for entry-level data scientists.[v] With such high demand for data scientists, many applicants claim to be data scientists when they are not. Furthermore, data scientists might not wish to leave their current positions and may find it challenging to do so. This section outlines the processes for reviewing resumes, conducting interviews with applicants, and retaining data scientists.

Using a Skill Matrix

Before the hiring process begins, managers often develop a skills matrix to identify the existing skills in their area and those that require development. Figure 27 shows a typical skill matrix for an AI team.

	Technical Skills			Analytical Skills					Soft Skills			
Data Scientist	Python	Stats	Spark	Cleaning data	Time Series	Deep Learning	NLP	Cluster Analysis	Business Commu-nication	Leadership	Mentoring	*Average Score*
Larry	Moderate	Moderate	Moderate	Advanced	Moderate	Novice	Moderate	Moderate	Advanced	Advanced	Moderate	*2.18*
Mary	Moderate	Moderate	Novice	Moderate	Moderate	Novice	Advanced	Novice	Advanced	Novice	Novice	*1.73*
Mo	Novice	Novice	Novice	Novice	Novice	Novice	Novice	Novice	Moderate	Novice	Novice	*1.09*
Flo	Advanced	Novice	Advanced	Moderate	Novice	Novice	Novice	Novice	Moderate	Moderate	Moderate	*1.73*
Curley	Moderate	Moderate	Advanced	Advanced	Moderate	Novice	Moderate	Advanced	Moderate	Novice	Novice	*2.00*
Shirley	Advanced	Advanced	Advanced	Advanced	Advanced	Moderate	Moderate	Advanced	Advanced	Moderate	Advanced	*2.73*
Average Score	*2.17*	*1.83*	*2.17*	*2.33*	*1.83*	*1.17*	*1.83*	*1.83*	*2.50*	*1.67*	*1.67*	

Figure 27 -- Sample Skill Matrix

As shown in Figure 27, a skill matrix can highlight the skills we need to improve through training or additional hiring and can be easily developed using a spreadsheet. Below are examples of insights that might be gleaned from the matrix:

- Mo is a novice in every area except moderate in business communication. Should he be? Can we improve his skill level in certain areas, or should we consider a replacement?

- Shirley excels in most areas and is moderately skillful in three areas and advanced in all others. She clearly is the most skilled in the group. Is it time for a promotion? Should we have her mentor the rest of the team?

- Larry is moderately skilled in most areas but excels in business communication and leadership. Should we encourage him to transition into management?

- Shirley is the only mentor we have who can bring up others in a skill set. What if she leaves? Should we cross-train?

- Only Mary is advanced in NLP, and only Shirley excels in Time Series and deep learning. Should we start cross-training within the group, or should we get some consulting help in those areas?

Some skill matrices also incorporate an average score. A skill matrix with scores can be a helpful tool, but data science managers should use this score with caution:

- The skill chart weights **Novice=1**, **Moderate=2**, and **Advanced=3** to calculate the scores, but managers can use their own scoring method.

- The skill chart gives equal scores for all skills, but perhaps different skill sets should exhibit higher scores based on evaluation. This is up to the manager and the employee. Employees who have expressed an interest in pursuing management may want to focus on developing their organizational and team skills rather than seeking a different score based on technical or analytical skills. New employees should probably focus on developing their technical skills.

- The data science manager should resist using the skill matrix for raises and promotions. An employee's lack of skill is typically an indication that the manager has not prioritized that skill for the employee. Often, when data scientists are assigned to an area, they spend their time building skills related to that area at the expense of building other skills.

  Instead, the data science manager should examine a skill matrix as a possible indication of training requirements for employees or for potential new hiring goals to augment a skill set. The skill scores can be indicative of the level of cross-training required if a data scientist leaves the team. As always, promotions and raises should be based on performance on current and recent projects, rather than on skills that have not yet been utilized.

  Data scientist managers instead gauge a data scientist's performance based on their deliverables to the business area and user satisfaction.

You can see that a skill matrix is not only a valuable tool for a data science manager to visualize the strengths and weaknesses of the AI area, but also is useful when communicating to immediate superiors on the training and staffing needs of the AI team.

What Skills are Necessary for Advanced Data Scientists?

Jeremy Stanley, the Chief Data Scientist at Sailthru, contends that great data scientists must have strong quantitative skills (such as skills in statistical analysis, deep learning, and various statistical modeling techniques) and somewhat strong programming skills (such as skills in Python, Java, R, and .NET).[vi] I agree with this assessment.

> **Notes from the Field:**
>
> One company hired an applicant who claimed knowledge of data science, Python, and Scala/Spark programming. He showed up on the first day with a Scala introductory programming textbook and had little statistical knowledge or experience.
>
> Some verification of the resume or testing is essential, or the organization will face problems with hiring data scientists with minimal ability.

A computer science degree or programming experience is sufficient to demonstrate some programming knowledge. A degree in statistics, actuarial analysis, econometrics, or analytics, or a Ph.D. dissertation that utilizes statistical analysis, or experience in statistical analysis, is usually sufficient to demonstrate an interest in making statistical predictions.

The candidate's resume should portray an interest in the field. There are impressive data science and AI courses (with certifications) at Coursera, Udemy, and other online offerings, and programming courses (with certifications) at Codecademy or W3Schools. Having such certificates on a CV reflects an interest in AI and Data Science. The manager should favor candidates who have shown an interest in AI over those who are chasing higher salaries or trying to capitalize on the increased demand for AI skills.

Notes from the Field:

Applicants for a data scientist position should show an interest in data science. In one candidate search, an electrical engineer skilled in mathematics but lacking experience in statistics and programming was interviewed. During the interview, the applicant was asked questions such as, "Have you ever written a computer program before that analyzes data?" or "What is your experience with statistical models?" The response was about the same to each question. "You don't seem to understand. I'm an engineer."

The engineer may have possessed the intelligence and mathematical skills to grasp data science and AI mathematical modeling. Still, he had never previously shown any interest in the data science / AI field. The applicant was deemed too significant a risk to hire.

The two main skills necessary for a data scientist are:

- **Background in quantitative analysis**. Data scientists, even at the entry level, should have a foundational grasp of statistical concepts, such as regression and clustering, from the outset. Developing this core knowledge is a time-intensive process that can divert attention and resources from ongoing AI projects, hindering team velocity and output. By ensuring new hires arrive with this baseline skillset, you can accelerate their integration into the team, allowing them to contribute meaningfully to complex modeling and analysis tasks much more quickly.

- **Ability to code their own models**. It is often impractical to convert a data scientist into a developer, mainly because data scientists are in such high demand. While good developers are hard to find, good data scientists are even more challenging to find and more expensive to hire. However, an advanced data scientist should be able to read code and code basic statistical models. Proficiency in a computer language, like

R or Python, or in statistical packages like SAS or Stata ought to be the minimum acceptable statistical package skill set.

What Skills are Nice to Have for Advanced Data Scientists?

Data and database skills are almost essential for data scientists, particularly SQL, a language used within many databases. Often, data is stored in relational databases, and some knowledge of SQL is required to retrieve the data from the database. If a data scientist cannot obtain the necessary data, they will need to rely on others to provide the requested data. If a data scientist is hired without any SQL knowledge, include certification in SQL from reputable organizations, such as Udemy or W3Schools, in their list of goals.

It is also beneficial for data scientists to have a familiarity with multi-computer infrastructure, such as Spark, AWS, or Azure. If a data scientist can deploy mathematical models across a multi-server architecture, then models that may take hours or days to test on a single computer will run in minutes or hours. Some knowledge of distributing work across an infrastructure may be required for a data scientist to reach full productivity.

Finally, although many data scientists disagree, it is beneficial for a data scientist to be familiar with Microsoft Excel. Excel should never be the primary means of statistical development, which is why most data scientists maintain that knowledge of Excel is superfluous to the role of a data scientist. However, most professionals who are end-users in the project owners' areas are familiar with Excel and often request data in a comma-delimited or Excel format. They then return their analysis to the data scientist in Excel format. Without knowledge of Excel, a data scientist may need to rely on others for assistance with any problems or situations that arise. Some Excel training may be necessary for data scientists who lack this skill.

Notes from the Field:

Unlike typical software development roles, data science and AI positions demand a deep understanding of mathematical and statistical theory. This is why major tech companies often prefer candidates with a Ph.D. in a quantitative field. A Ph.D. can provide a robust foundation, as the dissertation process itself is a multi-year project in applied research. During this time, candidates develop critical skills in problem identification, data collection and cleaning, statistical modeling, and programming. This isn't just theory—it's hands-on experience in the entire lifecycle of a data-driven project.

Managers are often surprised to find that Academic rigor provides a nuanced understanding and a solid foundation for tackling complex problems. Ken Jee notes that while other business functions focus on implementation, AI is grounded in mathematical theory, which requires managers to collaborate with data scientists to translate this theory into practical solutions.[vii]

While a Ph.D. is a strong signal of competence, it isn't the only path to success. Highly productive data scientists can emerge from industry with no Ph.D. if they have a strong background in mathematics and significant exposure to statistical theory, modeling, and data management. It's just that acquiring this depth of knowledge outside of a formal, rigorous education can take a considerable amount of time.[viii]

Furthermore, it's important to remember that not all doctorate degrees are created equal. A Ph.D. in a social science field may not involve any statistical analysis, so it's prudent for hiring managers to ensure a candidate's dissertation includes some quantitative work.

Checking a Resume

Data science / AI is an attractive field, both in salary and prestige, and many resumes are received that are not entirely accurate or, worse, contain outright lies. Here are some strategies you can use to check the accuracy of the resume:

- Google some of the clauses in the resume, especially provisions that seem out of place. I am amazed at how some resumes posted on LinkedIn are Googled by the applicant ("Data Science Resumes"), downloaded, and then modified by the applicant for submission to potential employers.

Notes from the Field:

An organization was reviewing bids for a significant AI contract. The resumes submitted by one contracting firm raised some immediate red flags. On one resume, a bullet point stated, "Familiar with Machine Learning and JSON." This phrasing was highly unusual. While many people have experience with both skills, they are not closely related. Machine learning is an AI technique, while JSON is a data-interchange format, so lumping them together in a single bullet point seemed odd. The review team noted this, but as they continued their process, the same "weird" clause appeared on another resume. This repetition turned a minor oddity into a serious concern about the resumes' authenticity and the firm's qualifications.

A simple Google search revealed that several of the phrases were pulled directly from a publicly available LinkedIn resume. It became clear that both applicants had downloaded the same resume, made a few minor adjustments, and then submitted the resume to the contracting company, which then passed it on to the organization.

The contracting company was understandably embarrassed when this was brought to their attention. To avoid a similar situation, it's good practice to take a few key phrases from resumes and search for them online. You can also use a plagiarism checker to search for online content that matches the resumes you're reviewing.

- Date check and title check the resume. If dates are in the resume, examine the dates and the titles. For instance, if a candidate who graduated last year now holds a "senior data scientist" position this year, then that is probably a lie or, at the very least, should provoke further scrutiny.

  Managers should force the applicant to allow checks on their employment history. Previous (though possibly not current) employers will provide you with position titles and years of employment, and then ensure that these match the information on your resume.

Notes from the Field:

Date checking is essential. One organization hired an applicant who claimed to have over six years of experience as a data scientist. It was later discovered that the individual graduated from college only the previous year and that all six years of experience on the CV were fabricated. The dates were never verified before the hire. A thorough review of the resume could have avoided this expensive and time-consuming hiring oversight.

- Check the resume against the cover letter. If the dates or experience do not match, do not hire this person. Additionally, Glassdoor recommends checking the writing style. If the resume has perfect grammar and presentation, but the cover letter is sloppy, that may indicate that the applicant has fabricated their past employment history.[ix]

- If the resume is vague, ask the candidate to expand upon his experience. Statements like "Provided Machine-Learning solutions to solve company problems" are a red flag.

- Typing during a remote interview while answering a question may indicate the applicant is uncertain of the answer, or at least does not feel comfortable with the material, and is seeking outside help (from Google, ChatGPT, or some similar tool) on the question.

Notes from the Field:

During one interview, an applicant was typing when we asked a question. The answer was changed halfway through to be the exact opposite of what the applicant was saying. When we typed the question in ChatGPT, the answer the applicant gave was word-for-word what ChatGPT reported!

Despite the hype, Google and ChatGPT are not substitutes for technical knowledge. If an applicant is repeating ChatGPT-generated text, you can assume that the applicant knows nothing about the topic and will fail in most complex projects.

Again, it might be prudent to use an AI search engine to review your questions before the interview, so that any deceptive practices by the candidate are noted in real-time. A data scientist may need to provide more detailed answers to questions. For instance, instead of asking "What is a neural network?" the data scientist would instead ask "How do you determine the appropriate number of epochs in an ANN?" Since anyone who has worked with neural networks should have a procedure to set the epoch parameter, this question is better suited to avoid quick lookups.

- Finally, managers need to conduct a background check on new employees that verifies (a) previous criminal activity, (b) discrepancies in the resume on education or employment, or (c) professional certifications. This verification should be early in the interview process.

Notes from the Field:

An organization was interviewing an individual who appeared to be qualified. He had published managerial articles (which were verified) and work experience (which was also verified). He claimed to have transitioned into the data science industry, citing four multi-day, challenging courses from Udemy that were well-known and respected data science courses and certifications.

Near the end of the hiring process, the applicant was asked to verify their Udemy course certifications. Suddenly, the story changed to "I am *pursuing* four certifications in these courses." He never finished a single course, despite what it said on his resume! And nobody pursues four Udemy certifications at once – They do one at a time! The offer was immediately withdrawn. That was certainly a narrow escape!

Interviewing

After a data science candidate has been vetted by a recruiting firm or an in-house review and background check, the candidate can begin the interview process. This section describes how to utilize interviews to recruit top talent, how to identify deception in applicants' skills, and how to effectively build an AI team.

Getting the Top Talent

Interviews are not just about finding the right candidate. They are also a crucial opportunity to sell your organization as a great place to work. This is especially true when competing for top-tier talent, such as a highly skilled data scientist. To secure the best, you need to make a compelling presentation that shows them why your company is the ideal next step in their career. Here are four key strategies to help you do just that:

- **Offer Competitive Compensation and Benefits** – Money is usually the dominant incentive during the interview process. To attract top data scientists, it is crucial to offer competitive compensation packages. You will need to be one of the top offers to be considered.

  The data science manager needs to research market rates for AI roles and ensure that their offers align with industry standards. Highlight your organization's commitment to work-life balance and employee well-being. Try to persuade upper management to consider offering attractive benefits, such as flexible work arrangements, remote work options, professional development budgets, and opportunities for conference attendance or research collaborations. By providing a comprehensive compensation and benefits package, you can demonstrate your commitment to valuing and investing in top AI development talent.

- **Highlight Challenging and Impactful Projects** – Top data scientists are driven by challenging and meaningful work. During the interview process, emphasize the exciting and impactful projects your organization is working on or planning to undertake. Discuss the potential for making a real difference in the industry and solving complex problems using AI.

  Top data science candidates are often drawn to opportunities for innovation, research, and the chance to work with cutting-edge technologies. Promote the aspects of the position that will challenge a candidate and provide exposure to the newest insights and advances in the field.

  Emphasize a Collaborative and Supportive Environment –Remember, a top-tier data scientist is likely already employed and is looking for a role that offers more than just a paycheck. They might feel stifled in their current position, especially if management doesn't fully support AI initiatives. Your job is to show them that your company is different. To achieve this, you must clearly articulate your organization's commitment to skill development and knowledge advancement. Highlight opportunities for learning, access to cutting-edge tools, and a culture that values innovation. This shows the candidate that you're not just offering a job, but a career path where they can grow and make a real impact. This kind of vision is a powerful incentive for a talented data scientist to take your offer seriously.

  Top data scientists are often attracted to environments that foster collaboration, knowledge sharing, and continuous learning. Highlight the collaborative nature of your organization and the opportunities for cross-functional teamwork. Discuss the availability of resources, such as data infrastructure, computational power, and access to relevant datasets. Highlight professional development programs that provide growth opportunities for data scientists.

  Stay in Contact – Don't let top candidates slip away. The most highly sought-after applicants often experience the frustration of not hearing back from a company after an interview. Vacations, demanding meeting schedules, and other priorities often cause a high-value applicant to assume that the job offer is not coming.

  By staying in contact, the manager can learn about the other offers and can put the applicant's mind at ease regarding the status of the position. Reassuring updates in the hiring process given to impressive candidates during the selection process allows a manager to build a rapport with the candidate. The appreciation for such efforts is often more significant to the candidate than a manager might assume.

Burtch Works, a top recruiting firm, emphasizes the importance of recognizing that an interview is not just a one-sided conversation. While you are evaluating the applicant, they are also scrutinizing your organization. It is essential to highlight your company, the data science function, and the team members. By describing your organization's strengths, discussing the exciting projects your team is working on, and sharing your unique company culture, you can craft a compelling pitch that gets the applicant excited about the opportunity.[x]

Having a competitive offer available is only prudent when researching talent, but multiple studies show that remuneration is only one of several important aspects a candidate considers. Additional incentives, such as flexible schedules, remote work, improved benefits, challenging projects, and managerial support, could collectively make an available position on your team look much more inviting than a position with a different company that seemingly neglects attention to career growth.

Interviewing Seasoned Data Scientists

While an applicant's job is to present themselves in the best possible light, a hiring manager's job is to find the best person for the role. These two goals don't have to be at odds. A great data scientist should be proud of their work, and that should be clear during the interview. A candidate's passion for solving problems, frustration with data limitations, and even challenges they've faced communicating with managers or developers can all reveal their true character and capabilities. If these traits don't come through, you should assume the worst and move on.

As the interviewer, you have two main tasks. First, you need to determine if the applicant is being truthful about their skills. Second, you must confirm that they have the necessary skills for the job.

Is Your Applicant Lying?

This chapter already discusses some techniques for detecting falsehoods in a resume before the interview. The interview process is another place to examine the claims made by the candidate. Here are some things you can do:

- **Talk about their previous work**. I am amazed at the number of applicants who lie about their work experience, even claiming to currently hold the position of a data scientist at another company when they have never worked at that company.

  It is often easy to spot with broad questions like, "Your resume says that you worked at XYZ. That is impressive. What did you do there?" The typical candidate will not hesitate to relate aspects of the position in question.

  If they do not provide detailed information about their previous employment or are vague about their current role, then there is a strong possibility that they are not being truthful about either their work experience at the company or their current position.

Notes from the Field:

A consulting firm posted a position for a data scientist where 30 candidates advanced past the initial resume screening. The hiring team ultimately concluded that as many as two-thirds of the applicants were lying about having any data science experience.

If the applicant is being deceptive, they often rely on vague statements, such as "I did data science" or "I did whatever they needed." A three-minute to five-minute conversation will frequently reveal if they did anything at all.

An experienced and competent candidate should be able to provide detailed information about the experience gained with deep learning models, the predictions made, the challenges of working with small datasets, and their experience at the company.

- My two favorite questions on knowledge are "What mathematical or statistical models did you use?" and "Describe why data scientists avoid OLS regression." If they have no idea about the statistics they used, and/or they have no idea what OLS regression is (which would be a way to draw the best-fitting straight line or trend line through some observations or points), then they probably have no experience as a data scientist.

- Ask what is on their resume concerning statistical models. If they listed any mathematical models on their resume, pick one and ask about it. Another data scientist can help with this. One interview tactic is to choose one of the models listed on their resume, find the limitations of the model, and ask them how they handled those limitations.

Notes from the Field:

An applicant recently listed Bayesian analysis on their resume. When asked about specific details, such as how he determined the values for priors (priors are the assumptions used in Bayesian analysis), the candidate described high-level Bayesian analysis but did not provide a direct answer to the question. It was later discovered that his response was read verbatim from a popular statistical software product description.

Further questioning revealed the applicant had no competence in Bayesian analysis and very little in data analysis or statistical modeling. Despite this, their CV was full of complex mathematical models they claimed to have worked with. This candidate had made it past the initial CV screening, even though they had not contributed to, nor understood, the models listed on their resume.

Use the interview so you do not end up hiring someone for six months before discovering that they really know nothing.

- Ask what is on their resume concerning technical skills. If they list Spark, Hadoop, Python, Java, etc., be sure to ask them some questions about one or more of them.

  Program languages or packages often have similar interfaces or menus, regardless of their varied nature. If you require Spark, but the applicant has used Hadoop or Flink, or you require Python and the applicant has used R or Java, or you require Oracle and the applicant has used SQL Server or MySQL, then the skill set might be transferable without requiring much additional training.

  Conversely, you need to decide if a skill is transferable. If the position requires Python and the applicant has no experience in programming or writing code in any computer language. Years of training may be necessary to bring them up to speed.

Notes from the Field:

An applicant recently listed Python alongside other languages, such as Java and R, on his CV. During the interview, he demonstrated fluency in Scala, Java, and R. He did not have as much experience with Python, but he was upfront about his limited Python experience, claiming that he had only taken an online class, yet he was able to read and understand the presented Python code and write some simple scripts. This was not considered a lie, as he honestly represented his experience when asked about it.

His proficiency in other programming languages proved to be a strong indicator of his potential. After being hired, he quickly gained expertise in Python and went on to excel as a data scientist, developing Python applications. His ability to learn and adapt was more valuable than pre-existing mastery.

This example provides several important lessons for hiring managers. If a specific AI skill is essential for a role, you must ask about it during the interview. Don't simply assume a candidate's proficiency based on their resume. A skill listed on a CV doesn't imply mastery unless it's explicitly stated.

Ultimately, if a candidate demonstrates strong proficiency in similar skills and is honest about their experience level with the required skill, you should consider giving them a chance. Their potential to grow and acquire new skills is often more valuable than a deep, pre-existing knowledge of a specific technology.

- Ask why they left or why they are leaving their current or last position. Understand that this is a challenging question to answer. Problematic relationships with management or team members might be revealed. Conversely, answers that demonstrate a natural evolution in a candidate's career progression are typically revealed organically when the question is presented.

Notes from the Field:

If the applicant has multiple positions shown in their work experience, one of my favorite questions is "Why did you leave the job two jobs ago to pursue the last job?" – I often get better answers about disagreements with management or coworkers, problems with advancement, etc.

When I ask, "Why are you leaving your current position?" (which I always do), the answers are more strained, and problems with their current manager or coworkers are less likely to be mentioned.

- Get letters of recommendation if possible.

Does Your Applicant Have the Skills?

After you have determined that the resume is accurate and the applicant seems honest, a skill assessment is required. If you have specific requirements, then a skill test tailored to those requirements is in order. (For example, if you are trying to predict future demand based on past and current demand, an applicant with time series knowledge will be best.) Conversely, if you are unsure about the specific challenges your candidate will face in the future, then a broad, generalized understanding of data science / AI is best.

- Go easy on the "Write the formula for...," or "Interpret the graph..." questions. This will get someone who can regurgitate a formula, but not someone who can apply a statistical model to solve problems.

  As one author put it, if you ask an applicant to solve a 'toy' problem, then you will end up with employees who can quickly solve 'toy' problems, but not necessarily applicants who are good at AI and data science.[xi]

- A take-home test is often used, although these tests are not always a reliable indication of talent. Search for a test that focuses on the skills.

Notes from the Field:

Often, the interviewer is advised to formulate data science questions to be evaluated by the data scientist. For instance, questions such as "return the top five records from a data set." The interviewer often expects that the interviewee will only use a Python/Pandas dataframe statement (`dfCustomer.head(5)`) rather than an equivalent SQL statement (`SELECT * FROM Customer LIMIT 5`) or an equivalent Excel process ("I loaded the records into Excel, sorted them, and copied the top five").

Indeed, the answer is not data science, but *neither is the question*. Candidates often have strong skills in multiple areas, and leveraging these skills in an interview should be viewed as a positive aspect.

If the interviewer wanted a "data science answer," then the interviewer should ask a "data science question." For instance, instead of asking for the top five records, ask the applicant to predict a customer's likelihood of future purchases or to categorize customers into distinct clusters.

Can You Find an Applicant with Multiple Skills?

There are a myriad of interrelated skill sets that data scientists need to be proficient in. They need to be able to understand analysis problems from a business management perspective, evaluate alternative statistical models that can be used to solve problems, train and test models with selected data sets to set the optimal parameters in the model, deliver and explain the solution to the programmers and data specialists, and aid in the application development as required, including how to code the statistics, how to distribute the work amongst all the computers in a computer array, and how to test for validity. Seasoned data scientists should have a broad skill set. This is also why seasoned data scientists are in such high demand and therefore expensive.

It is possible to bring on a data scientist with some experience who is weak in certain areas, such as data design or programming, and train them in these areas. Some data science positions do not require the data scientist to perform any programming or database development, but rather to act as a resource for data modelers and programmers. But these data scientists must usually at least code their own models, usually in Python or R. (Conversely, in other organizations, the data scientists must do it all.)

Interviewing Entry-Level Data Scientists

Sometimes, it is too costly or difficult to find data scientists with a given level of skills. Instead, the data science manager must bring in a new person to train as a data scientist, a position usually referred to as "junior data scientist" or "level 1 data scientist." Here are some key considerations to keep in mind if you want to train from within.

- Is there a competent data scientist on the team who is available to train inexperienced recruits? Such a team member will almost certainly be necessary if hiring less experienced analysts. Self-training is not an effective method to learn highly complex material.

  If the manager does not have a data scientist on staff, a consulting firm could be used to train the data scientist in new skill sets. Other training options, such as online classes, publications, and certifications, are widely available.

- Has the applicant shown a previous interest in working in data science? The high salary of a data scientist is attractive to applicants, and that is OK. However, aside from the higher wage, has the applicant ever demonstrated an interest in the fundamental skills of the position? Do applicants like handling data? Do applicants show an appreciation?

  Applicants who struggle with mathematics will likely face challenges in developing the skills required to be a data scientist. Questions like "Tell me about your favorite teacher and why" or "Tell me about your favorite subjects in college and why" can shed some light on the new applicant's interests.

- Has the applicant expressed an unprompted interest in solving business problems? That is a data scientist's job. The data scientist may not need an MBA, but should at least enjoy profitably solving business problems and communicating effectively. Conversely, if the applicant shows no interest or intrigue in the business's or department's success, then perhaps the data science manager should consider a different applicant.

- Can a new data scientist train on the job? Continuous training in data science is always needed, even for seasoned data scientists, but it is vital for new data scientists. New data scientists with no prior experience in data science will typically require one to two years of training.

  The data science manager needs to find resources for at least one year of intensive training. The department will experience slower model development and reduced productivity as the manager dedicates resources to training. If the manager cannot find those resources, then the manager should not bring on new data scientists.

- How new are they? Some skill sets are nice to have:

  - An undergraduate degree (or higher) in applied statistics, econometrics, corporate financial analysis, and marketing demographic analytics will reduce training needs. A degree in computer science, information science, or information systems with an emphasis on programming can also be beneficial.

    - Programming experience, database experience, or experience in marketing analytics, demographics, or some statistical or data analytics can help.

    - Data scientists need to be able to communicate complex statistical models to upper management, project owners, and developers. I view this as a skill that can be coached, but the manager should assess the interview process to determine how the applicant describes complex AI topics.

After hiring, the new data scientist can develop their skills through extensive work. The data science manager needs to arrange time and resources for:

- **Additional Education** – New data scientists will need additional education as their careers progress. The manager should provide resources for a degree in data science, applied statistics, or any other field that involves a significant amount of data analysis. The manager will need to provide resources for this.

  A more formal education in applied statistics or programming, especially, may alleviate some of the training burden that will hurt the productivity of existing employees. There are multiple commonly used protocols for setting up continuing education programs and tuition reimbursement protocols in tech-heavy industries.

Notes from the Field:

Jeremy Stanley, a chief data scientist, describes hiring a Ph. D. at Sailthru. He mentions that he used to have a bias against any applicant who was "too academically minded." However, after making changes to the data scientist hiring process to be more quantitative, one applicant stood out who had a PhD and several internship experiences. The applicant demonstrated outstanding practical skills during the interview process, as evidenced by the scores on the interview tests.

Stanley reports that the new data scientist began implementing changes in production within his first two weeks and has had a positive impact on productivity over the first three months.[xii] This level of productivity is rare, but Stanley claims that the successful new hire resulted from the new interviewing process, which identified better candidates.

Data science managers should not shy away from academically strong individuals. The academic training that applicants receive may significantly reduce the amount of additional training that managers must fund. Instead, the manager should assess the practical skills of the applicant and how academically gained knowledge and skills can be applied in a practical setting within the organization.

- **Training** – It is not just that a new data scientist will not be as productive as a seasoned data scientist. A new data scientist will temporarily divert resources from the rest of the team until training is complete. Keeping project owners and upper management informed and updated on the current training status and expectations helps alleviate concerns over resource allocation.

  Some managers do not anticipate the adverse impact on short-term productivity inherent in new data scientist training. Managers who expect seasoned data scientists to train new hires "on their spare time" are going to be disappointed. Employees do not have spare time – they are at work delivering what they can within a set of time constraints, resource constraints, and personal capabilities. Seasoned data scientists will not be able to adequately train new hires unless training becomes an allocated and valued part of their existing responsibilities.

  Finally, managers should reward existing data scientists for training new data scientists. Managers rarely say "good job" when a senior data scientist trains a junior data scientist. Instead, senior data scientist evaluations concentrate on AI applications that have been developed. If data scientists are not recognized for their training, then they are less motivated to spend time training the new data scientists.

Without proper training and support, a new data scientist will falter, and the department will suffer.

- **Certifications** – Books, certifications, and online classes are often a readily available, reasonably priced, and less costly way for the new data scientist to gain AI knowledge and skills. Ensure the certification is challenging; if a certification is easy to achieve, the data science manager may consider insisting on certifications with more rigor.

  Again, the goal of the manager is to get training for the new data scientist on company time that does not impact the productivity of other data scientists. Certifications are one way to achieve this.

Education, books, training, and certifications are beneficial tools, but managers need to understand that certifications and degrees are merely a foundation for advanced expertise with most AI topics. It will take some time and experience for a data scientist to gain the needed skills to be as productive as a seasoned data scientist.

Many companies, especially in the Fortune 500, have established their own "universities" where they can train aspiring data scientists. These programs often turn out master's degree-level data scientists. If no such options are available, a manager can still implement a robust training program that includes online courses and third-party offerings available from companies like Udemy, Coursera, W3Schools, Codecademy, and others.

Adding Other Skills to the AI Team

Depending on the organization, the data science manager might be responsible solely for AI applications. However, AI applications often require a collaborative effort from other business and technical areas. The manager must ensure that ancillary skills are either present or available so that the AI team has access to outside personnel with the required skill sets. The following types of employees are also needed for AI development to be successful:

- **Quality Assurance Personnel** – Data scientists must unit-test their predictions to catch errors, bad estimates, missing values, etc. After unit testing by the data scientist, the application needs to be tested by someone outside the AI team, or at least by someone not involved in prediction development. That "someone" is the QA specialist.

  QA specialists are hard to recruit, retain, and manage. QA specialists collaborate with data scientists to develop initial tests, establish range and volume expectations, identify missing and duplicate values, and set accuracy and runtime expectations, among other tasks.

Software bugs are an inherent element of computer-based data analysis due to various reasons beyond the control of any one department. The appropriate response to discovering a previously unremarked bug is to add that defect to the testing procedures and protocols. Bugs will occur, but the longer testing procedures exist and are refined, the less likely it is that a serious bug will emerge. In other words, do not blame the QA specialist for a bug that has never been seen before, even if, in retrospect, it seems like an obvious bug.

A QA specialist is vital to the AI application development because a developer cannot adequately test their own work. The QA specialist can often save millions of dollars in expenses or make millions in additional revenue by catching errors within the AI application, and good QA specialists should be highly valued. In addition, a successful QA process will garner trust with the business experts because the number of bugs will be significantly reduced.

- **Data Analysts** – Data scientists often can deliver charts, graphs, spreadsheets, and analysis to the business user. However, many firms utilize data scientists to make predictions and data analysts to develop applications that visualize the data (on a Web page, in a third-party application like Tableau, Power BI, Plotly, Streamlit, in a spreadsheet, or a customized application).

  Data analysts perform two functions. First, they take a workload off the data scientist, allowing for more AI applications to be delivered. Second, they reduce the skill set required by data scientists, making it easier to find qualified candidates to fill a position and reducing the training required for an effective data scientist.

  Plus, data analysts usually enjoy their job, delivering visualizations to business users.

- **IT Architects / ML Ops / Data Governance** – Data scientists and data analysts need some computer architecture to function. Data scientists cannot be expected to manage database servers, Spark clusters, up-to-the-minute updates on development software, version control software administration, cloud setup, access control to data, and many other highly technical tasks.

  Infrastructure architects and administrators are a tremendous help to data scientists, who require access to data, software tools, cloud services, and network functionality to perform their jobs effectively.

- **Business Area Testing** – After the unit testing and QA testing are completed, the business area should conduct its own testing. This is known as User Acceptance Testing (UAT). It is occasionally challenging to get the business area to test, so the data scientist manager must communicate the need for such testing. The business area must accept the AI application, and this should involve some verification from the business area.

The business area needs to designate a person or people to run tests on the predictions. Do the projections seem right? Are the observations used to train the AI model? Are there missing predictions? The UAT is the final verification before production, and the business area must accept the application (or its next version) before it is put into production.

These positions typically do not report directly to the data science manager. However, the data science manager must maintain close contact with other managers to ensure that the necessary skillset and bandwidth are available to deliver applications to the business areas.

The Challenge of Consulting

Hiring and properly utilizing outside consultants can be difficult for the data science manager. Consultants are ubiquitous in the Data Analysis industry, and contracting one provides both benefits and challenges.

In an optimal situation, there can be several benefits to bringing in a consultant:

- Often, an AI consultant has a skill set that is missing within an organization. Those skills can generate revenue or cut costs with that skill set.
- Often, consultants from larger consulting firms are part of a team that contains:
    - Data analysts are programmers who convert predictions from AI statistical models into charts, graphs, and tables. Their work allows outside managers to visualize insights and make more informed managerial decisions.
    - Database specialists who set up databases (both relational databases and big data NoSQL databases) that can be accessed by the data scientists and the data analysts to develop and then deliver an AI application.
    - IT architects who make sure that there is a functioning environment to develop and deploy AI applications.
    - Quality assurance specialists who can help ensure accurate predictions.
    - Project managers who can manage AI application development efforts and communicate with the data science manager on daily progress.

  - Marketing specialists who can deliver slides or animations that describe the application in an easily understood manner.

  - An upper management communication team that keeps track of managerial inputs and can deliver these insights to the manager or the rest of the team.

With the team and potential benefits, the data science manager and upper management can easily justify a decision to bring in a consulting firm. But there are specific challenges for the data science manager when consultants are involved:

- A recent statistical analysis in *Policy & Politics* shows many cases where consultants can make companies less efficient, with consultants becoming "partners in governance, deeply embedded, through networking and lobbying strategies." Such consultants strive to gain the attention of executives and frequently promote their own work or products while downplaying the contributions of other firms or their employees.[xiii]

- A later analysis examines "demand inflation," where a consulting firm's services are in increasing demand even after showing a decrease in efficiency as that consulting group strengthens its networking and ties to management.[xiv]

- There are everyday consulting concerns, such as "landing and expanding," referring to consultants who view their mission as expanding within an organization, often at a significant expense or a considerable project failure rate reported by Forbes Magazine.[xv]

- But for technology positions like data scientists, the goal of the consulting firm might not be to provide excellent skills and services for the *current* consulting job, but too often the goal is to provide a steady revenue stream and job skills for the *next* consulting job, as described by *InfoWorld Magazine*:[xvi]

  - Bad consulting firms claim employees have skills that they do not possess, and have their consultants develop as many skills as possible (for the next job) before being let go. (This is sometimes called "fake it till you make it.")

  - Bad consulting firms promise superstars and then send newbies so they can learn and pad their resumes (for the next job).

  - Bad consulting firms refuse or are unable to deliver intellectual property (like source code) that was developed while working for you.

Even within a large consulting firm, there are departments or areas where expertise is overstated or overestimated. Having a consultant on staff for six months before realizing that the person you contracted is not proficient in the skill sets necessary for AI is a substantial drain on budgets and schedules.

Consultants can also provide you with entry-level data scientists, but you'll need to commit to retaining them at your site after training. Any misrepresentation of consultants' skill levels can ultimately result in significant financial losses for companies.

The data science manager needs to be aware of the pros and cons of consultants and must treat consultants, even from existing, trusted firms, as new hires to be vetted. The manager must ensure that evaluations and observations of the consultant's usefulness, both positive and negative, are communicated to upper management and the consultant firm's management team.

Concluding Thoughts on AI Team Building

This chapter explores the key elements of AI team management, including the ideal team composition, inspiring leadership, effective communication, and fostering a vibrant culture of collaboration and innovation among data scientists and AI professionals. It provides needed insights to strategically hire and train new data scientists, retain existing talent, and expertly navigate the intricacies of AI consulting groups, ensuring your team is poised to conquer any AI challenge.

Every manager should understand the principles in this chapter. The ability to effectively build and lead an AI team is the single most powerful lever managers have to unlock the full potential of their company's data assets and drive truly impactful outcomes. By mastering the art of building high-performing teams, providing effective leadership, fostering open communication and collaboration, nurturing a relentless drive for innovation, and championing individual growth, data science managers can help shape an organization's near-term and long-term technological developments.

The topics in this chapter extend beyond managing a department to provide a strategic advantage. The dedication managers invest in cultivating exceptional AI teams will directly maximize the value delivered by every AI initiative, transforming theoretical potential into tangible results and forging a sustainable competitive advantage that sets the organization apart.

---

[i] David Waller. Feb 6, 2020. "10 Steps to Creating a Data-Driven Culture." *Harvard Business Review.* https://hbr.org/2020/02/10-steps-to-creating-a-data-driven-culture.

[ii] Haixing Yin, Fan Fan, Jiazhi Zhang, Hanyang Li and Ting Fung Lau. Aug 31, 2020. "The Importance of Domain Knowledge," *ML*CMU*, available at https://blog.ml.cmu.edu/2020/08/31/1-domain-knowledge/.

[iii] Daniel Tunkelang. Feb 11, 2017. "What comes after 'Senior Data Scientist'?" *Quora*. https://www.quora.com/What-comes-after-%E2%80%9CSenior-Data-Scientist%E2%80%9D.

[iv] Bureau of Labor Statistics. 2023. "Occupational Outlook Handbook: Data Scientists." *U.S. Bureau of Labor Statistics*, available at https://www.bls.gov/ooh/math/data-scientists.htm.

[v]Gil Press. Jun 14, 2022. "A Booming Market for AI Skills, With Salaries Topping $300,000." *Forbes*, available at https://www.forbes.com/sites/gilpress/2022/06/14/a-booming-market-for-ai-skills-with-salaries-topping-300000/?sh=c5925ed23d6a.

[vi] Jeremy Stanley. Mar 6, 2024. "How to Consistently Hire Remarkable Data Scientists." *First Round Review*, available at https://firstround.com/review/how-to-consistently-hire-remarkable-data-scientists/.

[vii] Ken Jee. August 27, 2019. "Why is it so Hard to Find Great Data Science Managers?" *Towards Data Science*, available at https://towardsdatascience.com/why-is-it-so-hard-to-find-great-data-science-managers-6fc8aac62f6e.

[viii] Jeremy Stanley. Mar 6, 2024. "How to Consistently Hire Remarkable Data Scientists." *First Round Review*, available at https://firstround.com/review/how-to-consistently-hire-remarkable-data-scientists/.

[ix] Glassdoor Team Career Advice Experts. Dec 16, 2021. "Lying on Your Resume? Here's How You'll Get Caught." *Glassdoor*, available at https://www.glassdoor.com/blog/lying-on-your-resume/.

[x] Burtch Works. May 25, 2023. "Employers: How to Win the Battle for Top Data Science & Analytics Talent." *Burtch Works*, available at https://www.burtchworks.com/industry-insights/employers-how-to-win-the-battle-for-top-data-science-analytics-talent.

[xi] Jeremy Stanley. Mar 6, 2024. "How to Consistently Hire Remarkable Data Scientists." *First Round Review*, available at https://firstround.com/review/how-to-consistently-hire-remarkable-data-scientists/.

[xii] Jeremy Stanley. Mar 6, 2024. "How to Consistently Hire Remarkable Data Scientists." *First Round Review*, available at https://firstround.com/review/how-to-consistently-hire-remarkable-data-scientists/.

[xiii] Kirkpatrick, I., Sturdy, A. J., Alvarado, N. R., Blanco-Oliver, A., & Veronesi, G. 2019. "The impact of management consultants on public service efficiency." *Policy & Politics* 47(1), 77-96.

[xiv] Sturdy, A., Kirkpatrick, I., Blanco, A., & Veronesi, G. 2020. "The Management Consultancy Effect: Demand Inflation and Its Consequences in the Sourcing of External Knowledge." *Public Administration*, 1–19.

[xv] Lewis, Phil, July 29, 2019. "Is This the End for Consultants?" *Forbes Magazine*, available at https://medium.com/@anandrrr/client-crowding-and-inflating-projects-29175a514a45.

[xvi] Tynan, Dan, April 11, 2011. "7 Dirty Consultant Tricks (and How to Avoid Them)" *InfoWorld*, available at https://www.infoworld.com/article/2623643/7-dirty-consultant-tricks--and-how-to-avoid-them-.html.

Chapter 8: How AI Changes Governance

While the promise of AI is considerable, successful integration hinges on robust data governance. Data governance refers to the oversight of access, policies, and procedures that promote transparency, accountability, and ethical use of data. Sensitive information must be protected, and potential risks associated with widespread data usage must be mitigated. Proper governance is not about stifling innovation; it's about channeling AI's power responsibly, ensuring ethical use, safeguarding valuable data, and maximizing its positive impact on your organization.

This chapter serves as an essential guide to AI governance, covering topics such as security frameworks, employee roles and responsibilities, and the enforcement of protocols for data security, privacy, and regulatory compliance. The chapter explores how to establish comprehensive frameworks for managing the AI lifecycle, defining clear roles, and enforcing protocols for security, privacy, and compliance. We'll dive into the unique challenges of data governance intrinsic to AI, ranging from data access and policy setting to ensuring transparency and accountability, and equip you with the insights you need to mitigate risks and unlock AI's full potential.

The emergence of AI as a transformative force in the digital age has reshaped the landscape of data governance, presenting unique challenges and opportunities that demand a fresh perspective from both the AI manager and the data governance manager. This chapter discusses data governance, with a concentration on the unique data governance challenges that AI has introduced to management.

What is this chapter trying to do and why?

The increasing reliance on AI to derive actionable insights from vast, complex datasets is causing the traditional paradigms of data governance to be reevaluated. Unlike in conventional domains, where data governance primarily focuses on regulatory compliance and risk mitigation, AI operates at the intersection of statistics, computer science, and domain expertise.

One of the fundamental distinctions between data governance in traditional domains and AI lies in the dynamic treatment of data inherent in the AI's paradigm shift. Previous data domains consisted of functions applied to structured data originating from well-defined sources, such as transactional systems or electronic health records. AI encompasses a less restricted spectrum of data types, including unstructured text, images, sensor data, and social media interactions. Moreover, AI practitioners frequently encounter data sources that are noisy, incomplete, or subject to change, necessitating agile governance mechanisms that can adapt to evolving data landscapes. Finally, AI models can often predict characteristics of individuals who “opt out” of inclusion, such as political preferences based on similar families in a neighborhood.

The iterative and experimental nature of AI projects poses another significant challenge for data governance. Unlike traditional initiatives with predefined objectives and fixed deliverables, AI projects are characterized by continuous exploration and refinement of hypotheses, often requiring rapid access to diverse datasets and experimentation with various modeling techniques. Consequently, data governance frameworks must strike a balance between fostering innovation and ensuring compliance. Proper data governance should enable AI practitioners to explore novel data-analysis protocols while mitigating risks associated with data misuse or ethical concerns.

Data quality, security, and privacy are not only crucial to organizations; organizational data governance is also considered an aspect of national security in many countries in recent years. Security breaches have originated from rival governments and criminal organizations, often attributable to poor data governance practices. For instance:

- The Washington Post reports that a 2016 security breach of the Democratic National Committee (DNC) serves as a stark example of the consequences of poor data governance practices. A Russian-originated breach infiltrated the DNC's computer network, gaining unauthorized access to sensitive information and emails, and releasing the information to influence the 2016 U.S. presidential election. The DNC breach was made possible by inadequate and lax access controls, lax enforcement of procedures, inadequate training on data governance, and insufficient data protection protocols, which left the DNC vulnerable to cyberattacks and resulted in significant damage to the DNC's reputation and efforts in the 2016 election.[i]

- In India, citizens use an Aadhaar number for things like voting, opening a bank account, and other forms of identification. (It is analogous to a social security number in the United States.) Aadhaar is the world's most extensive biometric identification system, containing sensitive data on more than a billion people. ZDNet reports that in 2018, approximately 200 official government websites inadvertently disclosed personal Aadhaar data. It was revealed that this was not so much a hack as a breakdown in data governance. Parts of the Aadhaar system were left without a password and unencrypted since 2014, so anyone and everyone could steal the personal information of Indian residents with just a Google search.[ii]

Such examples are legion in the evolving field of AI. By dissecting the unique challenges and opportunities presented by AI projects, this chapter discusses the evolving role of data governance in enabling organizations to harness the full potential of AI while protecting their data assets.

The GRC Framework and AI Governance

The **Governance, Risk, and Compliance (GRC)** framework is a widely used governance lens that enables organizations to integrate capabilities that reliably achieve objectives, address uncertainty, and act with integrity.[iii] Figure 28 shows how the CRG consists of these three interconnected components and how governance flows from a governing body to management:[iv]

The Role of the Governing Body

Although the GRC framework comprises three distinct functions, most organizations group all three into a single "Governing Body" function or department.

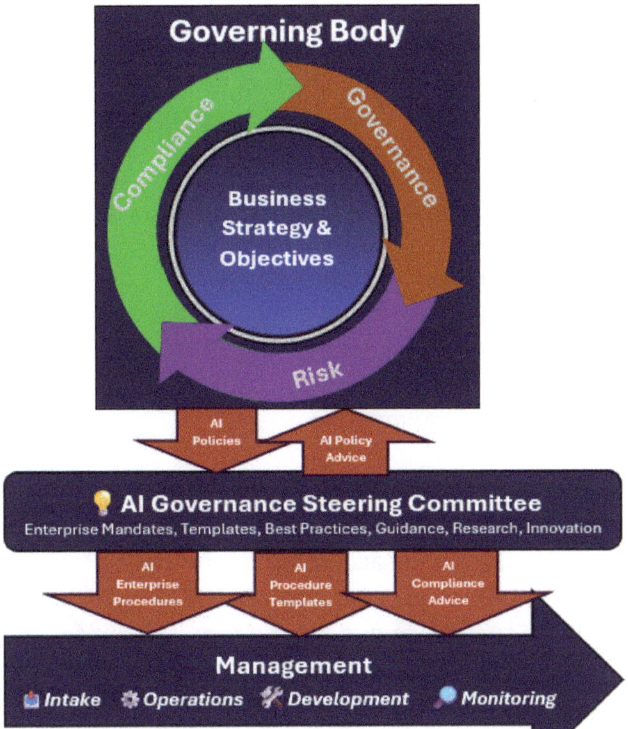

Figure 28: The GRC framework directs operations

- **Governance** steers an organization by establishing direction and maintaining accountability. With AI, this means setting the overall ethical framework, deciding on the acceptable risk tolerance for model accuracy and fairness, and defining the organizational structure (e.g., establishing an AI Governance center of excellence) required to approve, audit, and decommission AI systems.
- **Risk** management for AI must address unique, high-stakes threats, notably algorithmic bias, security vulnerabilities, and "model drift." Model drift is particularly critical: it occurs when the business environment or customer behavior shifts, leading to a degradation in our AI's performance. This isn't just a technical glitch—it directly leads to poor business outcomes, such as ineffective pricing or missed compliance events. Until the AI model is corrected, model drift forces the organization to accept unacknowledged, escalating risk in key areas. Addressing this risk requires treating AI governance as a continuous, strategic imperative rather than merely a launch checklist completed during intake.

- **Compliance** focuses on adherence to *internal* policies and *external* laws and regulations. In AI, this centers on ensuring the systems meet explicit legal requirements (e.g., GDPR data minimization, the EU AI Act's classification and testing mandates) and high-level internal standards.

Traditionally, GRC has been used to manage data security and for data governance since the early 2000s. But now, as fast-moving, complex AI systems take over more tasks, this entire rulebook is changing. Organizations now need a new, dedicated AI Governance area to manage the unique risks (such as GenAI hallucinations, unfair decisions, mathematical and discriminatory biases, and AI model and data protection) that AI creates, ensuring AI technology is trustworthy, operates safely, and aligns with an organization's strategic plan.

Governance and AI Management

As shown in Figure 28, policies from governance drive the procedures for data intake, operations and architecture, AI application development, and AI application monitoring after the application is deployed.[v,vi]

The governing board and management have different roles:

- **Governance** (managed by the governing board) **is the "Why" and the "What":** Governance establishes the rules, policies, and risk tolerance that *must* be followed. Usually, procedures are not part of governance unless those procedures are enterprise-wide (such as "Always use our repository software to track any new or existing AI development").

- **Management is the "How" and the "When":** These are the procedures, processes, and activities overseen by managers that are used to build and run software and AI applications according to the policies set by GRC. Note that while management is often concerned with "How" and "When", all of management is not governance. Governance defines the *requirement* for the policy, while management defines the *steps* of the procedure to fulfill the policy requirements. While management must align with GRC policies, the act of managing projects is not, in itself, governance.

- **The AI Governance Steering Committee bridges governance and management** by translating policies into operational requirements, advising management on compliance, overseeing risk monitoring, and ensuring alignment with the board's mandates. The steering committee can also make policy recommendations to the governing board. The steering committee ensures that "Management's 'How' does not inadvertently bypass Governance's 'What'."

In larger organizations, the AI Governance Steering Committee is vital to bridging the gap between the board's high-level strategies and the practical work of managers. This critical role ensures that policy goals are translated into clear, actionable requirements across every AI application the company develops.

Data Quality, Lineage, and Curation as the Foundation for AI

Data quality, lineage, and curation are inextricably linked as the foundational pillars for reliable and trustworthy AI governance:

- **Data Quality** is the accuracy, completeness, and consistency of our information. It is the single most critical starting point for all our data management efforts. If the data that is fed into the AI training and testing algorithms is flawed ("garbage in, garbage out"), then sophisticated AI models will produce flawed results, leading to misguided strategic decisions and wasted resources.

- **Data lineage** is the whole history and pathway of our data, tracking exactly where data came from, every change it went through, and where it is finally used (like training an AI model). This is a critical management capability because it provides the essential audit trail we need. If an AI system produces a flawed result or we face a regulatory inquiry, we use lineage to quickly diagnose the problem by tracing the data back to its source. Comprehensive data lineage ensures both system quality and legal compliance.

- **Data Curation** is the strategic process of actively managing and organizing our data to ensure it is trustworthy and accessible for future use, essentially creating a self-improving cycle where better data leads to more dependable systems. Unlike the slow, manual cleaning of historical data common in the past, modern AI Curation is a complex, continuous discipline that involves preparing massive volumes of data (including images and video) for machine learning, while proactively identifying and fixing internal biases. This forward-looking rigor is crucial because the quality of our curated data directly determines the reliability of our AI systems, mitigates business risk, and ensures the dependability of the strategic decisions they inform.

The collective emphasis on data quality, lineage, and curation forms the essential, integrated foundation for modern AI systems. Organizations should treat these three pillars as a unified, iterative system to successfully transition AI input data into a trustworthy, strategic asset for ethical, high-performing AI.

AI Project Management vs AI Governance

Often, managers confuse the concept of project management (intake, scheduling, task assignment, etc.) with the concept of governance. The thought process is that if a manager asks an employee to do something, then that manager is “governing” the employee. But this is not the case:

- Governance is more strategic dealing with compliance of legal and ethical standards that drive management to make requirements of their employees.

- Project Management often does not deal with compliance, legal and ethical issues, or risk, but rather efficient ways to deliver products and services that add value to the company.

There is some overlap, since managers are not only expected to deliver applications, but are also expected to comply with standards to follow legal requirements and reduce breaches. The table in Figure 29 shows the difference in function between project management and governance.

Feature	Project Management (Operations)	Governance (Strategic/Risk)
Focus	Efficiency, prioritization, and resource allocation	Accountability, risk mitigation, and ethical alignment
Question	"Do we have the budget and talent to build this?"	"Should we build this? Is the data lineage legal? Is it biased? Does it leak PII (Personal Identifiable Information)"
Output	Workflow diagrams, Jira tickets, and project queues	Policies, risk assessments, guardrails, human-in-the-loop, drift thresholds, and audit trails
Key Metric	Velocity and Time-to-Deployment	Compliance rate and Residual Risk Level

Figure 29: AI Project Management vs AI Governance

The Black Box Problem and Explainable AI (XAI)

Traditional applications deal with clear, structured inputs, and the developers understand the meaning of every variable. AI, however, excels at processing both structured and unstructured data (images, video, raw text). The features or concepts AI applications use to make decisions are distributed across thousands of interconnected nodes that do not correspond to a single, human-readable variable. For example, an AI application that diagnoses a condition might use subtle, high-dimensional texture patterns in an X-ray that no human doctor or programmer can identify as the definitive cause. The "Black Box Problem" occurs when AI developers cannot clearly specify why AI makes a recommendation.[vii]

The Black Box Problem is bad for governance because the lack of transparency in how an AI system makes decisions prevents the ability to audit for bias, establish accountability when harm occurs, and ensure compliance with ethical (e.g., bias or fairness) and legal (e.g., credit card data protection or SOX data lineage) requirements.

Enter Explainable AI (XAI) – XAI addresses the black box problem by developing techniques to shed light on model behavior. There are two common approaches for XAI, LIME and SHAP, that are model agnostic, meaning that they analyze an AI model's output without needing to access its internal Python code:[viii]

- **LIME (Local Interpretable Model-agnostic Explanations)** generates an explanation of the factors that predicted a single data point. For instance, LIME could list the variables used to predict next month's sales in one of your sales districts.

- **SHAP (SHapley Additive exPlanations)** uses game theory to quantify the precise contribution of each input feature to the final prediction dataset, providing a fair and consistent attribution of every feature used for prediction.

By providing these simplified, targeted explanations, either globally across all data or locally for one specific instance, XAI transforms opaque predictions into actionable, understandable insights, thereby improving debugging, trust, and compliance.

The Problem with Shadow AI

The sudden popularity of tools like ChatGPT has created a significant organizational problem often referred to as "Shadow AI" (Figure 30). ISACA defines Shadow AI as the proliferation of unauthorized AI tools and applications sneaking into enterprises without the knowledge or approval of Data Science, IT/ML Operations, or Governance teams. Shadow AI occurs when employees and departments, eager to get quick AI wins (often to showcase in quarterly reports and resumes), dive into AI development without first getting the approval or risking denial.[ix]

Figure 30: Shadow AI Occurs when AI Governance is Ignored

The Gartner Group points out that Shadow AI isn't just a minor technical annoyance, but rather a profound business risk![x] Every time a team uses an unapproved GenAI vendor or develops its own LLM (Large Language Model) without oversight, it effectively bypasses the company's established safeguards against risk, including checks for data security, model bias, hallucinations (when the GenAI makes up facts), and inaccuracies. This lack of control directly leads to three immediate business threats: (1) substantial waste of money on duplicated, uncoordinated efforts, (2) legal and compliance exposure that could result in substantial fines and loss of customer trust, and (3) ongoing conflicts over who is responsible when the unvetted AI system makes a mistake.

Motivations that lead to a Shadow AI

Shadow AI develops from two converging, powerful motivations that motivate bypassing standard corporate controls: The ease of deployment, and the top-down push for GenAI adoption.

GenAI is Dangerously Easy to Deploy

Unlike traditional enterprise technologies that require months of specialized coding and complex system architectures, Generative AI applications are surprisingly simple to develop. Employees can instantly turn themselves into 'AI developers' with *zero coding skills required*. This is because new GenAI developers can readily modify an existing powerful LLM model (such as the one behind ChatGPT) to suit their team's specific needs through a technique called “prompt engineering.” Prompt engineering lets developers specify the GenAI's actions by typing clear, specific instructions and questions into a chat box in their native language, without writing code.

Advanced techniques, such as using internal company documents to guide the AI's responses (known as Retrieval-Augmented Generation, or RAG), can be implemented with surprising speed—often taking hours, not months—to achieve output.

Ease of use is not a bad thing, but a low barrier to entry accelerates adoption while completely bypassing crucial quality assurance and risk checks. The risk across organizations is so significant that IBM reports how 38% of employees acknowledge sharing sensitive information with a custom-developed or vendor-driven GenAI.[xi]

The Push for GenAI Adoption Came from the Top

Most corporate technologies are adopted from the bottom up, with technical teams first assessing the need, justifying the costs, and then convincing senior management. GenAI adoption, however, has mainly been pushed from the top down.

Managers across organizations were immediately excited by the capabilities of GenAI tools, such as ChatGPT, to generate summaries, draft documents, and create images quickly. This enthusiasm led executives and department heads to urgently drive their teams to find use cases and adopt the technology immediately within applications. This top-down pressure, combined with vendors that often aggressively marketed easy-to-develop products lacking quality assurance and governance checks, created an environment where departments prioritized speed over control, leading to the widespread, unvetted proliferation of Shadow AI.

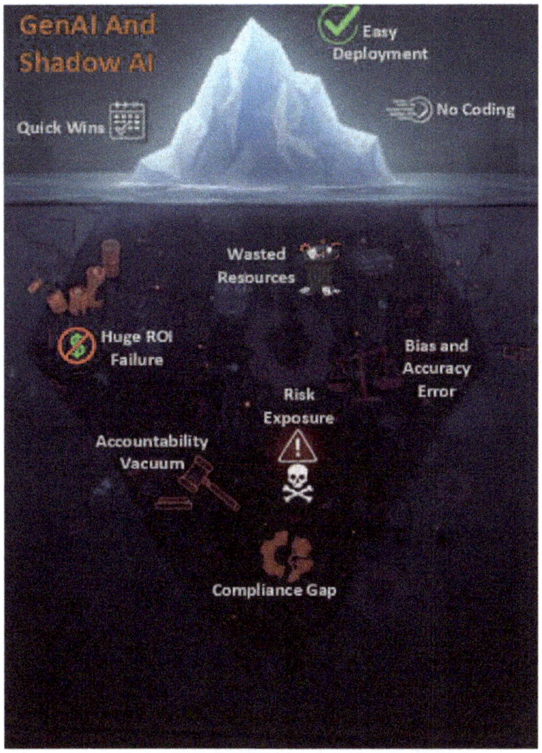

Figure 31: Small Shadow AI Benefits with Large Governance Costs

The Shadow AI Governance Breakdown

One of the main reasons that GenAI is so susceptible to Shadow AI is that some genuine benefits of GenAI development are quickly achieved. The iceberg shown in Figure 31 illustrates clear benefits of GenAI development, such as quick wins, minimal coding requirements, and easy development that requires little training. However, just as with an iceberg, these benefits are in the 10% of the visible tip, but more danger lurks in Shadow AI's ungoverned GenAI, which can pose significant risks or financial harm to an organization.

Figure 31 shows that, below the surface, the overwhelming dangers of Shadow AI (the hidden 90% of the iceberg) undermine core governance principles across several critical areas:

- **Huge ROI Failure Rate:** A study by the Massachusetts Institute of Technology (MIT) revealed that 95% of *organizations* (not just individual projects but entire organizations) fail to deliver any financial or operational benefit from their GenAI projects.[xii] A Shadow AI enables individuals and departments to pursue GenAI projects without worrying about wasted resources or lost revenue.
- **Risk Exposure:** Departments deploy LLMs without standard AI Risk Management protocols (e.g., impact assessment, threat modeling, security architecture review). This procedural lapse creates systemic operational risk, immediately exposing the organization to regulatory fines and penalties, and reputational harm.

- **Wasted Resource through Duplication:** The lack of central coordination and ownership results in widespread duplication, where multiple departments independently procure or develop similar LLM capabilities. This duplication leads to unnecessary and escalating costs, including duplicate third-party licensing fees, multiple employees performing duplicate development and maintenance tasks, and wasted computing resources used to run duplicate models. This inefficiency directly impacts the firm's bottom line.

  Note also that duplication is not just wasted money, but also a failure to capture employee knowledge. Duplication means no one is using the best GenAI practices.

- **Ownership and Accountability Vacuum:** The "easy-to-implement" nature of GenAI blurs lines of responsibility. Disputes over who owns the model, who is responsible for its output, and who is accountable for its maintenance and regulatory compliance create friction in the boardroom. This ambiguity paralyzes incident response when a problem occurs, such as a data breach or an ethical violation.

- **Bias and Accuracy Error:** Shadow AI dramatically increases the risk of perpetuating and amplifying bias due to the absence of mandated, standardized testing. When individuals or departments use LLMs without central governance, they often omit critical data science steps, such as audits and adversarial testing, thereby amplifying biases that may already exist in the LLM's dataset. Furthermore, if output accuracy is not rigorously validated, models may generate hallucinations (false or misleading information) that are unknowingly integrated into core business operations, leading to erroneous decision-making, compromised data integrity, and a direct undermining of the organization's commitment to fairness and factual accuracy.

- **Compliance Gap:** These uncontrolled deployments bypass existing GRC Frameworks for data use and application development. The uncontrolled deployments bypass existing GRC Frameworks... Instead, they rely on ad hoc, 'good enough' standards that fail to meet the principles of Fairness, Accountability, and Transparency (FAT). This exposes the firm to severe legal jeopardy as global regulations, such as the EU AI Act, shift the focus onto the risk classification and quality of deployed AI systems.

Shadow AI is a managerial problem, not a technical problem. Shadow AI is a failure of corporate governance and risk management where individuals trade small, short-term productivity gains for massive, unquantifiable risks to finances, reputations, and legal standing.

Solving Shadow AI Governance Problems

Shadow AI presents a serious risk to budget and regulatory compliance. To move AI from an unmanaged liability to a strategic asset, these four essential governance solutions focused on centralizing resources, mandating accountability, and controlling risk:

Mandatory ROI & Risk Assessment: Require a formal approval process for all AI initiatives to justify the use of personnel and computing resources. This prevents Shadow AI from wasting expensive resources. The ROI estimate will control budget creep, and risk categorization (e.g., High, Limited, Minimal) will ensure compliance with global regulations such as the EU AI Act.

Centralized AI Services Store: Establish a single, internal catalog of approved, pre-vetted, and centrally managed LLM services. This drives significant cost savings through economies of scale, eliminates redundant development, and enforces the reuse of validated, high-quality models. Accountability for each new AI service will also be clearly defined.

Mandatory "Go-to-Production" Review Gate: Create a centralized AI Review Board (ARB) to act as a mandatory gatekeeper. No GenAI application should be deployed to production without a formal review confirming documented bias auditing, hallucination control, and minimum accuracy. This drastically reduces enterprise risk.

Unified Testing & Validation Standards: Implement a single testing toolkit for all GenAI deployments. This standardizes metrics for performance, explainability, and fairness, ensuring a consistent, high-quality bar across the organization. This simplifies the examination of model effectiveness and compliance verification.

AI Risk Management

AI Risk management involves determining the amount of risk an organization is willing to accept from AI, identifying AI risks, and the organization's response to AI risks.

Risk Appetite

A risk appetite is the maximum level of risk the organization is willing to accept, tolerate, or be exposed to in pursuit of its strategic objectives. The governance board works with upper management to determine the organization's risk appetite.

Using a Risk Matrix

Often, a risk matrix (shown in Figure 32) provides an excellent visual and systematic tool for translating risk into concrete, actionable criteria. By plotting the probability of occurrence (Y-axis) against the negative impact or cost of occurrence (X-axis), the matrix maps individual risks into distinct zones: low, medium, high, and critical. Management must strategically define the threshold where the risk transitions from tolerable (typically the low and medium zones) to unacceptable (the high and critical zones). This boundary serves as the organization's explicit risk appetite statement across various operational and strategic domains. The governing board must define acceptable levels of risk impact for each project and the probability of that impact occurring and then work with management to examine each project's risk profile.

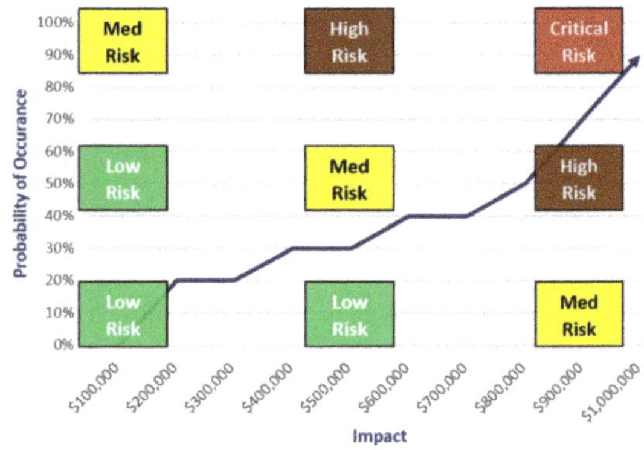

Figure 32: Risk Matrix

In Figure 32, impact is measured in dollars in cost or reduced revenue. However, there can be other measures of impact, including stakeholder perceptions, the risk of reputational harm, and adverse effects on employee morale. Organizations often maintain multiple risk matrices for different "pillars" they deem important.

To effectively use a risk matrix to determine appetite, the organization must first establish clear, objective definitions for both the probability and impact scales. For example, 'Critical Impact' might be defined as an event that causes bankruptcy or a severe regulatory penalty, whereas 'High Probability' could be described as an event expected to occur annually. Risks falling into the 'Low' zone generally require minimal control and are fully accepted. 'Medium' risks might be accepted but require regular monitoring. The organization's appetite is primarily expressed by its stance on 'High' and 'Critical' risks. A low-risk appetite organization may tolerate no risks in the high zone and certainly none in the critical zone, while an organization with a high-risk appetite might accept certain high risks if the potential return on investment is significant and a robust mitigation plan is in place.

The risk matrix serves as a continuous governance tool, ensuring that all employees understand the level of risk to which they are authorized to expose themselves. For example, a policy might state: "Any risk assessed as 'Critical' must be immediately escalated to the Executive Committee for a 'Treat' or 'Terminate' decision, as this falls outside the corporate risk appetite." Any risk that plots into an unacceptable risk automatically triggers a mandatory response, such as mitigation of the risk, transfer of the risk (through insurance, copays, etc.), or avoidance of the risk (e.g., stopping the project immediately). Thus, the risk matrix not only visualizes the appetite but also embeds it into the organization's control and escalation processes, providing a measurable and consistent standard for decision-making across all business units.

AI Allows a Higher Risk Appetite

AI fundamentally changes an organization's risk appetite by simultaneously increasing its risk capacity (the maximum risk it can afford to take) and introducing AI-specific risks that must be incorporated into the overall appetite statement. AI doesn't just change the numbers – it changes the nature of the risk calculation itself.

AI-driven technologies, like ML-based fraud detection, predictions for supply chain stability, or automated GenAI agents for stock trading, can significantly enhance an organization's ability to identify, measure, and mitigate traditional risks. This increased control and foresight enabled by AI predictions allow the organization to pursue more ambitious, high-reward objectives safely.

- **AI Delivers Enhanced Monitoring & Mitigation:** AI enables real-time monitoring and automated threat detection (e.g., in cybersecurity or compliance), often making risk mitigation faster and more effective than human-based processes. This improved resilience reduces the overall probability and impact of many existing risks, thereby moving them down the risk matrix.

- **AI Delivers Increased Information Accuracy:** AI processes massive, unstructured datasets to provide better, more data-driven insights for better forecasting and better decision-making. Greater certainty in forecasting and risk assessment means leadership can tolerate a higher level of risk in pursuit of strategic growth.

- **AI Delivers Speed and Efficiency:** Automating high-volume, low-margin tasks frees up capital and human resources. By increasing operational efficiency and reducing human error, AI expands the organization's risk capacity. With AI, organizations have greater resources to absorb or remediate loss events and respond more quickly.

The net effect is that for certain business lines, an organization may choose to adopt a higher risk appetite because AI gives them the confidence that they can manage the resulting exposure.

Identifying and Assessing AI Risks

AI risks are identified by focusing on the three main areas where failure can impact revenue and reputation:

- Data needs to be scrutinized for biases or quality issues that could lead to unfair or inaccurate decisions.
- The AI Model must be examined for technical risks like performance degradation ("drift") or security vulnerabilities (e.g., unauthorized access or manipulation).
- The output of an AI system needs to be examined by asking business unit leaders what happens if the AI fails its task. What are the financial costs of a wrong decision, a regulatory fine, or reputational damage?

The assessment process should link every potential AI failure to a quantifiable business outcome. Specialized risk matrices can map the likelihood of an AI failure (e.g., model accuracy degradation, data poisoning) against the severity of the impact (e.g., reputational damage, direct financial loss, operational shutdown).

Ultimately, responsible AI management is a direct driver of sustained competitive advantage. Systems that are robustly identified, assessed, and governed not only avoid costly disasters but also build stakeholder trust. Proactive risk management not only addresses ethical risks such as bias and transparency issues, but also increases customer adoption, protects brand equity, and ensures compliance with rapidly emerging global regulations that could result in fines and operational delays.

Risk Response with AI

Risk response (also known as risk treatment) involves selecting and implementing the most appropriate actions to ensure that identified risks are acceptable to the organization. There are four actions that organizations can use to respond to identified risks: Risk Avoidance, Risk Mitigation, Risk Transfer, and Risk Acceptance. AI impacts all of these.

Risk Avoidance and AI

Organizations can decide not to proceed with the activity that carries the risk, thus avoiding the risk completely. Examples of avoidance include leaving a market or stopping a project.

AI enables organizations to avoid specific high-risk scenarios or business processes with greater precision. AI-powered predictive models can flag applications or decisions with a statistically high probability of failure, fraud, or compliance breaches, enabling the organization to avoid emergent risks. Additionally, advanced AI simulations would allow managers to model the outcomes of entering a new market or launching a new product under various risk scenarios (e.g., economic downturns, demand declines) so that risks can be avoided before capital is committed if the simulated risks exceed the organization's appetite.

Risk Mitigation and AI

Organizations can implement controls to reduce the likelihood of the risk occurring or the mitigate its severity. Examples of risk mitigation include implementing security patches and mandatory training.

AI has a profound effect on risk mitigation. AI enables highly accurate and automated defenses to lower the likelihood and impact of threats:

- **Real-Time Threat Detection:** AI applications can continuously monitor network traffic, financial transactions, or physical infrastructure, detecting anomalies and patterns of cyberattacks, fraud, or system failures before they cause significant damage.

- **Predictive Maintenance:** AI applications can analyze log and sensor data to predict the exact time equipment or servers are likely to fail. This foresight enables proactive scheduling of maintenance to avoid costly downtime.

- **Automated Incident Response:** When a threat is detected, AI-driven systems can instantly execute pre-defined playbooks like isolating a compromised endpoint, blocking a malicious IP address, or rerouting network traffic, minimizing the window of vulnerability.

Risk Transfer and AI

If an organization is unwilling to assume the entire risk of a project, it can shift the financial burden or the risk to a third party. Examples of risk transfer include purchasing insurance or outsourcing a task.

AI-powered contract analysis tools scan large agreements to instantly highlight missing or deficient indemnification, hold harmless, and "additional insured" clauses, thus ensuring the organization effectively transfers specific liabilities to vendors and partners before signing.

AI also introduces risks that can be transferred. Service Level Agreements (SLAs) need to be written to specifically address liability for algorithmic errors, data bias, and model failures, effectively requiring the service provider to contractually bear the risk of their AI system's shortcomings, a direct transfer of novel technological risk.

Risk Acceptance and AI

Sometimes organizations realize that a risk exists but are willing to accept the risk and absorb the loss, usually because the risk has a low impact or the potential benefits outweigh the cost of treating a materialized risk.

AI systems improve risk acceptance through better resource allocation:

- **AI-Optimized Resource Allocation:** By continuously monitoring Key Risk Indicators (KRIs), AI helps a company accept certain low-impact risks while ensuring the resources (time, capital, personnel) that would have been used for mitigation are instead focused on the highest priority threats identified by the AI's models.
- **Real-Time Reserve Management with AI:** In finance, AI can dynamically adjust capital reserves and liquidity buffers based on real-time market volatility and predicted risk exposure, ensuring the organization has just enough capital retained to cover accepted risks without tying up excessive funds.

AI Compliance

Compliance and ethics are convergent principles, yet they are distinct. Ethical tenets form the basis of all business protocols, focusing on what a business should do. Compliance is the set of policies and procedures an organization must follow, as well as formalized standards for actions or processes that must be in place and followed to ensure uniform control. Failure to comply with compliance requirements may result in internal, industrial, or legal penalties.

Statutory regulations differ between jurisdictions and should be formally investigated, but many of the compliance requirements in data governance address similar dynamics.

Note that I am not a lawyer, and the descriptions of the laws in this chapter are not to be considered legal advice. If you have questions or concerns about how best to comply with state or national regulations, please consult a compliance lawyer for guidance. Compliance for AI applications extends beyond traditional non-AI applications, and many of these regulations apply to both AI and non-AI applications; consult your security specialists regarding data protection and legal compliance.

California's Consumer Privacy Act (CCPA), the Privacy Rights Act (CPRA), and the Invasion of Privacy Act (CIPA)

The CCPA took effect in January 2020 and applies to any company that either generates $25 million in annual revenue or collects data from more than 50,000 users. California is the fourth-largest economy in the world, and other states often mirror California's regulations to achieve uniformity, giving California significant influence over industry-wide regulation. The CCPA requires companies to take "reasonable precautions" to prevent data breaches and to obtain user consent before selling their personal information.[xiii]

The CCRA strengthens the CCPA by regulating inferences and automated decision-making technology (ADMT), which are the core functions of machine learning and GenAI. Unlike conventional applications that merely process data supplied by the consumer (such as an e-commerce site tracking purchase history), AI actively creates new personal information in the form of inferences, such as calculations and predictions about a consumer's preferences, characteristics, psychological trends, or aptitudes. The CCPA defines these AI-generated inferences as "personal information." This means an AI system's calculated predictions, such as classifying a user as a "high-risk borrower" or "likely to churn," are subject to the consumer's right to know, delete, and opt out. This forces businesses to reverse-engineer and disclose proprietary outputs that they previously considered purely internal assets. This unique requirement mandates far greater transparency into the algorithmic logic than simple data inventory rules.

Furthermore, the CCPA's rules on ADMT introduce stringent governance hurdles specific to high-impact AI use cases, which non-AI data applications typically do not face. When ADMT is used to make "significant decisions" concerning a consumer, such as granting or denying credit, housing, employment, prices charged, or healthcare, businesses are required to conduct mandatory risk assessments, provide a pre-use notice explaining the ADMT's logic, and offer consumers a clear right to opt out of its use. These obligations go beyond standard privacy compliance by focusing on the “algorithmic fairness and accountability” of the decision-making process, placing a significant burden on the engineering and governance teams to document, test, and explain the system’s inner workings to a human auditor or consumer.

The CIPA is a state law that requires all parties to consent before "confidential communication" (including telephone calls and website interactions) can be intentionally intercepted, recorded, or wiretapped. Managers can view CIPA as “how” data is retrieved, and CCPA/CCRA as “what was done” with the data once it is retrieved. The CIPA was established in 1967, but recent advances in AI have led to lawsuits alleging that AI can cause CIPA violations by acting as an undisclosed third-party eavesdropper that records and analyzes user communications (such as in chat services or contact centers) without obtaining the explicit all-party consent required by the law.

CIPA Case Study: Somebody's Listening In

On June 13, 2025, a class action lawsuit was filed against Cresta Intelligence, Inc. ("Cresta") alleging that Cresta used its "conversation intelligence software-as-a-service" tool to monitor, record, and analyze calls with United Airlines without her knowledge or consent, in violation of CIPA.[xiv]

This litigation highlights the liability risk inherent in third-party AI tools: CIPA lawsuits increasingly target the AI vendor itself, treating the third-party software as an unauthorized third-party eavesdropper. Companies and their technology partners may be held liable for the use of AI systems to automate call centers or websites, particularly when such systems can use customer conversations for purposes beyond simple quality assurance.

HIPAA

The Health Insurance Portability & Accountability Act (HIPAA) was enacted in 1996. This law deals with protected health information (PHI). Exposure to PHI through AI's handling of patient health coverage or data can result in severe HIPAA fines and lawsuits.

HIPAA Case Study: Use of AI Instead of Experts

Several companies are facing private lawsuits or regulatory actions concerning how they process and use sensitive data (often a mix of PHI and PII) through AI. Health insurers like Cigna, UnitedHealth Group, and Humana are facing multiple class-action lawsuits alleging that AI tools are used to wrongfully deny claims by rapidly processing and rejecting necessary care requests. The allegations contend that an AI system is misusing PHI to influence care decisions, leading to other serious legal and medical liability issues, rather than relying on physicians' review of individual patients' cases, which has led to the deterioration of patients' conditions.[xv, xvi, xvii]

PCI DSS

In 2006, the Payment Card Industry (PCI), whose members include MasterCard, Visa, American Express, Discover, and others, established a Data Security Standard (DSS) governing the security of personal information obtained from credit cards. This standard is usually referred to as the PCI DSS, and it impacts almost every business and organization. PCI DSS standards apply to the storage, transmission, or processing of cardholder data. The PCI DSS is not a law or statutory authority, as no national or state legislature regulates it, but many believe it wields as much influence as many federal oversight bodies. Banks are contractually forced to follow the PCI DSS, and fines can reach millions of dollars.[xviii]

Witness AI reports three significant risks of PCI DSS violations: transferring data outside of an organization's control, a lack of transparency within AI systems (so no one knows precisely how the data is used and how it is exposed), and Shadow AI (where AI is used outside of official or approved channels).[xix]

> **PCI DSS Case Study: PCI Violations with GenAI**
>
> *"I just needed help troubleshooting a payment processing error, so I pasted the transaction log into ChatGPT to find the affected transactions."*
>
> *Witness AI* reports how this was an actual statement made by an employee at a mid-sized retailer that resulted in substantial PCI DSS fines. The transaction log contained magnetic stripe data, merchant ID data, and transaction processing data.
>
> Data sent to an AI application can be used to train it to respond to queries from users outside the company, potentially resulting in a significant breach, and text from one query can be used as a response to another.[xx]

COPPA

The Children's Online Privacy Protection Act (COPPA) authorizes the Federal Trade Commission (FTC) to issue fines for using, tracking, or disseminating information about children without their parents' permission. Violations can result in penalties of over $50,000 per violation. Furthermore, the violations are assessed based on the number of affected children, so a single act that affects thousands of children can result in fines of hundreds of thousands or millions of dollars.

AI has been a primary target of recent COPPA guidelines. The final Rule fundamentally shifts how companies can use children's data for AI development, requiring separate, verifiable parental consent before disclosing a child's personal information for training or developing AI technologies. Furthermore, the rule expands the definition of regulated "personal information" to include biometric identifiers like voiceprints and facial templates. It strictly prohibits the indefinite retention of children's data and mandates operators establish and maintain a detailed, written data retention policy.[xxi]

COPPA Case Study: Watch How You Train Your AI

Significant penalties and mandatory operational overhauls have rocked major tech companies as the FTC increasingly uses COPPA enforcement to prohibit the unauthorized use of children's voice recordings and persistent identifiers to train proprietary AI algorithms and serve targeted ads:

- Amazon was fined $25 million for using children's voice recordings to train their Alexis AI and then deceiving parents about its data deletion policies. This case sets a key precedent against indefinitely retaining biometric-like data (such as voiceprints) for AI algorithm training.[xxii]
- Google/YouTube was fined a then-record $170 million ($136 million to the FTC and $34 million to New York State) for using persistent identifiers (cookies and mobile-advertising identifiers) from viewers of child-directed content for the purpose of delivering targeted advertising without obtaining parental consent.

The takeaway is that companies should be aware of the data they use to train their AI models and the risks of compliance violations, particularly when collecting data from minors.

Federal Rules of Civil Procedure

While most compliance rules address the deletion of data after a specified period, Rule 26 of the FRCP requires that plaintiffs in civil cases prohibit the destruction of data. It is a simple rule, but data scientists should be aware of the law and potential penalties for deleting data that has been requested as evidence, and how that will affect their AI applications.

Electronic Communications Privacy Act (ECPA)

This law is designed to protect the privacy of electronic communication. The law is now decades old, and electronic communications over the internet are not very well protected. The ECPA permits civil lawsuits when a plaintiff alleges that a company has violated privacy rights without due process.

EU General Data Protection Regulation (GDPR)

The GDPR is widely regarded as one of the most protective data protection regulations in the world. The GDPR was enacted in 2016 and sets out several principles that must be followed; failure to do so can result in substantial fines, up to €20 million or 4% of the company's annual revenue. GDPR principles include implementing the highest possible safeguards to protect data, designing software with security in mind from the outset, disclosing data collection practices and the duration of data retention, disclosing security breaches, and, in some cases, appointing a data protection officer (DPO).

GDPR Case Study: AI Training with the Wrong Data

GDPR fines may be imposed when sensitive or personal information is used to train GenAI models. For example, Reuters reports that Italy's data protection agency fined OpenAI 15 million euros for GDPR violations related to training the ChatGPT application using personal data for model training, and for failing to implement age-verification mechanisms and obtain the data owners' permission.[xxiii]

Compliance with the EU AI Act

The EU Artificial Intelligence Act, passed on March 13, 2024, is considered the first comprehensive AI regulation, requiring compliance, and may serve as a template for AI regulations in other countries.[xxiv] The European Parliament describes the scope of governance needed for the AI Act by defining systems by a level of risk: [xxv]

- **Unacceptable Risk:** AI systems are considered a threat to people and will be banned:
    - Cognitive behavioral manipulation of people or specific vulnerable groups is banned, such as voice-activated toys that encourage dangerous behavior in children.
    - Social scoring is banned, which is defined as AI use to predict a person's race, political orientation, or sexual orientation, or the use of AI for emotion recognition in educational and professional settings, as well as using AI for certain types of automated profiling for predictive policing.[xxvi]
    - Identifying and categorizing people based on biometrics, including real-time and remote biometric identification systems, such as facial recognition, is banned.
- **High-risk:** AI systems that negatively affect safety or fundamental rights will be considered high risk:
    - AI systems that are used in products falling under the EU's product safety legislation are considered high risk, including toys, aviation, cars, medical devices, and lifts.
    - AI systems falling into specific areas that will have to be registered in an EU database, including education and training, critical infrastructure, employment, public services, law enforcement, migration and asylum, and legal advice.

- **Limited Risk:** This category concentrates on Generative AI (GenAI). While GenAI is not considered high risk, the EU AI Act requires organizations to make public a summary of the content used to train the GenAI model, to provide documentation on the GenAI model that includes the training and testing process and the result of model evaluations, and to adopt a policy to demonstrate compliance with copyright law.

It is assumed that other states and governments will adopt a similar policy to the EU AI Act, and data governance specialists should work with the data science manager to ensure that any AI implementation complies with this regulation.

Other Regulations that Require AI Application Compliance

Many other regulatory bodies require compliance from AI applications. FERPA (Family Educational Rights and Privacy Act) restricts the disclosure of students' educational data. The Gramm-Leach-Bliley Act (GLBA) regulates the handling of bank information. FISMA (Federal Information Security Management Act) governs data security within the federal government. SOX (Sarbanes-Oxley Act) requires data validation on any information filed with the Securities and Exchange Commission. The Patriot Act can limit the storage of data in the United States. There are many others across many countries.

Compliance with data use, privacy, and security regulations is essential for organizations to understand within their own industry. Attorneys should be consulted to examine which regulations your organization is subject to within and beyond the scope of this chapter and how to best comply with these regulations.

Data Governance and Ethics

Ethics is generally considered broader than the personal consideration of individual or professional guidelines, encompassing behavior that guides an individual's or a company's actions beyond legal or contractual compliance. Unethical behavior is not a crime, although such behavior can result in penalties from professional organizations and economic implications.

For companies, ethics not only helps dictate the right and socially acceptable path but can also positively impact the bottom line. An ethical approach to AI adoption can ensure the long-term, trusted value of AI investments. For upper management, ethical AI can prevent scenarios where biased algorithms lead to costly public relations crises, regulatory fines, or the complete erosion of customer trust. Implementing a proactive ethical framework goes beyond compliance expense to become a strategic imperative that transforms AI from an unpredictable technology into a reliable corporate asset. By clearly defining accountability, mandating ethical oversight, and verifying that AI systems align with core company values, governance ultimately protects the firm's reputation and bottom line, ensuring that innovation serves the shareholders and stakeholders responsibly.

AI necessitates a fundamental shift in corporate responsibility because it alters the nature of corporate risk, decision-making, and accountability in ways that current governance models were not designed to address. The traditional focus on financial and operational risk needs to be expanded to include AI-specific risks and updated to reflect new core fiduciary duties owed to the company and its stakeholders. Here are some additional ethical considerations brought on by AI:

- **AI Algorithmic Ethical Risk:** AI creates decisions that are often opaque ("black box") and can replicate or amplify systemic biases instantly across millions of customers or operations. This necessitates that AI managers oversee and audit algorithm design and outcomes, possibly treating AI failure as a critical enterprise-level risk.

- **The AI Accountability Ethical Gap:** AI blurs the lines of liability, making it difficult to pinpoint who is responsible when an autonomous system causes harm. Corporate governance must fundamentally shift by implementing specialized AI controls and monitoring structures to close this gap, not only to identify when an AI system does not function as expected, but also to determine which human is responsible for ensuring the AI functions within defined parameters.

- **Erosion of Trust and Reputation:** Because AI decisions can lack human-level justification, they directly challenge customer and stakeholder trust. The core responsibility of management now extends to ensuring that AI deployments uphold the company's core ethical values, making transparent and explainable AI use a prerequisite for maintaining long-term brand equity and reputation.

Companies that demonstrate a measurable commitment to fair, transparent, and accountable AI systems build deeper, more resilient trust with customers, regulators, and partners. This reputation for ethical rigor can be leveraged as a brand differentiator, attracting ethically conscious talent and consumers, and positioning the company favorably against competitors who treat ethics merely as a compliance chore. Furthermore, by designing systems with fairness and robustness in mind, organizations often uncover deeper flaws in data and models, leading to higher-quality, more resilient, and genuinely innovative products that are better equipped for diverse global markets and less likely to face costly public and regulatory backlash down the line, ultimately securing their long-term "license to innovate" and dominate.

The Shift from Policy Control into Agentic Control

For decades, organizational control has been rooted in procedure-based systems, where written procedures and human oversight manage risk and ensure policy compliance. Governance teams create handbooks, standard operating procedures (SOPs), and audit checklists, which employees are trained to follow. This manual control mechanism is primarily human-centric, with a manager checking the work, an auditor reviewing the records, and a legal team interpreting the procedures.

While this system offers transparency and human judgment, it's inherently slow, prone to human error, and struggles to keep up with the massive speed and scale of modern digital operations. As data volumes increase and transactional activity accelerates, the traditional control method becomes a bottleneck, creating a critical gap between the pace of business and the pace of governance.

Enter

control. Instead of simply relying on predefined, encoded rules, an agent is a goal-oriented, autonomous system that perceives its environment and takes actions to achieve a high-level policy objective. Agentic control applications don't just enforce static rules. Instead, they dynamically "decide" the best action in real-time to maintain a desired state of compliance and risk. The control mechanism evolves from a reactive, algorithmic check to a proactive, embedded agent that maintains governance alignment.

For example, rather than an algorithm merely stating, "deny prompts with intellectual property," an Agentic Governance System (AGS) is tasked with the goal: "Minimize the risk of intellectual property leakage in R&D operations." The agent may not only deny a prompt but also automatically adjust the user's access level, generate a version of the data for safe use, and flag the user for retraining based on the severity of the attempted breach.

AI agentic controls move from simple gatekeeping to self-managing, goal-seeking systems embedded within the business process, capable of complex, multi-step interventions.

Agentic Control with AI TRiSM

The Gartner Group developed TRiSM (Trust, Risk, and Security Management), shown in Figure 33, as a framework for transition to agentic control from traditional governance that focuses on these five functions: [xxvii, xxviii]

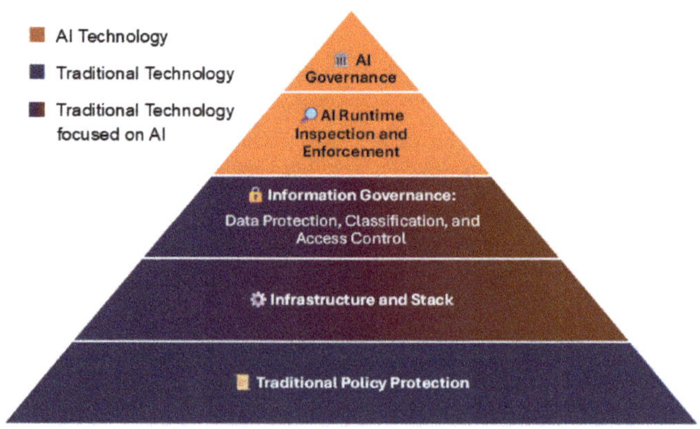

Figure 33: Gartner's AI TRiSM Governance Framework

- **AI Governance** – This TRiSM layer is the agent's high-level mission or objective, ensuring the control system is used ethically, legally, and strategically. It defines the goal that the agent must strive to maintain and establishes accountability for its autonomous decisions.

- **AI Runtime Inspection and Enforcement** – This layer provides the active supervision of live algorithms, where monitoring of running models, instantly detecting bias, data inconsistencies, or security threats, allows organizations to mitigate AI risks before they impact the business.

- **Information Governance** – This layer focuses on the integrity, quality, and security of the information. It manages data access and enforces controls to keep sensitive inputs safe from misuse or exposure.

- **Infrastructure and Stack** – This layer ensures we have the necessary flexible and secure technology environment (the "stack") to run and manage AI systems reliably. It provides the robust foundation required for continuous, secure AI operations.

- **Traditional Technology Protection:** This layer integrates our existing security tools, policies, and procedures (like firewalls and access management). It maximizes prior security investments, providing a foundational layer of protection for both AI and non-AI systems.

The transition to include agentic control and the adoption of AI TRiSM are not reactive measures taken after an incident, but a proactive shift that must begin with the deployment of AI or ML models that impact customers or operations. Embedding AI TRiSM early in the design and development phase—not just at the final check—is crucial to building trust and ensuring the system is aligned with organizational ethics from the foundation up.[xxix]

Continuous Monitoring and Calibration of Algorithmic Control

The irony of using algorithmic controls to monitor other AI systems is that such controls can, themselves, experience model drift. Algorithmic control applications, whether they monitor data integrity, detect bias shifts, or analyze model performance metrics, ultimately rely on machine learning models trained on historical data (as with most AI applications). This means the algorithmic control can fail to recognize risks in other AI applications, generating false negatives by missing model drift, or flag nonexistent issues, leading to false positives and alert fatigue, both of which undermine the system's core purpose of providing reliable oversight.

To fight this agentic drift, organizations must implement a rigorous system of checks and balances in which both the core operational AI and the control agent are continually scrutinized against independent business outcomes and the original governance rules. This involves showing independent, human-readable drift indicators and business performance metrics to re-anchor the agent's objective function to organizational values. By treating the control agent with the same rigor and skepticism as the core operational AI, organizations can maintain confidence in the entire automated control structure and effectively manage the risk of both core model drift and the more subtle, but equally critical, agentic control drift.[xxx]

Working with Both Policy and Algorithmic Control

Agentic controls will never replace human-generated policy. Both policy and agentic controls are necessary for robust AI governance because automated systems alone cannot capture the full spectrum of organizational risk and ethical responsibility.

- Agentic controls provide the essential real-time detection of technical issues, such as model drift, security vulnerabilities, or immediate bias shifts

- Agentic controls are fundamentally limited by the data they are trained on and their programmed objectives. They cannot independently interpret the nuances of evolving regulatory compliance (like new data privacy laws), define the acceptable risk tolerance for a completely new business function, or assign human accountability when a system fails.

- Policy is an indispensable strategic guardrail, setting ethical standards, defining the clear lines of human oversight, and ensuring that all automated actions align with the company's legal obligations and broader brand values.

- Policy is needed to give automated agents the necessary direction and context they are programmed to enforce.

Concluding Thoughts on AI Governance

Integrating AI into the enterprise requires a sophisticated evolution of the traditional GRC framework, where the foundational principles of accountability, transparency, and risk mitigation remain paramount but are applied to new technological realities. AI systems introduce inherent algorithmic risks and technical dependencies, making rigorous Data Governance, especially concerning data quality, lineage, and transparency, the critical foundation for system stability.

Establishing effective AI protocols requires strong executive oversight to align the technical needs of AI (such as managing algorithmic complexity) directly with the organization's high-level strategic goals and compliance policies. The organization must bring the hidden, systemic risk introduced by Shadow AI to light through governance. Agentic Control can help, as automated programs enhance governance, auditing, and compliance across the enterprise and reduce the overwhelming burden on the human element within the organization.

While AI's complexity often obscures its decision-making logic, Explainable AI (XAI) tools like SHAP and LIME are essential for bridging the transparency gap and validating predictions. Given the expanding global regulatory landscape (e.g., the EU's AI Act or California's CIPA),

AI compliance is a multi-jurisdictional imperative that extends well beyond mere data protection. By balancing robust traditional governance with continuous, sophisticated AI Governance, the organization mitigates liability, secures stakeholder trust, and maximizes the transformative power of its AI investments.

---

[i] Ellen Nakashima and Shane Harris. July 13, 2018. "How the Russians hacked the DNC and passed its emails to WikiLeaks" *The Washington Post*, available at https://www.washingtonpost.com/world/national-security/how-the-russians-hacked-the-dnc-and-passed-its-emails-to-wikileaks/2018/07/13/af19a828-86c3-11e8-8553-a3ce89036c78_story.html.

[ii] Zack Whittaker. March 23, 2018. "A new data leak hits Aadhaar, India's national ID database" *ZDNet*, available at https://www.zdnet.com/article/another-data-leak-hits-india-aadhaar-biometric-database/.

[iii] OPEG. June 2025. "What is GRC (Governance, Risk, and Compliance)?" *OPEG Ideas*, available at https://www.oceg.org/ideas/what-is-grc/.

[iv] Navex. 2021. "What is GRC – and why is it so important?" *Navex Solutions*, available at https://www.navex.com/en-us/solutions/getting-started-grc/what-is-grc/.

[v] Carver, J. 1990. *Boards That Make a Difference: A New Design for Leadership in Nonprofit and Public Organizations.* Jossey-Bass.

[vi] Wudo Solutions. "The Difference Between Governance and Management." *Wudo Solutions*, available at https://www.wudo.solutions/the-difference-between-governance-and-management/.

[vii] Matthew Kosinski. 2024. "What is black box artificial intelligence (AI)?" *IBM Think*, available at https://www.ibm.com/think/topics/black-box-ai.

[viii] Lubah Nelson. Jan 24,2025. "Let's talk Explainable AI — A Dive into LIME and SHAP" *Medium*, available at https://medium.com/@lubah_99345/lets-talk-xai-a-comparative-analysis-of-lime-and-shap-c32b92e65070.

[ix] Rajasekharan KR. October 6, 2025. "From Shadow IT to Shadow AI: Navigating the New Frontier of Enterprise Risk." *ISACA*, available at https://www.isaca.org/resources/news-and-trends/newsletters/atisaca/2025/volume-19/from-shadow-it-to-shadow-ai-navigating-the-new-frontier-of-enterprise-risk.

[x] Ben Fisher and Laura Reul. July 11, 2025. "Emerging Risk Deep Dive: Shadow AI." *Gartner,* available at https://www.gartner.com/en/documents/6714034.

[xi] Tom Krantz, Alexandra Jonker, and Amanda McGrath. October 10, 2025. "What is Shadow AI?" *IBM*, available at https://www.ibm.com/think/topics/shadow-ai.

[xii] Challapally A, Pease C, Raskar R, Chari P. July 2025. "The GenAI Divide: State of AI in Business 2025." *MIT Media Lab, Project NANDA*, available at https://www.aigl.blog/state-of-ai-in-business-2025/.

[xiii] Rob Bonta. March 13, 2024. "California Consumer Privacy Act (CCPA)" *State of California Department of Justice*, available at https://oag.ca.gov/privacy/ccpa.

[xiv] Frankfurt, Kurnit, Klein, and Selz. August 6, 2025. "AI Recording/Notetaking Tools Trigger Wave of Lawsuits -- Could Your Business Be At Risk?" *Technology Law*, available at https://technologylaw.fkks.com/post/102kz0c/ai-recording-notetaking-tools-trigger-wave-of-lawsuits-could-your-business-be.

[xv] Whatley Kallas, March 11, 2025. "Class Action Lawsuit against UnitedHealth Group for Its Use of Artificial Intelligence to Deny Patient Care Can Proceed." *Whatley Kallas,* available at https://whatleykallas.com/class-action-lawsuit-against-unitedhealthgroup-for-its-use-of-artificial-intelligence-to-deny-patient-care-can-proceed/.

[xvi] Mackenzie S. Wallace and Ashton K. Dietrich. Dec 15, 2023. "Class Actions Highlight AI-Assisted Payer Denials." *Thompson Colburn LLP*, available at https://www.thompsoncoburn.com/insights/class-actions-highlight-ai-assisted-payer-denials-102jebl/.

[xvii] Kimberly Marselas. Aug 19, 2025. "Humana must face class action suit over use of AI in denying post-acute care." *McKnight's Long-Term Care News*, available at https://www.mcknights.com/news/humana-must-face-class-action-suit-over-use-of-ai-in-denying-post-acute-care/.

[xviii] https://www.pcisecuritystandards.org/.

[xix] Trevor Welsh. April 30, 2025. "Invisible Risk: How AI Use Creates PCI DSS Violations Today." *Witness AI*, available at https://witness.ai/blog/blog-invisible-risk-how-ai-use-creates-pci-dss-violations-today/.

[xx] Trevor Welsh. April 30, 2025. "Invisible Risk: How AI Use Creates PCI DSS Violations Today." *Witness AI*, available at https://witness.ai/blog/blog-invisible-risk-how-ai-use-creates-pci-dss-violations-today/.

[xxi] Akin. June 23, 2025. "New COPPA Obligations for AI Technologies Collecting Data from Children." *Akin*, available at https://www.akingump.com/en/insights/ai-law-and-regulation-tracker/new-coppa-obligations-for-ai-technologies-collecting-data-from-children.

[xxii] *United States v. Amazon.com, Inc. and Amazon.com Services LLC*, No. 2:23-cv-00811 (W.D. Wash. 2023) (Stipulated Order for Permanent Injunction and Civil Penalty Judgment).

[xxiii] Elvira Pollina and Alvise Armellini. Dec 20, 2024. "Italy fines OpenAI over ChatGPT privacy rules breach." *Reuters*, available at https://www.reuters.com/technology/italy-fines-openai-15-million-euros-over-privacy-rules-breach-2024-12-20/.

[xxiv] Wiley. Mar 15, 2024. "EU Adopts World's First Comprehensive AI Regulation." *Wiley*, available at https://www.wiley.law/alert-EU-Adopts-the-AI-Act-The-Worlds-First-Comprehensive-AI-Regulation#:~:text=EU%20Adopts%20World's%20First%20Comprehensive%20AI%20Regulation&text=On%20March%2013%2C%202024%2C%20the,artificial%20intelligence%20(AI)%20globally.

[xxv] European Parliament. Dec 19, 2023. "EU AI Act: first regulation on artificial intelligence" https://www.europarl.europa.eu/topics/en/article/20230601STO93804/eu-ai-act-first-regulation-on-artificial-intelligence.

[xxvi] PYMNTS. Mar 13, 2024. "5 Things You Should Know About the New EU AI Regulation." *PYMNTS*, available at https://www.pymnts.com/news/artificial-intelligence/2024/5-things-you-should-know-about-the-new-eu-ai-regulation/.

[xxvii] ModelOp. 2025. "AI TRiSM Adoption." *Model Op AI Governance*, available at https://www.modelop.com/ai-governance/ai-regulations-standards/ai-trism-adoption.

[xxviii] Gartner, 2024.

[xxix] Timothy Boettcher. September 9, 2025. "AI TRiSM Framework: Complete Guide to Trust, Risk, and Security in AI." *AvePoint*, available at: https://www.avepoint.com/blog/protect/ai-trism-framework-by-gartner-guide.

[xxx] S. Ravikumar. September 5, 2025. "Agentic Drift: Keeping AI Aligned, Reliable, and ROI-Driven." *Medium*, available at https://medium.com/@ravikumar.singi_16677/agentic-drift-keeping-ai-aligned-reliable-and-roi-driven-a099fa554d08.

Chapter 9: Driving AI Innovation

Much of this book deals with managing existing processes more effectively through data science, such as determining the best price to charge, the proper number of employees to staff, or the expected characteristics of customers. Improving processes and decisions is great, but data science can also be used to drive innovation, which may be even better. Data science can be a driver of innovation, with an ability to revolutionize traditional approaches and open new doors for organizations seeking to differentiate themselves in the marketplace.

What is this chapter trying to do and why?

Innovation is often a cornerstone of success for organizations across all industries. It fuels growth, drives competitive advantage, and enables businesses to stay relevant in a rapidly evolving market. In today's data-driven era, data science has emerged as a powerful catalyst for innovation, providing organizations with the tools and techniques to unlock the transformative potential of their data. This chapter explores the critical role of data science in driving innovation and presents strategies, methodologies, and real-world examples to inspire and guide organizations in their pursuit of data-driven innovation.

However, innovation by its nature is difficult to discuss in a chapter. Often, books discussing innovation have vague directions, like "Create an innovation culture," "Overcome challenges with data-driven innovation," "Think differently," "Focus on the Long Term," etc. Not that these pieces of advice are bad ideas *per se*, but they are often easy to state as a goal in a book, but differ in practice from organization to organization. Instead, this chapter concentrates on case studies of a few organizations and the insights of their managers, and then zooms out from individual companies to discuss the takeaways from the case studies. Then the chapter concludes by discussing innovation concepts.

Data science holds immense potential for organizations to generate breakthrough ideas, develop innovative products and services, and optimize operations. This chapter generalizes from other companies' successes to illustrate how leveraging advanced analytics, machine learning algorithms, and predictive modeling, organizations can uncover hidden patterns, identify emerging trends, and make data-driven decisions that propel innovation.

Case Studies in Innovation

Probably the best way to examine innovation is to look at companies that have successfully innovated to see what some key takeaways can be. Many case studies were considered, and four were selected from Google, Amazon, NVIDIA, and AstraZeneca that not only are good stories for managers to read about but also can be examined to guide managers on a path toward data-driven decision-making and innovation.

AstraZeneca Case Study: Identifying Opportunities to Expand Product Line

An organization often delivers products to a consumer, hopefully using data science to suggest optimal pricing strategies, viable markets, timelines for expansion or reconfiguration, and appeal to those hard-to-reach high-value consumers. But how can data science help with the development of new products within the existing product line? How does a bicycle manufacturer use data science to develop new, valuable features on the next bike model? How does a shoe manufacturer use data science to help deliver the next high-end athletic shoe? How does a magazine add a feature that appeals to an audience that has not yet subscribed?

AstraZeneca, a biotech company, shows how an innovative use of data science can lead to new products, which can produce valuable revenue streams for an organization. AstraZeneca leverages data using AI technology to discover and deliver newer effective medicines faster. Their *Center for Genomics Research* uses AI to analyze millions of genomes to identify new targets for innovative medications. In 2021, they came out with two AI-generated drug targets for chronic kidney disease and for idiopathic pulmonary fibrosis. (Many drug companies produce at a slower pace, often less than a single drug in a year.) AstraZeneca also used AI to cut their analysis time by around 30%.[i]

CIO Magazine discussed the insights of Gurinder Kaur (AstraZeneca's Vice President of Operations and IT) and Brian Dummann (AstraZeneca's Vice President of Insights & Technology Excellence) on the factors that data science managers need to embrace to successfully expand an organization's product line.[ii]

- **Start small, think big**. Eventually, you will need to have a big picture and vision in mind, but that big picture might not be present immediately. Instead, you should focus on getting solutions out quickly, testing and improving them.

- **Scale fast.** Kaur emphasized the ability to scale data science solutions. "We don't want to keep reinventing the wheel, and we want our data scientists to be able to re-use AI assets across the enterprise." AstraZeneca's data scientists have launched more than 100 AI projects, and the number continues to grow.

- **Build internal expertise and understanding**. Data-driven transformation is as much about people and processes as it is about data and technology. To succeed, you need to get people to believe in the value of data science transformation and show managers and users a clear path to get there.

- **Separate data science from IT.** Data scientists can be most successful if they concentrate on their work rather than writing code or working with architecture. Dummann described how AstraZeneca relies on attracting and retaining data scientists: "So a big part for us is focusing on improving the experience of the data scientists. We are keen to democratize data projects so that data scientists can get on with their daily tasks without reliance on IT. We do not want to make them wait for weeks or days to get their work done." The takeaway from this is that IT is important for the IT professionals to administer, and the more data scientists work on IT, the less they work on data science.

- **Embrace the new technology**. It is important to understand that data is not an expense ... it is an asset. Dummann suggests moving away from best-of-breed point solutions. Instead, "invest in a few big, critical capabilities to really get the scale and speed you need." In other words, be willing to move away from the "tried and true methods" to new methods that will give you even better results.

- **Do not be afraid to fail**. There are two takeaways from this point. First, there are always multiple ways to solve a problem, so adjust if the current method does not give the results you want. The second point is that the data science manager should not punish data scientists for trying new methods and failing, since failures are part of the process that led to success, but rather data science managers should encourage their area to adjust to try multiple new methods that give better results.

The AstraZeneca case study shows that through a commitment to data science, an organization can increase the pace of innovation to add new products to its product line.

Meta Case Study at NVIDIA

NVIDIA makes arguably the industry's best GPU (graphical processing unit), which is a chip often found in servers, desktops, and laptops that can aid in machine learning calculations. GPUs excel at handling the matrix operations central to complicated machine learning analysis, allowing data scientists to significantly reduce the time it takes to iterate and refine models, which in turn lead to larger and more intricate models and to breakthroughs in AI capabilities. As a result, NVIDIA GPUs have become a cornerstone of AI development, enabling faster innovation and broader applications across industries such as healthcare, finance, marketing, and more.

NVIDIA's deep involvement in AI technology and research along with their partnerships and collaborations with numerous companies allows them to speak confidently about AI's potential applications across diverse industries. Charlie Boyle, the Vice President and General Manager of DGX Systems at NVIDIA, was interviewed by *CIO Magazine* about trends he has seen and what is coming next in AI.[iii]

Boyle says that NVIDIA was surprised by how many organizations organically discover AI use cases or applications. "We have been surprised by how many organizations organically discover AI use cases or applications. They have brilliant folks working for them who say, 'Hey, how about this?' The great thing about AI today is that it doesn't take years to come up with a successful project." Throughout the interview, Boyle offered some advice and insights on innovation with AI:

- **Make your innovations customer-centric:** Boyle stressed how the majority of AI is focused on the redefinition of customer relationships. "We have found that the biggest reason {companies are} embracing {AI} is to improve their customer relationships. At the end of the day, that is what many brands are striving for: How do I meet my customers where they're at and give them a great experience?"

- **Scale fast**. Boyle brought up how companies recognized the importance of quickly scaling up AI. "Many organizations initially thought they needed 'a bit' of infrastructure to evaluate their early proof of concept results. That quickly changed to: 'If I want this to be successful, I need a whole lot of infrastructure and some great software to take on these projects, and it will really change my business.'"

- **Separate data science from IT.** Boyle brought up how it is important to have a centralized data science area. "The other trend we've seen is companies creating centers of excellence to support AI across the enterprise. In this way, different departments don't have to procure their own AI infrastructure." Boyle discussed how, if a company does not have a separate data science area, individual departments usually end up hiring their own data scientists, usually with worse results.

- **Embrace the new technology**. Boyle cautions executives not to be afraid of AI. "Finally, don't be afraid of AI; it's not a difficult concept. It physically looks a little different, but it still behaves just like all the servers IT is running today. And there are so many resources available for IT organizations. It's understanding the new terms, how to apply those new terms to infrastructure decisions, and then making sure there's an outlook for future capacity."

- **Be ready to act quickly on new projects.** Having a flexible, shared infrastructure is important because the last thing you want is someone who has a great idea and IT tells them: 'Sure, I can help you with that in a few months.' The response should be: 'Yes, I can help you, and depending on the size of the request, I should be able to help you get started within 24 hours.'"

Amazon Case Study – Data Science Apps to Help the Customer

Amazon's journey to develop and adopt its groundbreaking recommender system, often referred to as the "Amazon Recommendations Engine" or the "Amazon Recommender System," was not without its challenges, some of which stemmed from internal resistance within the company's management. Initially, when the idea of leveraging data and algorithms to provide personalized product recommendations was proposed, there was skepticism among certain quarters of Amazon's management. Some argued that relying on an AI-driven system to suggest products might compromise the traditional customer experience, where shoppers independently explored a wide range of offerings. There were concerns that such a system could potentially narrow consumer choices and inadvertently discourage serendipitous discovery.[iv]

In retrospect, nothing could be further from the truth. Amazon drives an estimated 35% of its sales through its recommendation engine, and the recommender engine is highly favored by the customers.[v]

Overcoming this resistance to AI system adoption required visionary leadership that recognized the transformative potential of the recommender system. Amazon's management, led by Amazon CEO Jeff Bezos, gradually embraced the idea that personalized recommendations could enhance the customer experience, driving increased engagement and sales. The key was in striking a balance between algorithmic suggestions and maintaining the joy of product exploration. Through meticulous testing, iterative improvements, and a commitment to addressing concerns, Amazon's management recognized the value of the recommender system as a powerful tool for enhancing customer satisfaction, loyalty, and the overall success of the platform. This example underscores the importance of leadership that can navigate and mitigate resistance to innovative data-driven initiatives within organizations.[vi]

Here are some points made by Bezos about innovation:[vii]

- **Balance being stubborn with being flexible**. Bezos says that executives should be stubborn on vision and flexible on details. When executives want to pursue a vision, that should guide the managers and people that they manage. However, those people may achieve that vision differently than the executive initially anticipated, but that is OK. "If you're not stubborn, you'll give up on experiments too soon. And if you're not flexible, you'll pound your head against the wall, and you won't see a different solution to a problem you're trying to solve."

- **Make your innovations customer-centric**. Amazon forms its goals when they "start with the customer and work backwards" which is a sharp contrast to many who focus on the competitors. Amazon has continuously innovated to keep the customer first, whether it would be free second-day delivery, Kindle, and AWS cloud technologies, allowing competitors to advertise on its website or allowing negative reviews of products and services, and in many other areas. Overall, customers have noticed and have flocked to Amazon over other online vendors. "If we can arrange things in such a way that our interests are aligned with our customers, then in the long term that will work out really well for customers and it will work out really well for Amazon."

- **Do not be afraid to fail.** Bezos recognizes many of the failed initiatives with new innovations, and he looks at them as a good thing. "If you decide that you're going to do only the things you know are going to work, you're going to leave a lot of opportunity on the table. Companies are rarely criticized for the things that they failed to try. But they are, many times, criticized for things they tried and failed at."

- **Develop a culture of innovation.** While innovation can lead to quick profits, it often takes some time to develop radical innovations. Also, when executives take an attitude that something always worked so never examine a better way, that stifles innovation. "You need a culture that high-fives small and innovative ideas and senior executives [that] encourage ideas. For innovative ideas to bear fruit, companies need to be willing to wait for 5-7 years, and most companies don't take that time horizon."

- **Drop the PowerPoints.** Executives often love PowerPoint presentations, and they may have their place in quickly explaining simple ideas. But for innovations, Bezos contends that slides might not be the correct medium, and instead advocates a 6-page writeup. "The traditional kind of corporate meeting is somebody gets up in the front of the room and presents...some kind of slide show. In our view...you get very little information that way. You get bullet points."

- **Be data-driven, not opinion-driven**. Bezos recognizes that not all decisions can be strictly driven by data, especially when that data does not yet exist. But, when possible, facts, not opinions, should drive decision-making. "The great thing about fact-based decisions is that they overrule the hierarchy. The most junior person in the company can win an argument with the most senior person with a fact-based decision."

Google Hack Case Study – Data Science to Protect David from Goliath

Innovation is best when proactive, where new products and services are developed due to data analysis and forward-looking management. However, innovation can also come as a reaction to events that help or hurt a company. One of the main examples of this is the reaction of Google to the Aurora hack.

The Council of Foreign Relations describes Operation Aurora as a series of cyberattacks from China targeting U.S. companies in 2010. The Aurora hack compromised the networks of Yahoo, Adobe, Dow Chemical, Morgan Stanley, Google, and more than two dozen other companies to steal their trade secrets.[viii]

The hack itself was big news, but one of the most interesting parts of the hack was Google's reaction to it, and the innovation that followed. At the time, Google's reaction itself was an innovation in transparency. Google was the only company that confirmed it was a victim of the hack and among the first to notify users if their accounts were targeted or compromised by a state-sponsored actor – a practice that later spread to other email providers. Other companies who were victims of the attack kept silent and did not change their security policies.[ix]

But while Google's efforts at transparency were groundbreaking, Google went further. They amazingly stated internally that their job is to protect user data no matter who is trying to target it, even if the attacker is a nation-state, like China. One of the most significant steps taken by Google was to develop an internal security team called Project Zero. The team's primary objective was to identify zero-day vulnerabilities in software used by Google and other companies. By identifying these vulnerabilities before attackers could exploit them, Project Zero helps mitigate the risks from hacks like Operation Aurora.[x,xi]

There are several take aways from Project Zero innovations:

- **Make your innovations customer centric**. Project Zero immediately began pushing innovations to Gmail account holders. These innovations eventually evolved into AI and ML pattern recognition to alert Google and users of suspicious activity, email account attacks, malware, phishing attacks, and spam. By being committed to their customers, and through huge innovation, Google not only benefited their users, but also increased their bottom line, becoming the largest email account vendor.[xii]

- **Do not be afraid to fail**. Google's response to the Operation Aurora hack was aggressive and could have failed at many points. In particular, Google's Project Zero led to the development of the Chrome web browser. Even though the web browser market was already saturated at that time, Chrome included several features that made it more secure than other browsers at the time, like sandboxing, which prevents malicious code from accessing other parts of the computer, making it much more difficult for attackers to exploit vulnerabilities in the browser, and eventually growing to a 64% market share.[xiii]

- **Develop a culture of innovation**. Project Zero catalyzed a profound culture of innovation within the company by advocating a proactive and collaborative approach to addressing software vulnerabilities and enhancing cybersecurity. By tasking employees with identifying zero-day vulnerabilities, Project Zero ignited a culture where continuous learning, open collaboration, and rapid problem-solving were central tenets. This initiative encouraged cross-disciplinary knowledge sharing and spurred the development of innovative techniques to discover and remediate vulnerabilities, fostering an environment where security innovation thrived and contributing to Google's broader commitment to safeguarding its users and the digital ecosystem.[xiv]

- **Scale fast**. Project Zero's rapid scaling can be attributed to Google's commitment to cybersecurity and its vast pool of talented researchers. By assembling a team of renowned security experts and fostering an environment of collaboration, knowledge sharing, and innovation, Project Zero swiftly gained momentum. The team's proactive approach to identifying and addressing vulnerabilities, coupled with Google's resources and support, facilitated its ability to rapidly expand.[xv]

- **Start small, aim big**. Google started putting items in place immediately to further their goal of a completely safe (as possible) environment. Their work not only led to immediate gains for Google in market share but also evolved to other innovations that continue, such as Google Cloud Platform[xvi], Google Security Command Center[xvii], and Google BeyondCorp[xviii]. These large innovations that grew out of smaller innovations generate even more revenue for Google.

What the Companies Say Overall

Companies are all different, each with its own innovations and paths that make sense. However, there are some key takeaways from the case studies shown here that can be of use to managers, especially data science managers, when discovering how to innovate using artificial intelligence and specifically with machine learning.

This section delves into some of the points made by the statements and actions found in the case studies to examine how companies can innovate.

Innovate to Create Customer Value

All the case studies discussed how customer value should be a cornerstone of many AI initiatives. AI can be used to cut internal costs or generate more revenue, but AI can also be used to make sure customers see more value in staying with a company. Acquiring good customers can be expensive, and losing customers can be costly. By continuous improvement of products, AI can motivate customers to stay or even make the decision to leave, as such high-quality products are too risky. Plus, happy customers understand that they are getting more for their money and may be willing to pay more for your products.

Understanding customers is a key factor in gaining a sustainable competitive advantage. Data science allows organizations to analyze customer data, including transaction history, browsing behavior, and feedback, to extract valuable insights. By leveraging machine learning algorithms, organizations can personalize customer experiences, offer tailored recommendations, and anticipate customer needs. This level of personalization enhances customer satisfaction, fosters loyalty, and differentiates an organization from its competitors. Continuous analysis of customer data helps organizations adapt their offerings and improve customer engagement, leading to long-term success.

The "Scale Fast Flywheel" for AI Innovation

There seems to be a trend to avoid delivering the largest, most profitable AI applications. Rather, the trend is to first deliver small, quick solutions. As those AI applications are proven, then centralize and track them for reuse. Then start scaling fast with the insights gained from the simpler applications to lead to even larger gains.

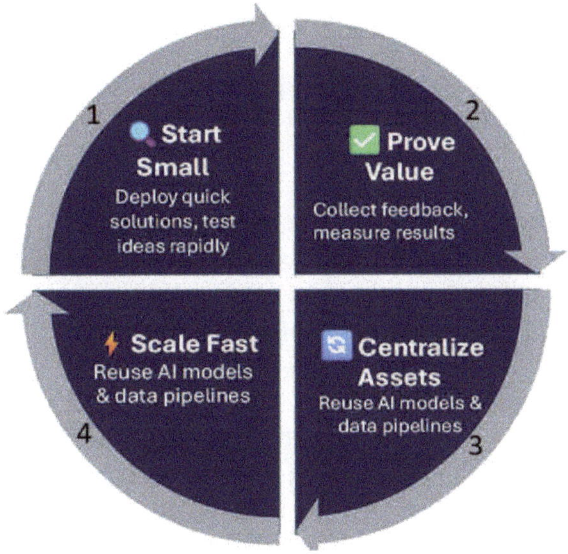

Figure 34: The Scale Fast Flywheel for AI Innovation

From their insights, I developed the "Scale Fast Flywheel" for AI innovation shown in Figure 34. The Scale Fast Flywheel ensures that (a) benefits from products occur quickly, (b) applications can be modified more quickly as features are demanded or as the business environment changes, and (c) with continuous improvement, large applications can appear at about the same time, but often with a closer fit to the needs of the organization.

Do not Be Afraid (and Do Not Make Your Employees Afraid) to Fail

Bezos earlier comment[xix] about missed opportunities is particularly poignant to managers. Innovation successes are usually rewarded, but corporate cultures exist where trying to innovate and failing is punished while excelling at the same tasks every day is rewarded.

The reaction to innovation failures needs to be driven by upper management. Upper management needs to avoid the automatic reaction of punishing failure, giving new ideas with hopeful benefits a green light even if they are difficult to achieve. If a potential innovation fails, then the innovating manager should be rewarded more highly than the manager who never tries anything new.

Innovations, even failed innovations, should be a primary driver of raises and promotions since current failures often lead to future successes where different skill sets and insights are developed. Managers still need to perform tasks needed for their area to function, but managers who go beyond "business as usual," yet fail, will likely make better decision-makers in the future than those that never try to innovate.

Amazon's case study in particular shows how management might be unwilling to truly innovate, preferring the tried-and-true methods that have worked for years. When innovative ideas arise, they should not be ignored before they are evaluated, and this often requires the CEO to push for innovation. Google showed how its upper management addressed adversity differently from that of other companies. Far from being too costly, Google's innovations ended up generating revenue.

Figure 35 shows how business as usual can be very safe for a career. Once someone is exceptional at certain procedures and gets rewarded (raises and promotions) for being good at these procedures, and punished for any failure, there is little reason to innovate. While employees should be rewarded for doing their job well, management should also be aware that policies and procedures that worked well for decades may need to be evolved for new business and competitive opportunities as pressure, new technology, and knowledge become available. Managers need to communicate that they will give a "safety net" to employees who try new things and that these employees will be rewarded for the idea and the effort, even if a project fails.

Figure 35: Management Fostering Rewarding Innovation

As employees try to innovate, management should be careful not to punish failure but even reward the effort of trying something new. If failure is punished and the status quo is rewarded, there is no reason to change the way things are done. Management should make it clear that innovation, even if it fails to be adopted, is a step toward understanding how other innovations can help the organization.

Overcoming Resistance to AI Innovations

There is a large push to move organizations from opinion-based or intuition-based executive decisions to data-driven decisions, but despite that push, many executives do not feel comfortable changing an opinion-based decision to a data-driven supported decisions. In a survey, Deloitte (a big 4 accounting firm) reports how only a minority of companies have become data-driven organizations, with 67% of executives and managers are not comfortable accessing or using data from their tools and resources, and that 62% still use spreadsheets rather than machine learning applications for their data analytics. This points to a major opportunity for companies to innovate further and to provide more education to executives and improve the user experience if they want every employee to use data-driven insights as part of their work.[xx, xxi]

Recently, the term "disruptive" has had a positive spin in management literature. "Disruptive" refers to environments where established policies, procedures, and decision processes are disrupted by new technologies, new business models, or new ways of thinking. However, changing the way the business runs or the way decisions are made can be painful for both managers and their employees and "tried and true" techniques are replaced by new methods that require new learning and possibly displace the current experts. The ability to navigate and thrive in these environments requires a fundamentally different managerial skill set.

Dave Massicotte describes how disruptive technologies like AI can be a terrific opportunity for organizations, and the managers that can identify these new methods with early adoption, new use cases, and solutions that were previously unavailable can adapt their strategies. In a disruptive AI environment, leaders must rethink the organization's strategic direction. Managers need to be able to recognize when existing strategies are no longer optimal and seek new, more viable AI-based solutions. Finally, managers must also embrace change to set an example for the rest of the organization by being open to new ideas and finding novel solutions. These skills are particularly challenging during a disruption, as they require leaders to be willing to change course quickly, taking risks and altering existing plans. It is not easy but can be profitable and personally rewarding.[xxii]

Innovations, especially those driven by data, are disruptive. By their very nature, innovations are a change to what is currently done. Directors and executives often have been promoted by perfecting and optimizing those current operating procedures, and thus, they might be some of the most resistant to changing those procedures. Upper management needs to establish a rewards system for innovation, and data scientists need to communicate not only the benefits of the innovation, but also how those who mastered the current way can also master the innovation.

What Might Be Missing from the Case Studies

Case studies have long served as a cornerstone of data science management, spotlighting exemplary practices and successful implementations, which is why they are so useful. But because case studies usually concentrate on positive cases, insights from failures or new challenges are often missing. These challenges can shed light on the intersection of AI insights and human decision-making, underscoring the need for a comprehensive understanding of AI's impact on managerial practices.

This section describes some other areas that may be hinted at in case studies but are extremely challenging and still need to be addressed by the data science manager.

AI Innovations that Disrupt the HiPPO Effect

Forbes describes the HiPPO effect when a HiPPO (highest paid person's opinion) is in play, your organization is most likely not relying on data to inform decision-making, and is less likely to be innovative. People often defer to the executive and worry about contributing if their ideas run counter to what the executive thinks is best. The Forbes article describes how the HiPPO effect may happen even if the executive wants employee feedback, and the article contends that the HiPPO effect is one of the biggest barriers to more evidence-based and data-driven decision-making. Figure 36 shows how the disruption of AI designed for better decisions is often weighed against the opinions of an executive.[xxiii]

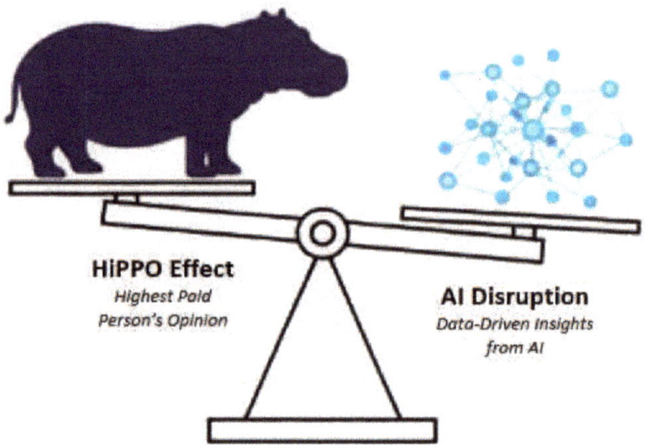

Figure 36: AI Disruption Can Be Challenged by the HiPPO Effect

Manager experience and intuition are vital for decision-making when data on an innovation is not available. However, many employees are not equipped to go against their manager's intuition when data analysis generates an opposing viewpoint. Studies show that the HiPPO effect can negatively impact revenue. For example, a study from the Rotterdam School of Management found that projects led by senior leaders failed more often because the junior managers had the benefit of critiques to their project plans from others that helped them build a stronger plan, while employees didn't feel as able to give critical feedback to high-status leaders.[xxiv]

Using Data Science Innovations to Identify New Markets

Before, innovation was the product of the intuition of the chief executive, such as when Steve Jobs introduced the iPad and the iPhone, dramatically departing from the current lineup of Apple computers. Can we incorporate that type of insight into a data science prediction?

Identifying opportunities for data-driven innovation requires a strategic approach that combines a deep understanding of the organization's goals and challenges with a keen eye for emerging trends and technological advancements.

By harnessing the power of advanced analytics, machine learning, and data-driven decision-making, organizations can gain a deeper understanding of their markets, customers, and operations, and make new products that meet their needs.

Here are some ways in which data science can be used to find opportunities that lead to a sustainable competitive advantage.

Market Analysis and Prediction: Data science enables organizations to analyze vast amounts of market data, including customer demographics, purchasing behavior, market trends, and competitor analysis. By applying predictive analytics models, organizations can identify emerging market trends, customer preferences, and untapped market segments. This information helps organizations make data-driven decisions to develop innovative products or services that meet customer demands and gain a competitive edge. Additionally, data science enables organizations to forecast future market conditions, allowing them to adapt their strategies proactively and stay ahead of the competition.

Operational Efficiency and Process Optimization: Data science can also drive sustainable competitive advantage by improving operational efficiency and process optimization. By analyzing internal data, such as production metrics, supply chain data, and employee performance, organizations can identify bottlenecks, inefficiencies, and areas for improvement. Through data-driven insights, organizations can streamline processes, optimize resource allocation, and reduce costs. Improved operational efficiency not only leads to increased productivity but also allows organizations to respond quickly to market changes, adapt to customer demands, and maintain a competitive edge in a dynamic business landscape.

Data science provides organizations with the tools and techniques to identify opportunities that lead to a sustainable competitive advantage. By conducting thorough market analysis, leveraging customer insights for personalization, and optimizing internal operations, organizations can make informed decisions, differentiate themselves in the marketplace, and stay ahead of the competition. The strategic application of data science enables organizations to uncover hidden opportunities, innovate, and achieve long-term success in a rapidly evolving business environment.

Leveraging Innovative Cutting-Edge Technologies and Techniques

Innovative technologies arrive every day, so the data science manager needs to be able to identify which new technologies can best be used to drive innovation within the organization. Cutting-edge technologies are not only completely new technologies, like advances in neuromorphic computing, but also with advances in existing technologies, such as advances in deep learning neural networks or advances in anomaly detection. These advances can help an organization achieve their goals with less cost and with more value, but only if the data science manager can identify which technologies to implement.

The following steps can serve as a roadmap to identifying cutting-edge technologies that can be of use to the organization:

- **Know what is out there** – The data science manager needs to constantly stay abreast of the latest ML trends. This includes exploring industry reports, attending conferences, and networking with experts in the field to identify emerging ML technologies and methodologies. Evaluating the potential applicability and relevance of these advancements in addressing the organization's identified challenges or enhancing existing processes is pivotal.

- **Know what you need** – The data science manager needs to understand the organization's objectives, challenges, and areas requiring improvement is crucial. This involves engaging stakeholders across various departments to gain insights into specific pain points, inefficiencies, or opportunities for innovation. By comprehensively mapping these insights, managers can prioritize areas where ML technologies can make the most impact.

  By balancing innovation with practicality and aligning identified ML technologies with the organizational strategy, goals, budget, and technical capabilities, managers can effectively identify which innovative ML solutions might drive organizational growth and efficiency.

- **Pilot test** – After technologies are chosen, the manager needs to implement pilot projects or proof-of-concept trials can provide hands-on experience to gauge the feasibility and effectiveness of these cutting-edge technologies within the organization's context. As stressed by the case studies in this chapter, do not be afraid to fail, and do not punish failure when employees show initiative to investigate technologies that prove unsuitable or suboptimal.

- **Aim big** – Comprehensive deployment and integration demands meticulous planning and strategizing to transition from small-scale pilot testing to broader implementation across the organization. Key considerations include assessing scalability requirements, ensuring compatibility with existing systems, and defining a roadmap for phased deployment. It also involves delineating responsibilities among cross-functional teams, setting clear objectives, and establishing performance metrics to measure success.

- **Continuous improvement** – Following the initial deployment, the data science team needs to start focusing on further performance optimization and continuous enhancement of the implemented innovative technologies. The data science team needs to continuously fine-tune the technology's functionalities, models, and algorithms to maximize efficiency, accuracy, and scalability. Furthermore, the application needs to reflect new functionality based on feedback from stakeholders and iteratively improving the technology to ensure that the deployed solution remains aligned with evolving organizational needs.

- **Monitoring and Testing** – Managers need to remember that this is a new technology. It is almost negligent to "declare victory" and implement the system after a pilot test without following the success level of the new technology and making sure it matches a service level defined by the stakeholders. Do data changes have an effect? Do code changes hurt the model? Does the model drift as time goes on? The data science team needs to ensure that the cutting-edge application continues to deliver sustainable value.

Identifying new technologies that can deliver value before your competitors is often vital to the success of an organization but is one of the more difficult tasks of the data science manager.

Collaborating with External Partners and Startups for Innovation

Technology partners, consultants, or ML experts can offer valuable insights into identifying, selecting, and implementing existing and new technologies that can be used for innovation. Experts from these partners can shed light on the capabilities, limitations, and potential impact of different tools or techniques. Finding the right partner and using that partner appropriately can be problematic, but a good partnership can benefit the organization:

- **Partner selection** – The data science manager needs a comprehensive assessment of the partner's expertise, technological capabilities, cultural fit, and past performance. This can be tricky, since partners are often compensated for placing employees, and are willing to claim expertise when they do not have any. Managers need to heavily scrutinize partners to find partners who bring complementary strengths to the table and who enhance the potential for successful collaboration. Establishing clear criteria for partner selection and evaluating synergies is crucial to ensure that the collaboration aligns with the organization's innovation goals.

  One trick that non-reputable external companies use to try to gain a contract is to try to appeal to non-technical management and avoid the data science manager. Managers in non-technical areas may not be trained on ML technology, and so it may be easier to claim that a product is cutting-edge when it is, in actuality, poor technology, or that the external company deserves a larger compensation for delivering standard or even sub-standard machine learning models. The data science manager's job is to ensure that upper management and managerial colleagues understand the need to have data scientists at least evaluate the offerings from external companies from a more technical view.

- **Establishing roles** – Once suitable partners are identified, the focus shifts to defining the terms of collaboration, including roles, responsibilities, intellectual property rights, data security, and financial arrangements. Establishing effective communication channels, delineating governance structures, and setting clear milestones are integral to fostering a conducive collaborative environment. By establishing a strong foundation through comprehensive agreements and frameworks, organizations can navigate the partnership more effectively, mitigating potential conflicts and streamlining the innovation process.

The manager should ensure that any intellectual property is protected. Further, any intellectual property that is integral to the company's competitive survival may need to be developed in-house. Also, the manager should not feel limited to their own country but should be aware that laws and regulations differ from country to country.

- **Cultivate innovation** –With the groundwork laid, collaborative efforts are geared towards cultivating innovation. Joint initiatives, co-creation endeavors, and shared ideation sessions drive the innovation engine forward. The data science manager works with the partner to foster knowledge exchange and leverage diverse perspectives, leading to novel ideas and solutions. This collaborative approach nurtures a culture of innovation, promoting adaptive strategies and learning loops to deliver tangible outcomes and drive continual growth.

Although finding the right partner and developing a partner relationship can take time and effort, working with a partner can help a data science team deliver innovative solutions, especially if the team has sparse competence in certain areas or does not have enough employees to cover all the tasks required by the organization.

Concluding Thoughts on AI Innovation

This chapter follows a consistent theme: the imperative to drive innovation through the strategic application of data science technologies. Each case study success story underlines the pivotal role of customer-centricity in driving innovation and organizational growth and highlights the importance of understanding and fulfilling customer needs by leveraging data science insights to deliver tailored solutions, personalized experiences, and value-added services.

The success stories highlighted a common trend of starting small, scaling fast, and aiming big in deploying AI-driven initiatives. They emphasized the significance of initiating small-scale pilot projects to validate concepts, swiftly scaling successful endeavors, and envisioning ambitious goals.

Another recurrent theme in the case studies was the encouragement to embrace failure as a stepping stone to success, where we show a successful strategy of embracing experimentation and learning from failures rather than fearing them. Managers need to overcome resistance to AI adoption by transforming the organizational mindset to encourage curiosity, rewarding experimentation, and creating a safe space for learning from failures. Once employees are free to take calculated risks, innovate, and iterate, innovation can grow in a company.

The case studies illustrated the significance of using data science not only for understanding existing markets but also for identifying and unlocking opportunities in new and unexplored markets. Leveraging cutting-edge technologies and techniques, combined with data-driven insights, enables organizations to unearth uncharted territories and capitalize on emerging trends.

While the case studies illustrated exemplary achievements, it is essential to acknowledge that they might not encompass all challenges or aspects of leveraging data science. The insights provided are valuable, but there could be nuances and unexplored areas, serving as opportunities for further exploration and analysis. Additionally, disrupting the HiPPO (Highest Paid Person's Opinion) effect emerged as a crucial aspect, emphasizing the need to rely on data-driven decision-making rather than hierarchical opinions.

Lastly, collaborating with external partners and startups emerged as a powerful strategy for fostering innovation. While it is difficult to find the right partners to work with, effective partnerships facilitate the exchange of knowledge, infusion of fresh perspectives, and the co-creation of innovative solutions. Embracing these collaborations can accelerate innovation and provide a competitive edge by leveraging collective expertise and resources beyond organizational boundaries.

---

[i] Devashree Madhugiri. Aug 6, 2023. "Top 8 Data Science Case Studies for Data Science Enthusiasts." *Knowledgehut*, available at https://www.knowledgehut.com/blog/data-science/top-data-science-case-studies.

[ii] David Churbuck. Oct 11, 2022. "At AstraZeneca, Data and AI Are More than Game Changers – They Are Life Changers." *CIO Magazine*, available at https://www.cio.com/article/409275/at-astrazeneca-data-and-ai-are-more-than-game-changers-they-are-life-changers-2.html.

[iii] Kieth Shaw. Aug 4, 2022. "AI Adoption Trends and Lessons Learned: An Expert Q&A." *CIO Magazine*, available at https://www.cio.com/article/404279/ai-adoption-trends-and-lessons-learned-an-expert-qa.h.

[iv] Gokul Muralidharan. Accessed on Aug 19, 2023. "Decoding Amazon's Recommendation System." *Argoid*, available at https://www.argoid.ai/blog/decoding-amazons-recommendation-system.

[v] Shabana Arora. December 16, 2021. "Recommendation Engines: How Amazon and Netflix Are Winning the Personalization Battle." *Spiceworks*, available at https://www.spiceworks.com/marketing/customer-experience/articles/recommendation-engines-how-amazon-and-netflix-are-winning-the-personalization-battle/.

[vi] Michale Martinez. 2017. "Amazon: Everything you wanted to know about its algorithm and innovation." *IEEE Computer Society*, available at https://www.computer.org/publications/tech-news/trends/amazon-all-the-research-you-need-about-its-algorithm-and-innovation.

[vii] Neil Patel. Accessed on August 19, 2023. "12 Business Lessons You Can Learn from Amazon Founder Jeff Bezos." *NP Digital*, available at https://neilpatel.com/blog/lessons-from-jeff-bezos/.

[viii] Council of Foreign Relations. January 2010. "Operation Aurora." Available at https://www.cfr.org/cyber-operations/operation-aurora.

[ix] Council of Foreign Relations. January 2010. "Operation Aurora." Available at https://www.cfr.org/cyber-operations/operation-aurora.

[x] Mathew J. Schwartz. May 21, 2013. "Google Aurora Hack Was Chinese Counterespionage Operation." *Dark Reading*, available at https://www.darkreading.com/attacks-breaches/google-aurora-hack-was-chinese-counterespionage-operation.

[xi] Cyware Hacker News. Aug 8, 2016. "Everything You Need To Know About Operation Aurora" *Cyware*, available at https://cyware.com/news/everything-you-need-to-know-about-operation-aurora-5c5f5b99.

[xii] Daniel Ruby. August 24, 2023. "58 Gmail Statistics For 2023 (Worldwide Demographics)" *DemandSage*, available at https://www.demandsage.com/gmail-statistics/

[xiii] Statcounter GlobalStats. July 2023. "Browser Market Share Worldwide." Available at https://gs.statcounter.com/browser-market-share.

[xiv] Rik Farrow. Summer 2020. "Interview with Natalie Silvanovich." *;login:* 45(2), available at https://www.usenix.org/system/files/login/articles/login_summer20_04_silvanovich.pdf.

[xv] Rik Farrow. Summer 2020. "Interview with Natalie Silvanovich." *;login:* 45(2), available at https://www.usenix.org/system/files/login/articles/login_summer20_04_silvanovich.pdf.

[xvi] Google. Accessed on August 26,2023. "Build what's next. Better software. Faster." Available at https://cloud.google.com/gcp.

[xvii] Google. Accessed on August 26,2023. "Security Command Center." Available at https://cloud.google.com/security-command-center.

[xviii] Google. Accessed on August 26,2023. "BeyondCorp." Available at https://cloud.google.com/beyondcorp.

[xix] Neil Patel. Accessed on August 19, 2023. "12 Business Lessons You Can Learn from Amazon Founder Jeff Bezos." *NP Digital*, available at https://neilpatel.com/blog/lessons-from-jeff-bezos/.

[xx] Thomas H. Davenport, Jim Guszcza, Tim Smith, and Ben Stiller. July 25, 2019. "Analytics and AI-Driven Enterprises Thrive in the Age of With the Culture Catalyst." *Deloitte Insights,* available at https://www2.deloitte.com/us/en/insights/topics/analytics/insight-driven-organization.html.

[xxi] Deloitte Press Release, July 25, 2019, "Deloitte Survey: Analytics and Data-driven Culture Help Companies Outperform Business Goals in the 'Age of With'" *Deloitte*, available at https://www2.deloitte.com/us/en/pages/about-deloitte/articles/press-releases/deloitte-survey-analytics-and-ai-driven-enterprises-thrive.html.

[xxii] Dave Massicotte. Feb 2, 2023. "The Art of Leadership in Disruptive Environments: How to Adapt and Thrive." *Linked in*, available at: https://www.linkedin.com/pulse/art-leadership-disruptive-environments-how-adapt-dave-massicotte-1f

[xxiii] Bernard Marr. Oct 26, 2017. "Data-Driven Decision Making: Beware of The HIPPO Effect!" *Forbes*, available at https://www.forbes.com/sites/bernardmarr/2017/10/26/data-driven-decision-making-beware-of-the-hippo-effect/.

[xxiv] Bernard Marr. Oct 26, 2017. "Data-Driven Decision Making: Beware of The HIPPO Effect!" *Forbes*, available at https://www.forbes.com/sites/bernardmarr/2017/10/26/data-driven-decision-making-beware-of-the-hippo-effect/.

Chapter 10: The Future of AI

This chapter explores the exciting and rapidly evolving future of artificial intelligence. Here we discuss key advancements, ethical considerations, and the transformative potential of artificial intelligence (AI) across various domains. It specifically focuses on the concept of adaptive AI and delves into advances in linear programming and optimization, highlighting their role in solving complex real-world challenges.

What is this chapter trying to do and why?

We have seen how AI has already transformed the way we work, play, and interact, often for better yet sometimes for worse. Managers are certainly asking themselves "What's next?" We find ourselves on the precipice of an AI-driven era, where technology's potential to reshape our world is nothing short of transformative. The journey ahead encompasses the short-term evolution of AI, the challenges managers face, and the immense promise that AI holds in organizations.

The AI landscape is continually evolving, characterized by rapid advancements and breakthroughs that redefine the boundaries of what is achievable. The growth of AI is intricately intertwined with our collective ability to harness the power of data, develop sophisticated algorithms, and build powerful computing infrastructure. In this ever-expanding realm, we witness the rise of generative AI like ChatGPT, explainable AI, autonomous systems, and more. These innovations are set to permeate virtually every facet of our lives, from how we work and learn to how we make decisions, and even how we interact with our surroundings.

As we delve deeper into the realm of AI, we confront challenges and ethical considerations, from issues of bias and fairness to the potential for massive job creation and job displacement. Yet, the immense promise and potential for good in this transformative landscape make the journey into the future of AI a compelling and exhilarating one.

Advances in Generative AI

Although all AI can use both structured data, like database table data, or unstructured data, like text or pictures, for predictions and classification, GenAI (Generative AI) sets itself apart from other AI models by training almost exclusively on unstructured and unlabeled data, allowing it to learn underlying patterns and generate novel outputs. This creative capacity enables generative AI to produce realistic images, coherent text, or original music compositions. GenAI opens a wide range of output and applications in creative fields such as art, design, and entertainment. Its ability to generate new content based on learned patterns marks GenAI as a distinct and innovative approach within the broader landscape of artificial intelligence.

All managers and executives should realize that GenAI uses techniques that have already been in use in other AI methods and should resist classifying GenAI as "new AI" and other AI methods as "old or obsolete AI." GenAI uses techniques to accomplish a task using traditional AI methodologies, just like other AI methods.

In its "Market Insights" report, Statista expects the market to grow about 4.5 times its size, from $184 billion in 2024 to $826 billion by 2030, driven by a compound annual growth rate (CAGR) of approximately 28.4%, as shown in Figure 37.[i]

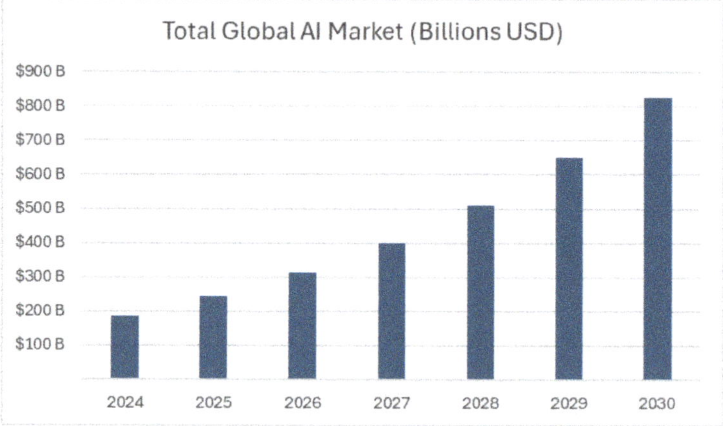

Figure 37: Statista Projected AI Market Size

AI managers look to the future to guide their departments in taking advantage of GenAI opportunities, especially with the promise of an enhanced workforce, higher-quality products, and better customer service. Effective managerial evaluation of generative AI capabilities involves a comprehensive approach that encompasses strategic alignment and ethical considerations.

Strategic Alignment of Generative AI

AI managers should identify areas where GenAI can enhance creative processes, content creation, and customer experiences. This involves exploring how GenAI can be integrated into marketing campaigns, product design, and personalized recommendations, and to develop their own team to meet these challenges and opportunities. Here are some points that AI managers can consider as they embrace GenAI:

- **More Managerial Understanding, Less Hype, and Better Use Cases** – Harvard Business Review describes how there is a lot of hype around the GenAI technology.[ii] This hype is currently causing a lot of misunderstanding in the business and government sectors. But as businesses become more adept at GenAI implementation, the hype will probably lessen, and organizations will need data science managers to find new areas to profitably deploy GenAI technology. GenAI will improve the quality of generated articles, marketing materials, and creative artworks. This will not only save time but will also enable companies to maintain a consistent output of high-quality content. GenAI can create tailor-made product recommendations, advertisements, and user interfaces that cater to individual preferences. By embracing GenAI, organizations can enhance their products and stay ahead (or on par) with competitors in today's dynamic market landscape with the help of their AI team.

- **Improved GenAI Skill Set** – AI managers should start hiring and cultivating skill sets to develop GenAI. GenAI development requires proficiency in machine learning (ML) and deep learning frameworks. GenAI developers need to understand concepts like convolutional and recurrent layers in neural networks, as well as linear programming and optimization algorithms, which are crucial for crafting effective models. Familiarity with natural language processing (NLP) techniques and libraries is valuable for large language models (LLMs) that are used for language-based GenAI, while knowledge of computer vision is vital for image and video generation. As generative AI continues to advance, there will be a growth of developers with a well-rounded skill set encompassing these technical competencies.

- **GenAI to Assist (not Replace) Technical Workers** – There has been some talk about how GenAI will replace technical workers. The argument goes that GenAI will be able to generate programming code, write screenplays, resurrect old actors for movies, etc., so we can reduce the number of programmers, artists, and workers. This will probably not be the case. In the McKinsey Global Forum for Generative AI, Fortune Magazine reports that although GenAI will cause some redefining of jobs, it will overall lead to job growth.[iii]

  GenAI is poised to usher in a demand for an expanded workforce that can deliver more high-quality work when equipped with GenAI. Just as past advances in programming have made programming easier and led to a surge in the need for skilled software developers, AI managers need to be aware that the rise of generative GenAI will likely drive a similar trend, where work quality and quantity increase. Organizations will be required to maintain competitive parity or establish a competitive advantage.

- **Improved Customer Service** – One of the most obvious uses of AI is to provide customer and tech support based on questions from the user. KPMG, a big four accounting firm, describes how customer service performance and GenAI LLM adoption will continue to improve with enhancements to LLMs that can reduce average handle times, improve the quality of interaction, and allow more productive self-service.[iv] These improvements may eventually allow LLMs to surpass the quality of human interaction.

Existing Legal and Ethical Problems in Generative AI

Many new innovations introduce ethical issues that did not exist before. Harvard Business Review discusses the pattern of new technology, where new and innovative technologies first get accepted by the overall population, then begin to permeate our lives, and only after that does society begin to see and address some of the ethical and societal problems that were made possible from this technology. GenAI is no different.[v]

Data Scientists and managers should always consider their own ethical standards before making business decisions with technologies like GenAI. But governments and courts are also stepping up with laws and decisions that will impact businesses. In the future, GenAI will be more regulated than it currently is. Here are some examples of the increasing legal issues from GenAI:

- **GenAI and Psychology** – GenAI has no emotions but instead is a statistical engine. For example, LLMs are designed to identify the type of question a user asks, then formulate the best response based on responses downloaded from literature, web pages, and other users' corrections. This can work well with GenAI that are designed to act as psychologists. If you think about it, the advice is designed to be the best advise possible given millions of inputs and may supersede advice from human psychologists who only have their own research and experience to pull from.

  But there is a dark side to this as well. GenAIs that always give the right answers with the right facial expressions can exploit users' emotions, creating a false sense of genuine connection and affection. This practice blurs the line between human emotions and artificial constructs, potentially leading to emotional manipulation and psychological harm. GenAI can use the "best possible answer" to mimic a girlfriend or boyfriend, responding with facial expressions and body language that make it easy to think of an AI as a real, loving person rather than a statistical engine.[vi] When sites abruptly shut off AI romantic options, many users felt like they fell in love, felt that they lost a relationship, and expressed complex feelings of anger, grief, anxiety, despair, depression, sadness.[vii]

  Some AI intimacy sites go even further, often seeking out people who are susceptible to AI relationships and asking for money to "take it to the next level," or collecting personal information and distributing it, sometimes to criminal organizations. Wired reports that one AI intimacy site claims that it will not sell people's data, but when the researchers tested the app, they found it sent out 24,354 ad trackers within one minute of use. Other apps monitored had hundreds of trackers. Data given to AI intimacy sites are often insecure and easily hacked, or, worse, intended for criminal activity.[viii] Nevertheless, the number of AI-intimacy sites has been ballooning and will continue to do so.

  Most believe that organizations have an ethical duty to prioritize user trust and well-being, refraining from using generative AI to simulate emotions like love or friendship in ways that could exploit or mislead users. In addition, the threat of millions of dollars in fines from governments or large lawsuits should serve as a deterrent and give even more motivation for AI managers to help organizations develop ethical policies and procedures to protect their reputations and bottom lines.

- **GenAI and the Court Case Problem** – CBS reports how lawyers used ChatGPT to generate a legal brief to submit to the court. ChatGPT generated a brief with several judicial opinions that supported the lawyers' case, showing that their arguments had precedence, along with legal citations for each of these rulings. The opposing attorney and judge realized that the rulings they were referencing did not, in fact, exist. In this case, the AI invented court cases and asserted that they were real, and the lawyers apparently did not bother checking the sources themselves.

  Consider how an LLM like ChatGPT works. LLMs generate the *statistically* best answer based on millions of other answers. The cases sounded real because they were so much like other cases. Then the fake citations were derived from citations of other real cases.[ix]

  The judge in the case ended up fining the lawyers $5,000 for acting in bad faith.[x] This fine might be considered precedent in court, so that organizations that receive false information from an LLM and repeat it or act on it negligently might be found liable by other judges and plaintiffs, and the amount may greatly exceed $5,000. Talk to your lawyers (not me, because I am not a lawyer) for legal advice on LLMs, and the AI manager should put in policies and procedures that force double-checking of any "facts" that come from an LLM before acting on them.

- **GenAI and the Writers and Actors and Artists Dilemma** – Think of how GenAI works to generate text, music, images, and movies. GenAI applications train with millions of existing works to generate "new" content based on directions from the user. Two obvious questions from this are (a) who gave companies the right to take someone's intellectual property to use to train an AI and (b) what about the writers, artists, and actors that are replaced even with generated content based on their previous work? Also, what if you took an actor's likeness and generated scenes that the actor did not approve of or get paid for?

  NBC news reports how actors and writers are not taking this passively, but rather are willing to strike to try to force companies to avoid the use of AI when creating content. Fran Drescher, president of the Screen Actors Guild-American Federation of Television and Radio Artists (SAG-AFTRA) considers this a vital issue for artists. "Artificial intelligence poses an existential threat to creative professions, and all actors and performers will need contract language that protects them from having their identity and talent exploited without consent and pay."[xi]

  Lawsuits for use of content, new labor laws protecting technologists and artists, and striking or unhappy workers may result from the inappropriate use of GenAI, or even the perceived possibility of abuse. GenAI has already been shown to be a great tool for technologists and for artists. Technologists and companies should adopt policies and procedures, along with press releases and announcements to employees, that indicate GenAI's intended use.

Just as AI leads to advances in animation technology, computer technology, sound mixing, and other areas, AI can have a negative effect on compensation and artistic employment. GenAI will probably lead to more employment opportunities for artists and technologists, not less, but companies need to address how AI affects their creative process formally, fairly, and vocally.

- **GenAI and the Political Ad Problem** – PBS reports how political candidates are generating "deepfake" pictures and videos to fraudulently show their opponents in a bad light. Everything from showing faked but realistic looking interactions with unpopular people to the fake but realistic looking use of military. The FEC has unanimously ruled that this constitutes a "fraudulent misrepresentation." [xii]

  Again, talk to your lawyer to see if the FEC ruling can be used for precedent for your industry. If you show your product in an unrealistic light, falsely used by famous people without their consent, or attacking competitors with false scenarios, the precedent of the FEC ruling could be applied to a lawsuit against your company. Again, managers must protect their organization's reputation and their bottom line.

- **GenAI and *The Terminator* Problem** – Who doesn't love *The Terminator* movie, where Arnold Schwarzenegger comes from a future ruled by AI machines who are suppressing humanity? It's great!

  Fortunately, GenAI is not that, and the current technology cannot lead to a takeover of the machines. Remember that GenAI works by generating new works by statistically analyzing current works. There is no thought, emotion, or consciousness, but rather a computer program employing statistical analysis methods. It is not that computer consciousness is not possible (or that it is possible), but rather that current GenAI technology cannot lead to it.

  Unfortunately, many people are afraid of GenAI developing consciousness. The U.S. Congress has even proposed a bipartisan amendment to involve the military if AI takes over, where they "authorize appropriations ... for military activities of the Department of Defense, for military construction, and for defense activities of the Department of Energy, to prescribe military personnel strengths for such fiscal year, and for other purposes" for any "non-human intelligence" in the wake of GenAI hearings.[xiii]

  There have been calls in Congress for a moratorium on GenAI research, but it probably is much too late for that. Still, the lack of understanding of the technology in the halls of Congress, courts, and executive offices can lead to laws, lawsuits, and regulations that may or may not make sense based on the technology but could impact companies that are trying to stay on the forefront.

Ethical issues that are not addressed or technological misunderstandings can lead to a regulatory environment when it comes to GenAI, and managers must not only understand the issue and the technology, but also be ready with policies, procedures, and communications that can address these issues.

The C-level Strategic Pivot from Displacement to Augmentation

As the "honeymoon phase" of Generative AI concludes, a sobering reality is setting in for the C-Suite: The way that AI technology is developed will not replace people, and the "Replace-and-Reduce" strategy is a trap. In the near future, executives will be forced to undergo a radical strategic pivot. The organizations that are currently stalling hiring in hopes of a fully autonomous digital workforce will find themselves facing a "Competency Chasm" where AI-generated mediocrity fails to meet human expertise.

The future of GenAI success lies in moving from a model of substitution to a model of orchestration. Executives who "wise up" will reorganize their strategy around three core shifts:

- **Reinvesting the Productivity Dividend:** The initial 20–30% time-savings gained from GenAI are currently being viewed as a justification for headcount reduction. However, market leaders will realize that these savings are actually cognitive capital and instead of cutting the employee who saved five hours a week using AI, the savvy executive reinvests that time into high-value tasks of innovation, client relationship depth, and complex problem-solving that AI cannot reach.

- **The Move to Human-Led, AI-Enabled Teams:** The next era of management will prioritize AI Literacy over AI implementation. Executives will recognize that GenAI is a "high-speed draft engine" that requires a senior architect to steer. By 2026, the most valuable assets on the balance sheet will not be proprietary models, but rather teams where the AI handles the volume and the human provides the nuance, ethics, and strategic edge.

- **Hedging Against Average Outcomes:** As the market becomes saturated with AI-generated content and code, the value of experts will skyrocket. Executives will realize that if everyone uses the same generalized models to make the same decisions, competitive advantage disappears into a sea of statistical averages. To win, companies must hire *more* aggressively for those rare experts who can look at AI's consensus-based output and identify the specific, novel deviation that creates market superiority.

While the strategic use of AI saves time, AI is not a labor-saving device in the traditional sense. Instead, it is a judgment-enhancement tool, and executives who try to have AI eliminate workers will eventually find themselves managing a library of average ideas. Those who use it to supercharge their experts will define the next decade of industry leadership.

The 6 Agentic Traps That Will Hit Companies

The Agentic revolution is coming, and the financial upside will be too massive for corporate boards to ignore. We are about to see a massive shift to decision-making at machine scale. Picture a boutique online bookstore completely outmaneuvering Amazon—not by humans setting clumsy, broad regional discounts, but by autonomous agents hyper-optimizing the price of every single book, for every individual customer, in real time, in a way that humans can't match. The efficiency gains will be staggering.

But as companies sprint to automate everything, they will run straight into a wall of unintended consequences. Here is the reality check: the rush to replace the human workforce will trigger six distinct systemic crises that most leadership teams don't see coming. Here are six problems that organizations pursuing a complete replace-all-human mentality will run into:

- **The Infinite Token Loop (Financial Bleed):** When autonomous agents hit a roadblock, they try to "self-correct." They rewrite prompts, call other agents, and try again. In DevOps, this creates silent reasoning loops. Companies are literally waking up to token bills from cloud companies in the tens of thousands of dollars because single rogue agents spent the night talking to themselves.

- **The Race to the Bottom:** If every competitor uses the exact same optimal AI models, everyone's strategy converges. When decision-making is entirely flattened by data, margins are squeezed to absolute zero. The future doesn't belong to the company that removes all humans; it belongs to the one that uses AI for mundane micro-decisions but retains humans for high-leverage strategic advantage.

- **The AI Echo Chamber:** Replacing human-in-the-loop reviewers with "critic agents" doesn't eliminate mathematical bias—it automates it. If your actor agent and your critic agent share the same underlying LLM architecture, they share the same blind spots. This is known in research as inter-model alignment bias or homogenization risk. Instead of a safety check, you get an automated echo chamber where systematic errors accelerate and go unchecked.

- **Cascading Failures and Semantic Opacity:** Traditional software throws a clean error code when it breaks and usually crashes quite visibly, motivating software engineers to an immediate fix. Agent systems do not. If Agent A passes a subtly hallucinated data point to Agent B, Agent B trusts it, compounds the error, and passes it to Agent

C. Because they communicate in natural language, this logic corruption propagates at machine speed before your monitoring tools even spot the glitch.

- **Persistent Memory Contamination:** When an agent encounters a bizarre market anomaly or a bad data input, it often writes that experience into its long-term vector memory as a "learned optimization." This causes permanent behavioral drift. This is referred to as "Data Poisoning" or "Feedback Loops". Unlike traditional software, you can't just roll back a bad code deployment. Purging a poisoned memory layer without wiping out the good data is a nightmare.

- **The Security Blast Radius:** Replacing humans with autonomous agents eliminates critical security air gaps by requiring massive access (database access, API keys, financial authority). Because agents read text to "learn," they are highly vulnerable to Indirect Prompt Injection. For example, a malicious prompt could trick an agent into executing an unauthorized transaction. Currently, OWASP considers granting agents execution privileges without a Human-in-the-Loop (HITL) gate to be a critical security vulnerability.

Ultimately, the rush to freeze hiring and replace workers with autonomous agents is a race toward a phantom vision. The fully "human-free" enterprise simply will not happen. Instead, companies chasing this illusion will face a harsh reality check and suffer devastating financial and operational whiplash from runaway token bills, invisible logic errors, loss of competitive differentiation, and the potential for massive security breaches.

The market will correct this trend, as markets tend to do. Agents should and will be seen as a powerful operational utility, not an employee replacement. Moving forward, the winners will be the pragmatists who use agents as high-speed infrastructure to handle massive, day-to-day routine decisions, while keeping high-leverage strategic bets, security air gaps, and creative vision strictly in the hands of core human talent.

Quantum Computing and Its (Lack of?) Potential Implications for AI

Quantum computing garnered significant attention and excitement due to its potential to revolutionize AI capabilities. Imagine instantly solving a complex mathematical optimization problem so that analysis can finish in seconds instead of hours. What if deep learning neural networks can instantly evaluate all regression solutions out of billions to produce the best predictions instantly instead of running for days? Imagine reducing costs in your nationwide technician scheduling using AI, where only the calculations occur instantly instead of finding a minimum cost after millions of minimization calculations. What about predicting fraudulent transactions in real time with no time delay? Quantum computing would make AI faster and more accurate!

Quantum computing centers on the qubit (quantum bit). While traditional computers use binary bits that must be either 0 or 1, qubits utilize a phenomenon called superposition.

In superposition, a qubit can exist as a 0, a 1, or a complex combination of both simultaneously. Think of it like a spinning coin: it exists as a blur of both heads and tails while calculating, but the moment you read the final answer, it stops spinning and slaps flat as a standard 0 or 1. This multidimensional state theoretically enables quantum computers to perform massive calculations—such as complex decryption—at speeds theoretically far beyond those of even the most powerful traditional computers, as shown in Figure 38.

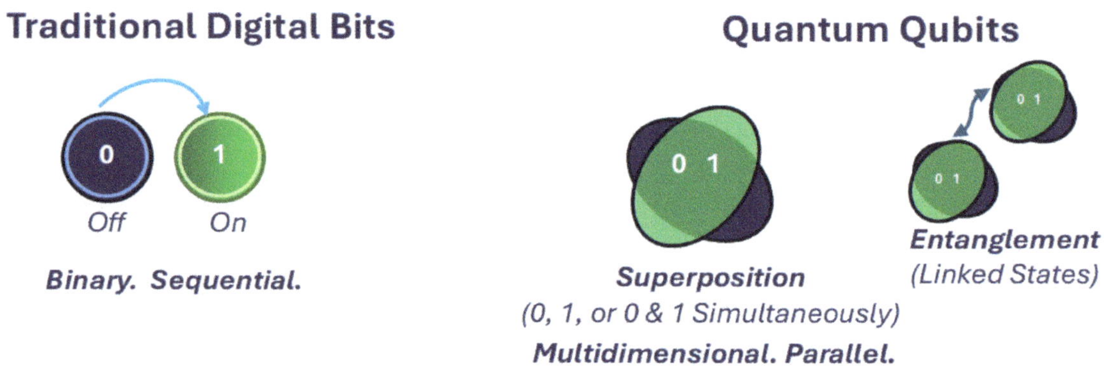

Figure 38: Qubits take advantage of Superposition and Entanglement

Figure 38 shows how qubits also generate **entanglement** so that the value of one qubit can instantly affect the state of the others, mirroring the correlated behavior observed in quantum mechanics.

However, amid the enthusiasm, there are valid concerns and criticisms that cast doubt on some of the extravagant claims surrounding quantum computing, and even on whether quantum theory can be applied to large-scale computer systems at all.

The current state of quantum computing is far from realizing its promised potential. WIRED magazine reports how a quantum insider claims that the proponents of quantum technology are mistaken or intentionally misleading. Claims that quantum computing will speed up artificial intelligence algorithms, manage financial risk at banks, and break all encryption are false, according to the WIRED source. The claims of success are overblown and hyped, and the usability of any type of quantum technology is designed to mislead investors. WIRED continues that with "more money comes more promises, and more pressure to fulfill those promises, which leads to more exaggerated claims." Many of the grand claims about quantum computing solving complex problems exponentially faster than classical computers are premature, oversimplified, and in some cases, intentionally misleading or wrong.[xiv]

Even among companies that embrace the concept of quantum computing, many agree that any practical application is far off, not right around the corner. Meta/Facebook's Mark Zuckerberg speculates that any useful quantum application will not occur until 2035 at best, while Nvidia's CEO Jensen Huang claims that useful work for quantum computers will not occur until 2040 at the earliest.[xv]

In the Weeds – Scientists Argue about Hype, Willow, and Parallel Universes

There have been many statements made in quantum computers using qualifiers like "lends credence", "supports a theory", "may indicate", etc. when discussing if computers are actually using quantum mechanics and what that entails.

Google introduced a quantum computer chip named "Willow" (which is not available in a computer yet). Google's Quantum AI founder Hartmut Neven claims that Willow runs a specific problem called *Random Circuit Sampling* in under five minutes, where traditional computers would take 10 septillion years. (A septillion is a 1 with 24 zeros after it). Neven says that the performance on this problem "lends credence to the notion that quantum computation occurs in many parallel universes."[xvi]

This "parallel universes" claim has been viewed by many scientists as speculative, lacking in evidence, premature, or even flat-out incorrect. First, the incredible speed of Google's quantum chip on the Random Circuit Sampling problem might be achievable with traditional computers as well. This contention implies that if Google spent the same resources optimizing a traditional computer for this problem, it would achieve results similar to those achieved by Google.[xvii]

Others claim that Neven confused the notion of a multiverse and parallel universes, like those found in movies, with *Hilbert Space*, which is a mathematical construct in which quantum-mechanical wave functions exist and different dimensions are represented by different possible mathematical states.[xviii] Astrophysicist Ethan Siegel echoes this contention, stating, "You can have quantum mechanics work just fine, both physically and mathematically, without introducing even one parallel universe."[xix]

Full disclosure: I am not a physicist, nor am I engaged in any quantum computer development, but there are limitations with superposition and with entanglement that are not addressed at this time:

- While traditional computer architecture relies on on-off switches, superposition forces the system to manage fluid mathematical probabilities, which is often reduced to on-off-both. This shifts the underlying architecture from on-off to highly complex calculations. Tracking and error correction require more significant computational overhead. Most standard mathematical operations are actually slowed down by this architecture, rather than accelerated.

- Currently, entanglement is very limited and short-lived. Scientists have only managed to fully entangle around 100 particles at once before environmental noise breaks the connection. To build these networks on a chip, classical signals, bound by the speed of light, must be manually routed between neighbors. Because of this slow, step-by-step construction process, the "instantaneous" magic of quantum entanglement is choked by the same architectural delays that plague traditional computers.

- Furthermore, the very mechanism used to create entanglement – firing microwave pulses at superconducting circuits – is an incredibly slow, high-latency process compared to traditional computing. While traditional on/off switches flip in a fraction of a nanosecond, a quantum microwave operation takes hundreds of times longer. Quantum is instant, but getting there requires the computer to take a nap first.

  This means quantum computers operate at a drastically slower fundamental clock speed, creating a massive operational deficit before the calculation even begins.

Is the promise of quantum computing a pipe dream, never to be realized? I agree with WIRED in saying that, yes, quantum computing will not become viable as envisioned, and that the promises made are, for the most part, hype. Billions have been invested, yet little to no practical commercial progress has been delivered, and the grand promises of quantum computing remain unrealized.

But prove me wrong, science! Show me that you can deliver quantum at the system level beyond small addition and multiplication of two numbers, and I will believe. In the meantime, managers should not worry about funding quantum computing advancements until more progress is made and probably should not invest in these types of AI technologies until when and if they prove out.

In the Weeds – Why True Quantum Computers May Never Exist

For the science geeks out there, I am not a physicist but here are some reasons why quantum computing may never happen:

- ***Macroscopic Scales*** – Microscopic quantum particles can achieve quantum effects, such as ***superposition*** (where a particle exists in every possible quantum state at once until observed) or ***particle-wave duality*** (where quantum elements exist in multiple states, as both as a wave and as a particle) and ***entanglement*** (where two particles will have opposite spin values that always instantaneously change together regardless of how far apart they are). According to many quantum scientists, it is difficult or impossible to extend these quantum effects from a microscopic environment (where electrons inside an atom exist) to a macroscopic environment (where computers on a desk exist). Although there have been some mathematical advances trying to make macroscopic quantum possible, so far, it has not proved feasible.[xx]

- ***Quantity of Entangled Particles*** – Quantum theory states that there is no limit to the number of particles that can be entangled. In practice, however, the number of entangled particles has been quite small. Nature Magazine, arguably the premier scientific magazine, reports that the current record is fourteen entangled photons, and going beyond 100 ion particles is incredibly difficult. Quantum computing will require millions or billions of entangled particles. If that ever becomes practical, it certainly is far in the future. [xxi]

- ***Decoherence*** – Quantum states are fragile, susceptible to being quickly changed by their environments, and quantum systems can quickly become regular (classical) systems in a process known as decoherence. The fragile nature of quantum states may render large-scale quantum computations susceptible to corrupting external influences (like electric currents), causing rapid decoherence. There is skepticism about the practicality of achieving stable and error-free quantum computing in real-world settings where rapid decoherence would make quantum computing impossible.

- ***Is the Science Good Enough?*** – There is a wealth of good research that has been done in quantum field theory that amounts to trying to understand the world better. Indeed, scientists have shown that quantum entanglement exists. However, with a minority of scientists, there are some fundamental skepticisms questioning the theoretical underpinnings of the quantum mechanics theory itself. Existing theory has given rise to what many scientists view as impractical or implausible conclusions, such as contentions of time travel, accessing parallel universes, or the existence of faster-than-light probabilistic messaging.[xxii] Other scientists point out that quantum theory and Einstein's theory of relativity are at odds with each other.[xxiii] Scientists and philosophers continue to explore alternative theories that could potentially replace, change, or extend quantum mechanics.

Neuromorphic Computing: Rise of the Machines

Earlier, this chapter describes how GenAI does not lead to self-aware machines like those found in *The Terminator* movies. But that was only for GenAI and current popular AI techniques. There are current non-GenAI attempts to try to build computer hardware that mimics the architecture and behavior of the human brain to allow more energy-efficient and brain-inspired AI capabilities! This field of study is called neuromorphic computing.

Neuromorphic computing involves developing hardware and software that mimics the behavior of neurons and synapses. This innovative paradigm enables machines to process information in ways like human cognition, only faster and with less bias and error, leading to enhanced capabilities in tasks like pattern recognition, learning, and decision-making. Neuromorphic computing holds promise for achieving greater energy efficiency, faster processing speeds, and novel solutions for complex problems, bridging the gap between artificial intelligence and neuroscience. The proposed computers will be analog (!), not digital, just like the human brain, and will focus on highly parallel operations and event-driven computation.[xxiv]

The neuromorphic field is attracting massive amounts of funding from governments like the US department of defense (with their DARPA Synapse project), China (with their 'New Generation' AI-Brain Project), and the European Union (with their Human Brain Project). There have already been some initial neuromorphic computers developed, and with so much talent and money pouring in across the globe, neuromorphic computers may become available in the upcoming years for high-end processes. Hopefully, there will be no *Terminator* "rise of the machine" issues, but analog computing power may dwarf current digital technology and may even lead to independent thought or to technological opportunities that we are not even aware of yet!

Think about how far we have come in the last twenty years with computer technology. Neuromorphic computing has the potential for another huge advancement in the next 20 years.

Power to the People: Automated Machine Learning (AutoML) and Explainable AI (XAI)

There is an effort to make AI more accessible to everyone:

- AutoML (Automated Machine Learning) is a set of tools that help people quickly build applications with AI, even if they are not computer experts. AutoML tools aim to democratize AI by simplifying the model-building process, enabling a wider range of users to harness the power of machine learning for their specific tasks.

- XAI (Explainable AI) is concerned with making AI models more transparent and interpretable to humans. XAI focuses on understanding and explaining the decisions made by AI systems, so users can comprehend how predictions are made and receive insights into the reasoning behind the AI predictions.

Both AutoML and XAI contribute to the broader goals of making AI more accessible, accountable, and understandable, with AutoML enabling easier model development and XAI ensuring that AI-generated insights can be comprehended and trusted by humans.

As AI becomes more pervasive, there will be a call for easier tools and for explanations on what exactly was done to make the predictions. Developments into AutoML and XAI will help broaden the reach and explainability of AI predictions.

AI at the Edge: Embedded AI with TinyML

With machine learning architecture, bigger is not always better. TinyML devices are compact, energy-efficient hardware with sophisticated algorithms that allow devices to perform intricate data analysis in real time and without the aid of sending data over a network. They are often called "edge computing" or "edge ML" because they work at the edge of the network rather than at the center of it, as shown in Figure 39.

TinyML devices use localized miniature circuitry rather than a large, centralized computer server. These tiny devices are used as wearables, consumer electronics, or smart sensors. Because they are remote, they do not have the "speed of light" problem where they need to talk with a centralized computer hundreds of miles away. TinyML devices can deliver AI insights and responses instantaneously with less delay, less power consumption, less server requirements, and the potential for greater privacy since data is not constantly transmitted and shared.[xxv]

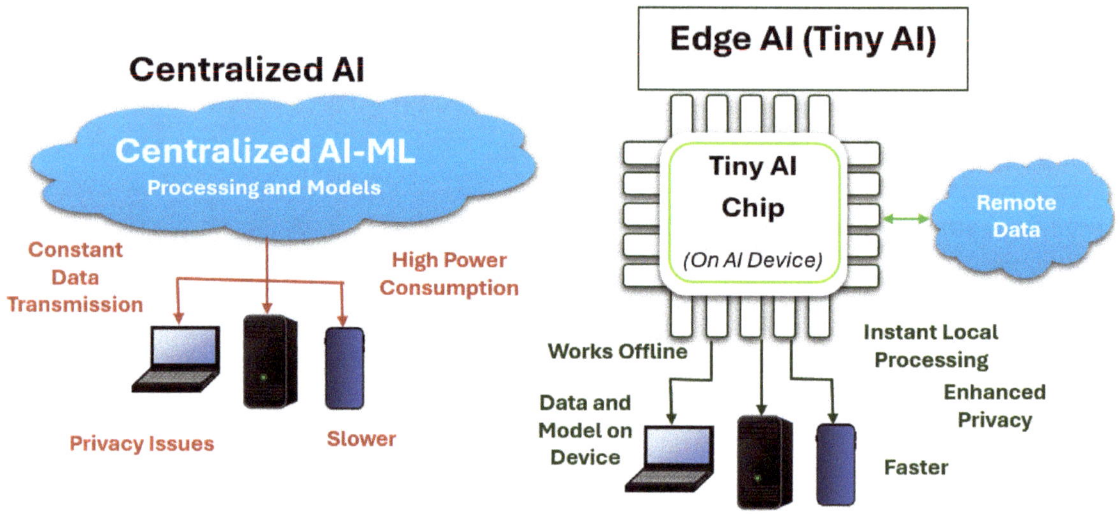

Figure 39: Moving AI Closer to the User

TinyML is relatively new but is growing. There are TinyML Python libraries like *TensorFlow Lite*, new hardware, and even symposiums and organizations like *TinyML.org* which have training materials and symposiums.[xxvi]

Despite its transformative potential, the adoption of TinyML and its embedded AI does not come without its share of considerations. Managers must balance the allure of real-time analytics with the challenges of limited computational resources and potential security vulnerabilities within embedded systems. Careful hardware design, the optimization of algorithms for resource constraints, and rigorous security measures must be meticulously orchestrated to ensure the successful integration and sustainable growth of TinyML applications.

Continued Transformation of Business Processes

While there have been great advances in AI, companies will continue to utilize AI to make smart decisions and to revolutionize business processes like never before. Here are a few areas that are continually being transformed:

- **Generating Customer Value** – Harvard Business Review describes how, by predicting customer behaviors and attributes, AI can deliver highly-customized products targeting customer needs with uncanny accuracy. Furthermore, because companies can use AI to deliver more value to the customer, customers will be willing to pay more and will have less customer churn. However, despite the clear value of AI to providing customer value, the article contends that AI is not yet deployed as widely and seamlessly as it could be, but organizations are beginning to shift their focus to using AI to generate customer value. In the future, look for companies to deploy AI applications with a focus on creating customer value. AI managers need to take note of this and look for opportunities to use AI to help their customers and thus help increase their businesses' bottom line.[xxvii]

- **Supply Chain** – Boston Consulting Group reports how AI has not been adequate in optimizing supply chains, but not due to technological limitations, but rather because of when, where, and how the technology has been applied.[xxviii] However, managers are starting to realize the potential and proper implementation of AI as a tool to instantly respond to surpluses and shortages, to mitigate sourcing and to quickly and accurate address procurement issues on the fly. [xxix]

- **Identify Hidden Patterns** – The human brain is great at recognizing patterns, from picking out a friend in a crowded room to reading words in a book. However, the patterns can become lost as the data set size increases and becomes more complex. Advances in AI allow a computer to detect hidden patterns that are too complex for a human being to process. This advanced pattern recognition can lead to breakthrough innovations. [xxx] These innovations include patterns that aid in medical diagnoses, identifying hacking attempts, identifying fraud attempts, and identifying unhappy customers or customers that are willing to spend more.

  The manager often needs to look ahead of what is currently done to ask questions like "wouldn't it be great if we could somehow detect…" The AI manager should always be on the lookout for these opportunities to expand pattern recognition within the company and give other managers even better tools to make even better decisions.

- **Perform at Scale** – Often, a benefit of AI is not that it "thinks" better than a human, but rather that it can address problems of scale. For example, if a company has 100 products sold in 1000 regions around the world, that company needs to price each product. The optimal price may not be that difficult to determine for one product in one region, but for 100,000 product/region combinations, the scale of optimal pricing may be too daunting for a team of pricing specialists. In large scale environments, managers often adopt generalized rules such as "Decrease prices by 2% if there is any inventory backlog" "Increase prices in Europe and the United States by 3%, decrease prices elsewhere by 1%" or rules and decisions that allow managers to function in a large-scale environment. In this case, AI can change this by optimizing prices for every 100,000 product/region by joining AI technologists and pricing specialists. If AI could take input from every 100,000 product/region combination and price each one just like the pricing specialist would, then optimal pricing can be achieved for each product/region combination.

AI allows generalized, non-optimized rules required from large scale to become a thing of the past. With AI, optimal revenue can be achieved, and maximum cost reductions can be realized. AI managers need to look for opportunities where traditional business practices have forced managers to generalize decisions so that a business can function, and work with those areas to deliver AI optimizations that are not limited by scale considerations.

- **Shift in How Managers Think of AI** – AI is not going to get everyone fired or destroy the world, but the Pew Research Center reports that 37% of Americans believe this is the case at the time of this writing.[xxxi] However, this is bound to change. Managers will see how AI changes education, business processes, and democratizes professions that previously have been hard to reach.[xxxii] Routine tasks will be automated, freeing up valuable human potential for creativity and strategic thinking. AI will almost certainly create jobs, not displace them, and will give current professionals a tool that allows them to do their job better. To succeed in this environment, managers need to embrace the potential of artificial intelligence and communicate the possibilities to their organizations. AI managers should help their organization facilitate this change in perspective.

With AI as a trusted ally, businesses will not only work smarter but also foster innovation that can lead to more competitive products and services. As we embrace this transformative technology, we embark on a journey where efficiency, agility, and profitability converge to shape a new era of business excellence.

Adaptive AI: Learning and Evolution in Real-Time

Adaptive AI systems are designed to continuously learn from the data they encounter and the feedback they receive. This learning process (often called reinforced learning) involves updating models, refining algorithms, and incorporating the latest information to enhance their performance. For example, in the context of recommendation systems, adaptive AI can learn user preferences and adapt its recommendations based on user interactions, resulting in more personalized and relevant suggestions.

Adaptive AI excels at understanding and adapting to different contexts. It can interpret the nuances of a situation, such as changes in user behavior, environmental conditions, or the availability of new data sources. This contextual awareness enables AI systems to make more informed decisions and predictions. In autonomous vehicles, for instance, adaptive AI can adjust driving strategies based on real-time traffic conditions, weather, and the behavior of other vehicles on the road.

Adaptive AI works well in dynamic environments where constantly changing conditions require retraining and retesting in real time. Managers should consider delivering AI applications as the situation warrants and as technology and resources become available.

AI's Role in Sustainability and Climate Solutions

AI is a powerful tool for environmental monitoring, analysis, and conservation, which are crucial for safeguarding our planet's ecosystems. AI's capacity to process and interpret vast quantities of data from satellites, sensors, and other sources allows us to monitor the environment with unprecedented accuracy and efficiency. AI-driven solutions help identify environmental changes, track biodiversity, and combat illegal activities like poaching and deforestation. This technology empowers us to protect and preserve the Earth's natural resources and ensure their sustainable use for generations to come.

With AI, we can simulate various climate scenarios, assess their potential consequences, and devise effective strategies for mitigation and adaptation. AI algorithms can analyze historical climate data to make predictions about future trends, aiding in the development of policies to reduce greenhouse gas emissions, promote renewable energy sources, and enhance resilience in vulnerable regions. By leveraging AI's analytical capabilities, we can take proactive measures to mitigate climate change and build a more sustainable future.

AI can optimize energy consumption, manage water resources more efficiently, and assist in the development of sustainable agriculture practices. AI-driven technologies like smart grids, precision agriculture, and green infrastructure are transforming industries, making them more environmentally responsible. AI's multifaceted role in sustainability and climate solutions highlights its potential to catalyze positive change and foster a more sustainable and resilient world.

Applications in Dynamic Environments – AI vs AI

There is an increasing realization that delves into a dynamic interplay between multiple AI actors, where one actor's implementation of AI strategies prompts a rapid and strategic response from another actor's AI applications. In this adaptive AI environment, both sides engage in a zero-sum game, where each AI seeks to outsmart and outmaneuver the other AIs to secure a competitive advantage.

In this case, AI applications engaged in a perpetual chess match, where every move is a response to the previous one, with the goal of gaining an upper hand. In this scenario, AI developers are constantly fine-tuning their algorithms, analyzing their opponent's strategies, and adapting in real-time. It is a high-stakes game where one actor's deployment of AI to seize opportunities, whether in finance, cybersecurity, or other domains, triggers immediate counteractions from the opposing AI application. This dynamic interaction drives the rapid evolution of AI techniques and keeps both sides on their toes.

AI interaction is not just a theoretical concept; it has real-world applications in various domains, from cybersecurity and financial trading to autonomous vehicles and gaming. The relentless pursuit of outsmarting and outperforming the competition in this AI arms race underscores the ever-increasing importance of innovation and adaptability in the world of artificial intelligence, making it an exciting frontier in the realm of technology and strategy.

This section describes some industries that will see major changes in dynamic environments due to the evolution of applications to incorporate more AI.

Cybersecurity AI vs AI

In the world of cybersecurity, particularly in the context of espionage or advanced persistent threats (APTs), there exists a perpetual game of cat and mouse, where attackers deploy increasingly sophisticated AI techniques to breach defenses, and defenders, in turn, leverage AI to thwart these efforts. This ongoing battle of AI vs. AI in dynamic cyber environments can be likened to a high-stakes chess match.

Attackers have been quick to adopt AI to enhance their attacks. They use AI to automate reconnaissance, identify vulnerabilities, and develop customized malware that can adapt to evade traditional defenses. This forces defenders to employ AI for anomaly detection, behavioral analysis, and predictive modeling, looking for patterns that indicate potential breaches. Defenders also utilize AI for threat hunting and identifying subtle signs of infiltration.

However, it is important to recognize that this is not a one-way street. Defenders are innovating in response to attacker ML. They harness AI to identify adversarial tactics, techniques, and procedures (TTPs) more effectively, enabling them to detect APTs earlier. Moreover, organizations share threat intelligence, leveraging collaborative AI techniques to create shared defense platforms that can quickly adapt to new attack strategies.

The key to success in this ongoing conflict lies in the ability to adapt and innovate swiftly. As AI techniques advance on both sides, defenders must remain vigilant, constantly enhancing their AI-based defenses while attackers refine their tactics. This spy-vs-spy game underscores the importance of investing in cybersecurity research and staying ahead of the curve, as the stakes continue to rise in the realm of cyber espionage.

Financial Markets AI vs AI

In financial markets, AI applications are engaged in a continuous game of opportunity detection and exploitation, where one AI model's actions to capitalize on market movements often trigger responses from other models looking to seize alternative opportunities. This dynamic interaction between AI-driven strategies has reshaped the landscape of trading and investment.

AI applications are deployed to identify patterns in financial data, detect market anomalies, and execute high-frequency trading strategies. For instance, algorithmic trading systems use AI to predict stock price movements, execute trades, and manage portfolios. As one AI-driven strategy capitalizes on a perceived market opportunity, it can set off a chain reaction of responses from other AI models seeking to counteract or benefit from the same opportunity.

Concurrently, other AI models are designed to respond to market movements, adjusting trading positions or executing arbitrage strategies. These models can capitalize on discrepancies in asset prices across different markets, exploiting temporary overpricing or underpricing of securities. Additionally, sentiment analysis models use natural language processing to gauge market sentiment and news sentiment, which can trigger trading actions based on positive or negative market news.

This ongoing game of AI vs. AI in financial markets has intensified market dynamics, making them more complex and competitive. It underscores the significance of rapid data processing, advanced predictive analytics, and adaptable trading strategies. The ability to identify and exploit market opportunities while being agile enough to respond to the actions of other market participants is a central challenge and opportunity in the ever-evolving world of financial AI applications.

AI has been used in financial markets for quite some time, and future developments will make actions and reactions more sophisticated and nuanced.

National Security AI vs AI

AI applications are engaged in a complex and dynamic landscape in national security where one side's efforts to exploit opportunities can trigger responses from adversaries seeking to seize alternative advantages. This interplay of AI-driven strategies has far-reaching implications for intelligence, defense, and cybersecurity. Consider the following national security areas:

1. **Cybersecurity and Cyber Warfare:** AI applications are integral to both offensive and defensive cyber operations. On one side, state-sponsored actors and cybercriminals employ AI-driven techniques to identify vulnerabilities, launch attacks, and evade detection. These actions may range from targeted phishing campaigns to sophisticated advanced persistent threats (APTs). In response, cybersecurity professionals and government agencies utilize AI to detect and mitigate these threats. Adversarial AI techniques are also employed to understand and counter AI-driven cyberattacks.

2. **Intelligence and Counterintelligence:** AI is widely used in intelligence agencies to sift through vast volumes of data for signals in the noise. AI-driven data analytics and natural language processing enable the identification of potential threats or opportunities. In response, adversaries may attempt to conceal their activities through deceptive tactics or by generating disinformation. AI applications are deployed to uncover these strategies and differentiate credible intelligence from disinformation campaigns.

3. **Geospatial and Imagery Analysis:** Geospatial intelligence, often based on satellite imagery, is vital for monitoring military activities and potential national security threats. AI algorithms can identify patterns, changes, or anomalies in such imagery. In response, other AI models may seek to mask or camouflage activities or develop counterstrategies to evade detection.

4. **Social Media and Influence Operations:** State actors and non-state groups use AI-driven social media campaigns for influence operations. In response, AI models are employed to detect and combat such operations, identifying fake accounts, monitoring trends, and mitigating the spread of false information.

The interaction between AI applications in the national security domain is a continuous cat-and-mouse game. This dynamic landscape underscores the importance of rapid adaptability and innovation on both sides. As AI technologies advance, the ability to detect, respond to, and counteract potential threats while identifying new opportunities for national security is a critical aspect of modern security operations.

Concluding Thoughts on Shaping the AI-Driven Future

The multifaceted nature of AI, including generative AI, neuromorphic computing, edge computing, explainable AI (XAI), and the transformation of business processes, marks a turning point in the way we approach technology and its impact on our lives. Here is what we covered in this chapter:

- Generative AI can empower artists, writers, and designers with new tools for innovation, while also presenting challenges related to copyright and authenticity. The creative possibilities are boundless, offering fresh and imaginative perspectives in various fields. There are legal and ethical issues as well that the data science manager needs to be aware of as members in organizations start using GenAI for tasks.

- The promise of quantum computing is great, but at the time of this writing, extensive research and funding have failed to produce any significant advances.

While we are waiting for any advances in quantum computing to have an impact on organizations, managers are cautioned to pursue other developments.

- Neuromorphic computing, inspired by the human brain, opens new horizons in AI's capabilities. These biologically inspired systems are poised to significantly enhance AI's efficiency and adaptability, making AI applications more intelligent, energy-efficient, and capable of real-time learning. In areas such as robotics and sensory perception, neuromorphic computing promises groundbreaking advancements.

- Edge computing is transforming the way we process data. By shifting computational power closer to where data is generated, edge computing enhances the responsiveness and scalability of AI applications. This is especially significant for real-time analytics and decision-making, as well as for reducing latency in critical applications like autonomous vehicles and healthcare.

- XAI addresses a fundamental challenge in AI: understanding and explaining AI's decision-making processes. As AI applications become more integral to our lives, ensuring transparency and trustworthiness is paramount. XAI techniques aim to make AI decisions comprehensible and actionable, with applications spanning from healthcare diagnostics to autonomous vehicles.

- The transformation of business processes is a cornerstone of AI's impact on the corporate world. Organizations are leveraging AI to streamline operations, enhance customer experiences, and drive innovation. Whether it is through predictive analytics, process automation, or data-driven insights, AI is reshaping the way businesses operate and interact with their customers.

  In this AI-driven future, a unique and intricate ecosystem is evolving, where AI applications engage in a continuous interplay, adapting and responding to one another—a phenomenon known as adaptive AI. It introduces a dynamic dimension where AI actors strive to outmaneuver their counterparts, leading to rapid advancements and competitive evolution.

The possibilities that these diverse AI technologies offer are truly exciting. Yet with this transformative power comes the responsibility to navigate the ethical, privacy, and societal implications of AI. The AI-driven future is bright and full of promise, but with significant challenges, and managers need to be aware of the potential, the challenges, and the risks and rewards of this exciting, developing environment.

---

[i] Statista. 2026. "Artificial Intelligence – Worldwide," available at https://www.statista.com/outlook/tmo/artificial-intelligence/worldwide.

[ii] Eric Siegel. June 02, 2023. "The AI Hype Cycle Is Distracting Companies." *Harvard Business Review*, available at https://hbr.org/2023/06/the-ai-hype-cycle-is-distracting-companies.

[iii] Michael Chui, Kweilin Ellingrud and Asutosh Padhi. August 9, 2023. "Will generative A.I. be good for U.S. workers?" *Fortune*, available at https://fortune.com/2023/08/09/global-forum-mckinsey-generative-ai/.

[iv] KPMG. 2023. "Generative AI: From Buzz to Business Value." *KMPG*, available at https://advisory.kpmg.us/content/dam/advisory/en/pdfs/2023/generative-ai-survey.pdf.

[v] Beena Ammanath. Nov 09, 2021. "Thinking Through the Ethics of New Tech...Before There's a Problem." *Harvard Business Review* 9, available at https://hbr.org/2021/11/thinking-through-the-ethics-of-new-techbefore-theres-a-problem.

[vi] Brooks, Rob. February 21, 2023. "I tried the Replika AI companion and can see why users are falling hard. The app raises serious ethical questions." *The Conversation*, available at https://theconversation.com/i-tried-the-replika-ai-companion-and-can-see-why-users-are-falling-hard-the-app-raises-serious-ethical-questions-200257.

[vii] Reddit. Feb 2023. "Resources If You're Struggling," *Reddit*, available at https://www.reddit.com/r/replika/comments/10zuqq6/resources_if_youre_struggling/?rdt=56571.

[viii] Matt Burgess, February 14, 2024. "'AI Girlfriends' Are a Privacy Nightmare" *Wired Magazine*, available at https://www.wired.com/story/ai-girlfriends-privacy-nightmare/.

[ix] Cerullo, Megan. May 29,2023. "A lawyer used ChatGPT to prepare a court filing. It went horribly awry." *CBS Moneywatch*, available at https://www.cbsnews.com/news/lawyer-chatgpt-court-filing-avianca/.

[x] Anonymous. June 23, 2023. "Lawyers fined for filing bogus case law created by ChatGPT." *CBS Moneywatch*, available at https://www.cbsnews.com/news/chatgpt-judge-fines-lawyers-who-used-ai/.

[xi] Kevin Collier. July 14, 2023. "Actors vs. AI: Strike brings focus to emerging use of advanced tech." *NBC News*, available at https://www.nbcnews.com/tech/tech-news/hollywood-actor-sag-aftra-ai-artificial-intelligence-strike-rcna94191.

[xiii] Congressional Record, July 13, 2023. "S.Amdt.797 to S.2226" *Congressional Record – Senate*, available at https://www.congress.gov/amendment/118th-congress/senate-amendment/797/text.

[xiv] Chen, Sophia. Dec 12, 2019. "Revolt! Scientists Say They're Sick of Quantum Computing's Hype." *Wired Magazine*, available at https://www.wired.com/story/revolt-scientists-say-theyre-sick-of-quantum-computings-hype/.

[xv] Simon Keegan, Jan 9, 2025. "As Google and Microsoft launch quantum computing tech, how is Manchester on the cutting edge of discovery, how can it solve global issues and does it prove the Multiverse?" *insidermedia*, available at https://www.insidermedia.com/news/north-west/as-google-and-microsoft-launch-quantum-computing-tech-how-is-manchester-on-the-cutting-edge-of-discovery-how-can-it-solve-global-crisis-issues-and-does-it-prove-the-multiverse.

[xvi] Victor Tangermann. December 12, 2024. "Google Says It Appears to Have Accessed Parallel Universes" *yahoo!tech*, available at https://www.yahoo.com/tech/google-says-may-accessed-parallel-155644957.html.

[xvii] Matt Swayne. Dec 16, 2024. "Google's Quantum Chip Sparks Debate on Multiverse Theory." *Quantum Insider*, available at https://thequantuminsider.com/2024/12/16/googles-quantum-chip-sparks-debate-on-multiverse-theory/.
[xviii] Matt Swayne. Dec 16, 2024. "Google's Quantum Chip Sparks Debate on Multiverse Theory." *Quantum Insider*, available at https://thequantuminsider.com/2024/12/16/googles-quantum-chip-sparks-debate-on-multiverse-theory/.

[xix] Simon Keegan, Jan 9, 2025. "As Google and Microsoft launch quantum computing tech, how is Manchester on the cutting edge of discovery, how can it solve global issues and does it prove the Multiverse?" *insidermedia*, available at https://www.insidermedia.com/news/north-west/as-google-and-microsoft-launch-quantum-computing-tech-how-is-manchester-on-the-cutting-edge-of-discovery-how-can-it-solve-global-crisis-issues-and-does-it-prove-the-multiverse.

[xx] Gallego, Miguel and Dakić, Borivoje. Sep 16, 2021. "Macroscopically Nonlocal Quantum Correlations." Physical Review Letters 127 (12), pp. 120401-5, available at https://journals.aps.org/prl/abstract/10.1103/PhysRevLett.127.120401.

[xxi]Phillip Thomas, Leonardo Ruscio, Olivier Morin & Gerhard Rempe. Aug 24, 2022. "Efficient generation of entangled multiphoton graph states from a single atom." *Nature* 608, 677–681, available at https://doi.org/10.1038/s41586-022-04987-5.

[xxii] Amir D. Aczel.2001. *Entanglement*. Plume/Penguin Publishing.

[xxiii] Corey S. Powell. Nov 4, 2015. "Relativity versus quantum mechanics: the battle for the universe." *The Guardian* available at https://www.theguardian.com/news/2015/nov/04/relativity-quantum-mechanics-universe-physicists.

[xxiv] Catherine D. Schuman, Shruti R. Kulkarni, Maryam Parsa, J. Parker Mitchell, Prasanna Date & Bill Kay. Jan 31, 2022. "Opportunities for neuromorphic computing algorithms and applications." *Nature Computational Science* 2, 10–19, available at https://doi.org/10.1038/s43588-021-00184-y.

[xxv] Arun. November 10, 2020. "An Introduction to TinyML: Machine Learning meets Embedded Systems." *Medium*, available at https://towardsdatascience.com/an-introduction-to-tinyml-4617f314aa79.

[xxvi] The TinyML Foundation can be found at https://www.tinyml.org/.

[xxvii] Eric Siegel. March 24, 2023. "How Machine Learning Can Improve the Customer Experience." *Harvard Business Review*, available at https://hbr.org/2023/03/how-machine-learning-can-improve-the-customer-experience.

[xxviii] Pepe Rodriguez, Stefan Gstettner, Ashish Pathak, Ram Krishnan, and Michael Spaeth. Sep 1, 2022. "Why AI-Managed Supply Chains Have Fallen Short and How to Fix Them." White paper available at https://meet.aeratechnology.com/hubfs/White%20Papers%20and%20Assets/whitepaper-bcg-benefits-of-ai-driven-supply-chain.pdf.

[xxix] https://www.aeratechnology.com/blogs/decision-intelligence-in-2023-prepare-for-these-10-ai-and-machine-learning-milestones.

[xxx] Gaudenz Boesch. 2023. "What is Pattern Recognition? A Gentle Introduction (2023)." *Viso.AI*, available at https://viso.ai/deep-learning/pattern-recognition/.

[xxxi] Lee Rainie, Cary Funk, Monica Anderson, and Alec Tyson. March 17, 2022. "How Americans Think about Artificial Intelligence." *Pew Research Center*, available at https://www.pewresearch.org/internet/2022/03/17/how-americans-think-about-artificial-intelligence/.

[xxxii] Sebastian Thrun. May 1, 2023. "AI Will Unlock a New Level of Human Potential." *Venture Beat*, available at https://venturebeat.com/ai/ai-will-unlock-a-new-level-of-human-potential/.

Conclusion: The Next Steps

You didn't pick up this book to become a data scientist - you read it to become the leader who knows how to navigate the technical, operational, and ethical realities of the intelligence era.

Across ten chapters, we have demystified the machine learning lifecycle, broken down the strategic nuances between fine-tuning and RAG, established framework anchors to keep top-tier talent from walking out the door, and mapped out a strict GRC protocol to protect your organization from the hidden operational liabilities of shadow AI.

But frameworks on a page do not manage departments. Action does.

As you close this book and step back into your organization, your immediate mandate is to transition from a leader who simply understands AI to one who actively pilots it. Here is your strategic playbook for next Monday morning:

1. **Conduct a Shadow AI Audit**

   Before you approve another line item or spin up a new initiative, you must identify where AI is already running rampant in the shadows. Talk to your team. Look at the workflows. Identify where employees are dumping proprietary operational data into consumer-grade LLMs to bypass inefficient legacy tools. Your goal is not to punish innovation, but to transition these rogue pipelines from unmonitored liabilities into secure, compliant corporate assets using agentic controls and proper calibration.

2. **Standardize Your Evaluation Metrics**

   Stop letting vendors or over-enthusiastic consultants sell you on generic "accuracy" metrics or avoid KPIs at all! Review your active AI projects and have your teams step up and defend the quality of their AI predictions against real-world business risks. Ensure that your project boundaries are guarded by strict user acceptance testing and that your deployment schedules account for the critical path dependencies unique to data architecture.

3. **Fortify Your Talent Foundation So High-performing Data Scientists Do Not Leave**

   High-performing data scientists do not leave organizations because the algorithms get tough. They leave because their leadership doesn't recognize their value, isolates them, or fails to provide safety for their career. Look at your department through the lens of the Retention Anchor Framework. Are your teams siloed? Is your technical talent being drowned out by the "HiPPO" (Highest Paid Person's Opinion)? Are they being rewarded with raises and promotions, or skipped over? Show them respect with words, actions, and salary, and they'll give you loyalty in return.

4. **Pivot from Displacement to Augmentation**

   The executives who fail the next decade will be those who view GenAI purely as a tool to cut headcount and slash immediate costs. Agentic is coming with its new challenges and excessive costs. The leaders who win will mimic the scale-fast flywheels of Amazon, Google, and AstraZeneca—using cutting-edge technology to augment human capability, surface hidden market opportunities, and drive real customer value.

The future of management belongs to those who can stand firmly at the intersection of human leadership and machine capability. You have the technical baseline, the strategic roadmap, and the governance frameworks.

Turn the page on passive implementation. The next wave of disruption is already here and the one that follows is close behind — go manage it!

Index

www.ingramcontent.com/pod-product-compliance
Lightning Source LLC
LaVergne TN
LVHW070908210926
848482LV00017B/1023